Studies in Lechery

Studies in Lechery

CAL LOUISE PHOENIX

atmosphere press

Published by Atmosphere Press

Cover design by Senhor Tocas
Author photo by Nicole Spacek

Atmospherepress.com

Contents

Prologue

"Damnit!" Jack shouted. His arms hesitated in midair; instead of overturning the coffee table, he grabbed a lone pencil from its top. He shot up and stomped around the sofa. Between his fists, the pencil cracked.

I bit the insides of my cheeks. My knees bent until I was cowering on the floor. Watching him might fuel his storm, so I stared into my lap, tracing the plaid of my thrifted skirt. Slivers of tissue tore between my teeth as I suppressed a wave of nervous giggles. I wondered if I appeared to him as small as he made me feel.

Tuesday evenings marked our weekly rendezvous. Each visit began with a predictable chain of action. Jack lived in an upscale townhouse four blocks from my decrepit childhood home. I always traveled there on foot, always after seven PM. He'd leave the front door ajar (even though I had a key) and rise from one of two sofas to greet me with a kiss. I'd kick off my shoes, drop my purse, and slip off my headscarf. He'd offer to fetch me a glass of water or adjust the ceiling fan's speed, and I'd refuse these kindnesses. I could see to my needs without troubling him.

We'd settle into each other in front of the television. Jack would lower the volume and report on his activities and the complaints he'd gathered over the week. I listened intently and gave advice when it seemed appropriate. Mostly, I remained reserved. It wasn't my place to question him or pry. It never had been.

This particular visit had followed our pattern until it was my turn to speak. I started by describing an experimental essay I was writing about our relationship. I'd been rereading my diary for source material.

"It's just crazy to read the entries from the beginning of

this year, or even five months ago, because things have shifted so much between us, with everything that's happened."

I expected Jack to chuckle in agreement and maybe apologize for the inconsistencies on his part—to remind me of his love and commitment. But, his body stiffened in response. I lifted my head from his chest to watch his eyes shrink and darken behind his glasses.

"Jack, what's wrong?"

"I just feel like a scumbag," he grumbled. "I'm upset with myself. I hate disappointing you." He was exploiting me, he said. Our relationship was exploitative.

I'd recoiled, punched by the remark. My mouth filled with rust and salt. *What the hell—he can't say that if I've already said that.*

That tiny rumble in my belly perked up. It was mostly dormant unless Jack was acting out, as he had over the summer. I could never quite make it out, though its message was clear: *this feels wrong*.

My knees now burned where they dug into the carpet. The pencil splintered into smaller and smaller bits in his hands. Straining not to laugh, I sat as dumb as a golem.

Jack ranted. The secretive nature of our relationship forced me to be someone I was not, he declared. It made him feel like a bastard, like he was taking advantage of me. He worried that if our relationship carried on and if it finally *did* end, he was terrified of how it would affect me. "I feel like something explosive is going to eventually happen," he concluded.

My lips parted, but he interjected, clapping a hand over his chest. "And this—me, right now—this is a labor of love! Do you understand? I am a burden to you, and pushing you away is my way to make sure you'll be okay."

I did not understand. I'd always found the depth of self-loathing ridiculous and frankly, exhausting.

With a steadying breath, I implored, "Please Jack, I don't see you as a bad person—and I don't feel exploited now. We've *talked* about this. If I still felt that way, I wouldn't fight so hard to stay close to you or to take care of you."

"But, I don't *want* you to take care of me! I never did! It's exploitative of you!"

"It cannot be exploitative if I'm *willing*, Jack!"

"Cal, why can't we just go back to being friends? I just want to be a friend and mentor to you."

"Haven't we already tried and *failed* at it? You can't keep your hands off of me!"

He groaned at the ceiling, rolling back the breadth of his shoulders and throwing up his arms. "You're not listening! These are my feelings and they're real to me!"

"Goddamnit, Jack!" I whacked a sofa cushion with a frustrated hand. "I didn't risk *everything* just to be your friend!"

His eyes shimmered. "Don't you understand how you saying that removes my agency?"

"Your *agency*?" I scoffed. "Everything between us has always been on *your* terms! And that makes sense because of your workload and your health problems. I've told you I'm willing to be accommodating, and I *have* been accommodating—this whole time."

His pacing resumed. Fragments of yellow wood and graphite fell from between his fingers and littered the rug, the tweed upholstery of the sofa.

I tried again. By now, I was used to exercising a lot of patience with him. "Jack, do you love me?"

"You know I love you. I've always told you this." He leaned into the sofa's backrest. "Look, it sounds so cheesy, but—you're like a light. It's your soul I love so much and I just feel like I'm tarnishing it." He swiped at tears and murmured, "Surely others see that in you too."

"No," I whispered, "no one else sees me the way that you say you see me."

Jack straightened. "Oh, fuck you! Fuck you—come here!" He circled the sofa, plopped down, and extended his arms.

I submitted. His face disappeared into my shoulder. Dazed

by the emotional helter-skelter of the last few minutes and unsure of what else to do, I buried my face in his neck and gulped along with him.

Eventually, I heard him say, "Look at me," but I shook my head. The next thing out of his mouth might be our undoing.

He gently squeezed my arm. "Come on. It's okay. Look at me."

I obeyed. One hand hovered over my mouth to guard against the nervous laughter that still scratched at my esophagus.

"I'm having a freak-out," Jack said. "I shouldn't be making any decisions right now. Can we meet again later this week to talk about this further?"

Yes. We agreed to meet on Thursday after my shift at the tutoring center. I had no way of knowing it wouldn't happen and I'd be in his home only once more before the illusion crumbled.

I collected my things, and we embraced. As I descended the stoop outside, Jack lingered through a crack in the door as he always did, waving and blowing me kisses.

WORD FOR THE YEAR IS *SURREAL*

"How bold one gets when one is sure of being loved."

—Sigmund Freud

"Personal problems are public issues. Given this, many say that sociology is the dismal science—a dark and pessimistic discipline. Don't hang around with sociologists, they say, because the trade of sociologists makes them pretty gloomy people."

—Ken Plummer

"Perhaps you will say to me – 'I no longer take the slightest interest in you Miss Charlotte – you no longer belong to my household – I have forgotten you.' Well Monsieur tell me so candidly – it will be a shock to me – that doesn't matter – it will still be less horrible than uncertainty."

-Charlotte Brontë, to her professor

December

14 December 2015

Current mood: grumpy
Current music: Ben Howard, "Black Flies"

I've started a quilt of denim squares. Two years ago, [my ex-fiancé] Cody set aside several pairs of work pants to throw out. I salvaged them, convinced I could repurpose the denim somehow. Then, confined to bed with a chest cold last month, I remembered the old jeans, packed in a trash bag at the back of my closet.

[My cats] Filburt and Gojira pinned me to the mattress with their warm round weight. Movies played on my laptop, which was propped on a book near my feet. I smoothed pant legs over a large art book, traced the squares in pen, and cut them out. I've purchased a huge length of fleece for the base. My plan is to sew squares of four until I have enough to cover the fleece. Then, I will sew these into rows.

People say I'm torturing myself by doing this all by hand and that it will take forever, but I'm in no rush. I find it relaxing—usually.

The fall semester has ended. Now comes winter break, which is long and unstructured. Not needing to be anywhere, nor to wake up or go to bed at any time for any reason—it always throws me off. When there are no expectations of my presence, I start to feel helplessly aimless until I can think of something to occupy my hands, my head.

Besides the quilt, I *do* have something to keep me busy over the next six weeks. It's quite a tale, actually.

My adviser in the sociology department is Dr. Jack Blair; we students call him JB for short. When I decided to declare a second bachelor's in sociology, he'd said something like,

"Obviously, I'll be your adviser, if you're okay with that."

Uh, *obviously.* He's taught the majority of my sociology classes since I took Intro with him in the fall of 2009.

At this point, JB and I are really close. He's gifted me books over the years and told me about his health, which has been poorly for a while. I've revealed my history with self-harm, disordered eating, and alcoholism, and even talked to him about being polyamorous. He knows much more about me than I know about him, though he's been less reserved lately. Maybe he feels he can confide in me more now that I'm stronger in my studies, sober, and generally more focused and serene.

After some maneuvering, JB and I have mostly nailed down my final semester. I'll be doing an internship and retaking British Lit 2. Since JB forgot to get me enrolled in Race and Ethnic Relations last semester—and it's only offered in the fall—I'll complete it as a directed readings course over winter break. This way, I can focus on my other classes once the spring semester starts.

We're still trying to resolve the algebra requirement. JB seems confident I'll get an administrative waiver for an alternative course designed to use mathematical concepts through a sociological lens. He and some other professors specifically developed the course for another student with dyscalculia (a learning disability defined by severe difficulty in comprehending numerical signs and arithmetical calculations). That student went on to graduate—no problem.

If I can't read clocks, tell my threes from eights or sevens from nines, or make sense of division, fractions, decimals, or percentages, then surely I can't be expected to take—and pass—college algebra. I'll be vibrating with anxiety until it's sorted out. Graduation is only five months away.

Today, JB is meeting with Susan, director of student disability services, to get the ball rolling. I'll send him a text message later to ask him how it went.

Right, his phone number. He gave it to me on Wednesday (the 9th). Since I only have a few weeks to complete the Race/ Ethnic Relations coursework, I think he assumed this would be the best way to stay in touch.

On Shabbos, he texted to say my internship was approved. He also suggested we meet soon. In the past, I've baked cookies for the English department and given muffins to my favorite professors during finals week. I've never had the chance to do something like this for JB. So, I offered to make him soup or bake a casserole—something to nosh while we review my homework. He said that'd be lovely.

The text exchange continued from there, and I wondered if the tone wasn't flirtatious, especially after something he'd said on Wednesday.

We were in his office when his phone rang. To amuse myself, I began surveying his bookshelves. JB cupped his hand over the receiver and encouraged me to browse. I flipped through a couple of books on religion and feminism. After hanging up, he apologized, and I sat back down, saying, "No worries!"

Then, he said, "You know, and pardon me for saying so—I don't mean to be a creep—but *you look good*, you know? You look great."

I paused, unsure how to receive his comment. He knows I've battled an eating disorder and has complimented my appearance before, saying I look healthy or look good. I figured this was his way of expressing support for a troubled student. But, this was different. His words carried an unfamiliar inflection.

Finally, I just said, "Thanks."

"I'm sorry," he rushed. "I don't mean to sound like a creep."

"No, it's fine. You're not a creep. I always appreciate an honest compliment."

He asked how "all that" was going—referring to my disordered eating patterns—and I said it was fine, which is true. The conversation moved on, and I just brushed it off—until the text messages from Friday night. I wish I'd saved them.

Here's the thing: I have no idea if he's *actually* flirting with me. It's probably nothing. But, maybe I want to think JB's flirting with me—an odd thing to admit. I've never been one to romanticize my teachers. JB's different though, and not because I'm attracted to him, but because I'd like to be *closer* to him. He's said he views me more as his peer than his student. He makes me feel special, and I think he's a special person too.

Could I be interested? He's so brilliant, understanding, and has a great sense of humor. He's also played a very important role in my life. I'd be a very different person if I hadn't taken that first class with him, which inspired me to eventually embrace a second bachelor's.

The obvious problem: such a prospect is completely inappropriate.

Who knows? Still, it's been on my mind since Shabbos.

JB definitely has fans. Students adore him, swarm him, flow in and out of his office in erractic tides. There's a consensus among us and yes, we all love JB, and yes, we would all marry JB, blah blah blah, isn't he just the best? It's probably too much, too boundary-defying.

Case in point: my friend Kayla. For a while, she'd talked about an accountant she was seeing named Bob. He wasn't religious, but was open-minded about her background. He'd even toured a new church with her. They were affectionate, but never had sex because of her beliefs. Things between them stalled or became tense, and Kayla broke up with Bob, or so she told me. Then, while going over an assignment with JB in his office—this was some years ago—he asked if he could share something, "just between us." He said Kayla was being "stalk-y" toward him: hanging around his car in the parking lot and even showing up at his house.

The phone rang and he glanced at the caller ID. "It's Kayla. I knew it would be. She always calls around this time." He didn't pick up, but said we would need to speak quietly now.

Because he hadn't answered, she'd be sitting in the foyer, mere steps from his door.

Finally, JB asked if I knew about Kayla's boyfriend Bob, how she described him, and did I know where he was going with this?

Sure enough, when we wrapped up our conversation, and he opened the door, Kayla was there, waiting to see him.

It immediately clicked. Bob was JB. Kayla had been describing a fictitious relationship, over-exaggerating the nature of what was happening with "Bob." What kind of delusional bullshit is that?

To be sure, I sought out our mutual friend, Mikki, who was closer to Kayla. After hearing my appeal for the truth, Mikki sighed and admitted to having known all along, sworn to secrecy. She'd tried to talk sense into Kayla about being in love with her professor and making up a relationship as a cover to explore her attachment to him—or whatever.

I confronted Kayla about it through Facebook Messenger. I didn't care about the subject of the lie; I just couldn't tolerate being lied to by a friend. I've not spoken to her since. So, that's some shit. And I'm not interested in getting conflated with that kind of *meshugas*. No fucking way.

17 December 2015

Current mood: confused

Current music: Diary of Dreams, "Butterfly:Dance! (Ooea Version)"

At Dr. Blair's house, I found myself unable to look at him for very long. I thought, *My god, is this my life? How did I get here? How will I get out of this?*

He gave me a tour, beginning on the ground floor, then upstairs, and finishing with a glance into his garage basement.

The first floor is modern with the living, dining, and kitchen spaces blending together, separated only by a counter. Upstairs is the laundry nook, then the second bedroom (which serves as a library), the linen closet, and at the end of the hall is the master bedroom. I peeked around the basement with him, seeing exercise equipment—a bench press and the like—closely arranged in front of the carpark, as well as a drafting table and some other arts supplies. He noted that he keeps his paintings in a closet down there.

It was odd seeing him in casual clothes instead of the usual collared shirt and black V-neck sweater. He seemed larger than normal and confidently spilled over his side of the sofa, his stout arms and chest comfortably rounded open. In comparison, I felt microscopic, balled up on the other end of the sofa, with a throw pillow clutched in my lap.

We discussed the political pop-art he's hung in his living room. We flipped through some books together. We talked. It was pleasant, easy-going, though I was nervously self-conscious. What matters most is that he enjoyed my company. I'd arrived around eight PM, but didn't leave until two o'clock in the morning.

I have four more book reviews to do. Classes resume in a month, which seems very close. My anxiety is crushing, and I can't stop thinking about JB. What stupid madness.

27 December 2015

Current mood: groggy

Current music: Dustin Tebbutt, "The Breach"

On Xmas Eve, I visited JB again so he could look over my first two book reports. To my relief, he said they were excellent. We fell into hours of conversation. By midnight, JB looked sleepy. "You're wilted," I observed. "I should leave you be."

He told me to wait until the end of the TV show we were only half-watching. Then, he said, "So, we're getting to know each other more—were there any additional questions you had for me, anything you wanted to ask me?"

I stared as if he'd read my mind. "Well, yes, actually," I said. "There is something I've wanted to ask you that's been giving me a little anxiety over the last week, and I'm a pretty direct person..." Blah blah blah—I don't remember my exact words. "Are you sexually attracted to or sexually interested in me? I get this *vibe* that might be the case, and I just want to know for sure."

"Oh, yes, *totally*," he answered. He knows there exists the obvious relationship of student and professor, and yet, "I've had many dirty, dirty thoughts about you."

Uhhh oh my god are you serious?! Outwardly calm, I said, "Oh, okay! I just wanted to know for sure. I like to know what a person's intentions are if I'm spending time with them."

He said he hoped his response didn't make me uncomfortable. I said, no. It didn't. The problem was that the feeling was mutual (being that I'm interested in—well, more *curious about*—him), and since there's a glaring power imbalance, those feelings are complicated.

"You have my future in your hands," I said. "I can't risk compromising my academic career by doing *anything* that might sour our dynamic so close to my graduation. And most of all, it just wouldn't be ethical." I told him if he wanted to wait five months, we could explore something then. Or, we might develop a friendship we wouldn't want to muddy with sex—who knows?

Though he nodded in agreement, he added, "With all that being said, I absolutely want to eat you out."

Eep! I thanked him for his honesty. He also made it clear that while he praises my work, he does so because he genuinely feels it's exceptional and not because he's trying to get into my pants.

Our goodbye hug lasted a little longer than normal.

Yesterday, I outlined my conversation with JB to [my long-term partner] Alex over the phone. He's in Florida at his mother's for the holiday, and although I would have liked to relay this to him in person, I know he prefers timely updates.

I expected the conversation to be difficult, but I hadn't expected Alex to interrupt and chastise me. I was offended, as if I'm still the same emotionally brash woman-child he'd started dating eight years ago. Too annoyed to hear anymore, Alex ended the call prematurely. I stood dumbly in the kitchen with my phone, quivering with cold and worry until my cigarette died out.

Does he actually think I'd allow sex to compromise my college career—*my life*? I've worked too damn hard. No—no, no, no.

It doesn't matter anyway. *Talking* about sexual interest is not the same as *doing* sexual things.

29 December 2015

Current mood: depressed

Current music: My Dying Bride, "Roads"

An impending wave of depression has been nipping at my fingertips and tugging at the clumps of hair beneath my headscarves. Today, it finally pulled me under its heavy cover.

I've been tempted to cut myself, but can't be bothered. I've struggled to concentrate on my assigned reading. It could be the cold or the anxiety of the upcoming semester. It could be these mad, swirling thoughts about JB that I'm not ready to confront.

January

13 January 2016

Current mood: resolved
Current music: Clan of Xymox, "Jasmine & Rose"

Last Thursday (the 7th), I arrived at JB's around seven PM with my denim quilt rolled up inside a canvas bag. When I'd described it, he seemed impressed, so I wanted to show him. Selfishly, I also needed a surface to spread out the fleece base; then, I'd know how many more squares of four to sew before starting on the rows. And unlike the grimy, unfinished wood floors at my house, JB's are clean and carpeted.

We unfolded the fleece in his spare room and lined the four-squares on top. JB helped me tally how many more squares to assemble. It was exciting to see how much I've accomplished, though I have more left to do than I'd estimated.

"It's an art piece," he praised. "I could see this being exhibited."

I identified the denim sources. Cody's work pants, battered and stained from carpentry. Vintage denim from [my best friend] Amber and scraps from [my niece]'s cut offs. Alex's frayed, old jeans, and my own, from before I lost weight, quit drinking, and lost more weight.

Before we went back downstairs, JB led me to his bedroom. He scooped through his dresser and handed me two pairs of Levis, both in good condition. I began to protest, but he assured they were too big now and he was eager to contribute.

Fast-forward. Around two AM, my quilt and his jeans were folded and stuffed into my bag. I stepped outside. JB followed.

It was raining. We huddled under the tiny roof above the stoop and shared an awkward, lingering exchange. It was the most perfect moment for a first kiss. I wonder if he'd thought so too, which was why he hung at my side.

Something eventually had to give, right? If he turned me down, then I would know to pull back, suppress the anxious churning, and limit my contact with him. If he accepted... Well, I guess we'd figure it out?

So, I asked if I could kiss him.

"Yes, please do."

His head lowered. My toes lifted. Our mouths met. I held my breath. Lights flickered behind my eyelids.

Pulling away, I said something like, "Glad to get that out of the way"—because enough already. Bomb the levees.

"I've been wanting to do that for a long time," he confessed. I could've fainted. He couldn't be serious.

We kissed again, and he hugged me for a long time before I dashed home.

Last night, we watched President Obama's last State of the Union address, and JB bent my ear with some scandalous university gossip. "On that note," I said, "we should discuss this, whatever this is," and signaled to the two of us.

He said he wants to keep seeing me and wants a relationship. *Eek!* Okay, but how does that work, exactly?

"Would we be required to report our relationship to someone?" I asked.

"Yes, that's the protocol," he answered. But after discussing the matter further, we decided to conceal our affections.

I'm not proud of this. It's not ideal whatsoever. It is, in fact, remarkably terrifying because there's *a lot* at stake.

As he's explained, there's no university policy about student-professor relationships, except in situations where students are trading sexual favors for good grades or are sexually harassed by professors. It's up to [the university] to decide how they want to deal with consensual student-professor relationships, on a case-by-case basis. JB said ours, in particular, could be dealt with very seriously.

If we were discovered, he said it could hurt his reputation and "stigmatize" my character. My academic standing would come under investigation, and it could severely delay my graduation plans. It would ruin my ability to get this waiver for the alternative math course. My transcripts could fall under administrative review. Because I've taken most of my sociology courses with him and consistently got good grades—grades I haven't always deserved—I could be forced to retake *all* of those classes with different professors. Worse yet, JB said some record of our involvement could follow me into graduate school!

So, I've given this a lot of thought—*now what, okay okay, this could work I think, oh holy hell*—and I genuinely feel I can adapt. Honestly, what else can I do? JB said he can keep the personal and professional separate, and I think I can do the same, though I'm fucking scared. There are an infinite number of things that could go wrong. But, I trust him, and this consoles me.

Oy, why all of this now? Why didn't he just wait until after I'd graduated to hit on me, to start inviting me to his home?

Well, whatever. Here we are. And of course, we've agreed to keep things secret.

JB said he understands this to be unnatural on my part. He knows me to be proudly self-expressive and honest to a fault, which are qualities people—himself included—admire about me. So, he's sorry I'll have to be guarded about our relationship, as I am usually an open book.

We also agreed to just allow things between us to develop organically, for which I'm grateful. I'm still getting to know him, still coming to terms with his humanity. I've put him on a pedestal, which is easy to do when someone is a well-liked authority figure. To touch him outside of casual hugs is *surreal*. I've never viewed myself as his equal. It's like touching a sculpture or painting I've only ever observed through a pane of protective glass.

That previous boundary is astonishingly difficult to navigate now. Last night, I was hesitant to touch him. We didn't kiss again until hours after I arrived, and we'd been cuddling on the couch, holding hands.

Already, we've discussed a few pertinent topics, such as the threat of sexually transmitted illness and how my other partners feel about the situation. I also asked whether he'd had much exposure to polyamory. He said he'd dated a polyamorous woman before, so he's familiar with my romantic lifestyle.

Most importantly, has he ever done this before: dated a current student of his?

"Oh god, no," JB answered. There'd been a couple of students—one he'd dated briefly and another one-night-stand, but both situations occurred after they'd graduated and only after they'd approached him first.

Hearing this was a huge relief. If I was just another notch on a student-lover bedpost, I'd been out of there in a flash. The opposite is true, according to him. I'm exceptional. He's never felt this way about a student before.

The age difference is a little odd, but not a deal breaker. He'll have just turned thirty-nine when I turn twenty-nine this summer. Still, as he likes to say, I have an old soul.

Before we get too carried away, there's one more significant detail: JB is *technically* dating a colleague. While he says the relationship has ceased to be rewarding and they haven't been intimate in months, they still need to officially end things. I told him I wasn't comfortable progressing sexually until he's broken up with her. Absolutely not.

I'd better start my trek to the mechanic's shop. They say my car is leaking "from every possible system" and the transmission is on its way out. I can't afford another car right now and I need transportation to get to and from [the city] to see Alex and attend synagogue. I wasn't anticipating this (which seems to be the theme of late).

15 January 2016

Current mood: okay
Current music: Sóley, "Devil"

JB is actually *twelve* years my senior. We came across his passport in a kitchen drawer last night. He looks tired in the photo. I think my head looks big in mine.

When I first arrived, he greeted me with upsetting news regarding the college algebra requirement. Apparently, administration feels my learning disability case is weak, given one of the clinicians who diagnosed me with dyscalculia was my mother—fair enough. Also, I've only attempted one basic algebra class—years ago—and withdrew after seven weeks because I was already failing pitifully.

There's some discussion about the possibility of a computerized algebra course, designed to integrate information slowly. But, JB said this suggestion is bogus. I have a clinical diagnosis. Why should I prolong my graduation just to prove how inept I am? He has the syllabus and readings for the alternative sociological math course ready to go. All we need is administrative permission to begin. He even called the student law clinic. He asked if my family had a lawyer.

JB tromped around the living room, almost yelling as he informed me of these matters. I meekly perched on the sofa, lips gummed together, intimidated by his display of frustration. Eventually, I bid him to sit down. He grasped my hands, promising to fight to the end on my behalf, and not to worry; sometimes, all it takes is a letter from a lawyer to get the university to bow. Then, he dropped the subject.

Magda—the colleague he's dating—has been [out of the country] for a class trip. JB picked her up from the airport yesterday. He plans to end things, but it wasn't the right time, just after she's returned from a trip abroad. Pending that necessary conversation, we're holding off on "the hot and heavy stuff," as he called it.

It didn't stop us from kissing until my lips were chapped and peeling. It didn't stop his hands from slipping beneath my clothes to stroke my stomach or clutch my ass. It didn't stop us from, somehow, becoming entangled on the kitchen floor, my legs folded around his waist, face lost in his neck. From there, JB stood, carrying me, a whimpering little doll, back to the couch.

He encouraged me to snooze, but I resisted, saying I'd crash once I got home. He said he would do the same once I'd left, after "taking care of something." I joked that I could leave my knickers for him to smell while he masturbated, but he'd have to remove them himself.

Locking eyes with mine, he reached for the button on my pants.

"You're *serious*? You want to do that?"

He didn't reply. My back arched as he unfastened my jeans and slowly pulled them and my underwear down together.

"Oh my god," he marveled, running his hands over my legs. "You're so beautiful, so sexy. Brains *and* beauty—wow." He kissed my bare feet, tucking a toe briefly into his mouth.

I giggled and swayed my knees. He untangled my underwear from my jeans and smelled them—*argh!* Then, he helped me back into my jeans and kissed my stomach.

Our time spent wasn't entirely spent testing our boundaries. We talked for hours. I'm thrilled to learn about him, his work and experiences on campus. He says he loves having me over, that I make him feel more alive than he's felt in a long time.

I'm so glad. I've loved this man as a role model and mentor for years; I'm finding it easy to love him in other ways, which is daunting and a little disorientating, but feels almost natural. What matters most is that I can be myself around him.

Last night, I asked how long he'd been attracted to me.

"Since your first class with me, in Intro." He described how he'd admired my forthrightness and grasp of the concepts. He'd also found me physically appealing and liked how I dressed: my black clothes and, more specifically, my striped socks.

He had to be joking. Back then, I was a twenty-two year-old, irreverent little shit!

"So, why *now*?" I pressed. "Why didn't you wait until May?"

JB winced and his tone became somber. "I'd been so sick last year. At times, I thought I was going to die. I wanted you to know how I felt while I still had the chance—before something happened to me or before you moved for graduate school."

Though my chest constricted with sympathy, I was somewhat confused. "I thought I'd told you I was only looking at low-residency programs."

He laughed. "Oh, no. I thought you'd go anywhere to get the hell out of your parents' place."

Ha! His presumption was a sound one. God knows, I've complained enough about living in the unsettling aftermath of Dad's hoarding and domestic negligence. Still, I corrected him, explaining how I hoped to move to [the city] and live with Alex.

JB smiled, saying he didn't want to step on Alex's toes, but he could definitely see us cohabitating—if all goes well, of course.

How is this my life? This feels like a movie.

16 January 2016

Current mood: stressed

Current music: Sóley, "I'll Drown"

My god, *this* text exchange from yesterday:

> JB: Leaving school—Good progress made today on the math stuff… But enjoy your weekend and don't fucking worry about that nonsense (peace out).
>
> *Me: No use worrying over that which I have no control, so I'm planning to enjoy myself this weekend. Thank you for all of your help, doc.*
>
> *This cold weather sucks. I woke up feeling like I wrestled a bear all night, which I guess I kind of did :P*
>
> :) :) …At least until the wee hours of the night …Yes it's super cold today (starting a trash can fire now).
>
> *I'm cutting up your jeans right now. Absolutely never stopping to bury my face in them and smell. Not me :)*
>
> You make me blush :) …It's not like I have an article of your clothing that I carried with me all day.

My jaw flopped open. I was in bed with [my cats] Filburt and Gojira and gasped so loudly it startled them; they jerked their heads and blinked at me.

> *…all…day, Jack? Like, with you?*
>
> I know, I'm creepy …It was balled up in my pocket (felt like I was carrying your positive energy with me today—I meant it to be more sweet than sexual) :) ..
>
> *No. I'm delighted. And flattered.*
>
> :) ;) …Yes, feeling a bit smitten, I am …Kisses for you.

Graciously accepting of your kisses. I am a smitten kitten, as well

Well, fuck. Dr. Blair, with my underwear in his pocket. Dr. Blair, enamored with me, his adoring pupil.

And yet... However fun and naughty, I know it's not justifiable. I'm brutally aware of this, even as I try to fool myself into believing that succumbing to the affair is the better choice. Jack—I should start using his proper name—is far more concerned about me than himself. He's reiterated that if we're discovered, though it would affect his reputation, the worst of the damage would befall me.

So far, I'm not apologetic. The threat of being caught, ruining my life, and staining his career, is terrifying. But, I'm not sorry. It was my idea to kiss him. I don't believe he would've touched me if I hadn't presented it as an option, made the first move.

I don't condone lying. I'm raw and forthcoming, a brazen, passionate force. My clothes are black with flashes of color and pattern, stretching taut to contain my shapeless body. Tattoos grin across my flesh. Nose and lip piercings dot my face, with a dozen more in both ears. And in an incongruent attempt at cultural modesty, I cover my head in public—*oy*.

Were I a quiet, mousy woman, but that isn't me. Not in the presence of others anyway. In private, my confidence is suspended and my insecurities rule me. I forget how to be brave and apologize for my very existence, suddenly convinced of how obnoxious I must be.

I won't survive this if I don't learn to conceal truths. Every speck of me brays in protest—but whatever is developing between me and Jack... I hope it's worth it.

All considered, I'm an emotional wreck. The ambiguity about the algebra class is especially overwhelming. Surely, something can be done. If my graduation is delayed over this or for any other reason, it would *completely* sabotage my designs for the immediate future.

Graduate in May. Take a year off. Write. Submit. Do some volunteer work in the summer. Take on a seasonal, part-time job in the fall to build up my savings. Start applying to MFA programs in the winter. Get accepted somewhere. Start during the summer session. Find a decent job in [the city]. Move in with Alex (finally). Finish grad school. Start teaching. Boom.

These plans have been my lullaby, and I'm determined to see them through. Otherwise, what do I have to show for everything I've ascended over the last eight years?

23 January 2016

Current mood: cold
Current music: Daughter, "Youth"

Jack finally saw me without a headscarf. We were seated on his bed, talking—taking breaks to hungrily kiss and paw at each other. His hands circulated over my sweater and tank top, which I finally pulled off. I straddled him and with a swipe, I removed my headscarf.

He gasped, awed. "I haven't seen your hair in *so long*." His fingers dug into it, tugging the locks until our mouths met, until my mouth met his penis, until my folds cradled him, until he began to come, and I met him again with my mouth, swallowing.

No coming back from that, my absolute nakedness. Outside of family, no menfolk see me without a headscarf unless we're lovers. And goddamnit, I'm in love with Jack.

Classes start on Tuesday. I went by the library to see if the tutors were scheduled. My supervisor turned me away with a shrug and a smile. No one was around. Outside, it was snowing.

I walked to Jack's. He was almost giddy as he ushered me inside.

It was the first time I'd been to his house before nightfall. I remarked on the warm glow of sunlight slinking in through the window blinds. After a pause, I asked, "Jack, can I make a confession?"

"Sure, of course."

"I'm falling in love with you. You don't have to say anything, but that's how I feel."

He hugged me. "Thank you for telling me," he said, adding that his own emotions are both exciting and challenging. He'd need to be certain before he expressed the same sentiment. I appreciate that he's being cautious. The prospect of love is complicated for us both.

I prepared myself for a difficult phone call with Alex. I've kept him informed, tip-toeing around the exact nature of what's happened with statements like, "we've kissed" and "we've fooled around." He doesn't like to be privy to frank details anyway, regardless of the lover.

All I had to say was that things with Jack had gotten "more serious." Alex knew what that meant and wasn't pleased. "You can forget about me visiting this weekend," he declared. "I don't want to see you right now, or talk to you for a while"—click.

Oy, meyn harts.

Some hours later, Alex rang back. He sounded close to tears. My *kishkas* swelled with guilt. I took my phone downstairs and walked circles in the kitchen, fiddled with items on the counter and sucked on a cigarette.

He echoed all of my fears about what Jack and I are doing, the risks involved. He emphasized how important academia is to me and couldn't believe I'd do something that could jeopardize my goals. "If he really wants to protect you, then why didn't he just wait until you've graduated?" Alex demanded. "It's fucking *impulsive*. He can't honestly give a damn about you if he's allowing this to happen now—and you can tell him I said that."

Alex was further annoyed by how calm I stayed during the call, but how else should I react? He's absolutely right. All of his concerns are legitimate. I know this is inexcusable. Jack knows it too.

What was I supposed to do? This thing was like a red-hot, speeding train. Once it began to move, there was no stopping it. As soon as Jack hit on me, what should I have done? Brushed him off? Ignored him and his text messages?

How does one reject their academic adviser five months before graduation, while enrolled in four classes with him—someone they've looked up to for years? Feigned disinterest or ignorance? At what cost? Argh! It just *is* what it *is*. And because I'm a sap, I've fallen in love, so it's all the more *fakakta*.

Alex said we had to come up with an alternative plan. "I just can't sit here and know this is going on and be anxious all the time for you," he fretted. "I feel like I care more about your future than you or he does right now, and it pisses me the fuck off."

I tried to assure him, but it was pointless, like confronting the wind with breath.

The following morning, I turned up early for my tutoring shift and told [my close friend and fellow tutor] Naomi I was going by the sociology department to grab a cup of coffee. She responded with a mischievous wink.

While the coffee brewed, I stood at the reception desk to chat with [my friend] Troy, who works in the department. Jack walked in, surprised to see me. I greeted him coolly to keep up appearances. He asked if I had a couple of minutes to talk.

Once he'd shut the door to his office, he launched into an update on my learning disability case. I guess some administrative staff have begun to ignore his calls and emails.

"I feel like I'm either going to have a heart attack or start ripping out people's throats," he grumbled. But besides that, how was I doing?

"I talked to Alex last night, and he gave me an ultimatum," I whispered.

"Oh. He doesn't like that there's a new person?"

"No, it's not that it's a new person, but who that person *is*. Am I still coming over tonight?"

Yes, I was. Cool.

We shared a quick, silent kiss before I left.

Jack was still keyed up that evening. As soon as I arrived, he began outlining what he'd done to help my case that afternoon, which included calling disability advocates with legal services and speaking to the university's ADA coordinator, Linda Barrow.

The school would provide accommodations to disabled students, Dr. Barrow stated, but bypassing a general education requirement wasn't an option. He reminded her we were trying to pursue an alternative course. He said something about how the way she interpreted the law wasn't shared by other legal professionals. Dr. Barrow then threatened if a lawsuit was filed, his relationship to me would be subject to investigation.

For the love of Hashem, no. No, Jack.

"If we came under investigation, we would be *fucked*." I pleaded for him to stop—stop until we've heard from Susan in student services. On Wednesday, she'd said she was preparing a final statement for the committee assigned to review my case. Wait, I urged. It'll get figured out.

Given the fear and defeat hanging in my face, Jack submitted. He coaxed me into his lap, where I momentarily relaxed before describing my conversation with Alex. Jack grew sad and fidgety. He said he cares about how my other partners feel because he worries about me getting hurt. "So, we need to find a middle path that would appease Alex."

"Yes, and what does that look like to you?" I asked if I should limit my visits.

"No way." Though, if we have to hold off until graduation,

he said he'd be willing to do so. "But once the summer hits, I don't care; I'm taking you on a trip."

"Jack, you're already planning to go to Iceland this summer." For research.

"Then, I'll take you to Iceland with me."

From there, he divulged how surprising the magnitude of his feelings are for me, how he's often felt the need to check himself because it's *so much*. Yet, he's prepared to practice distance if our situation called for it.

So, that's where things now stand. On Friday, [department head] Dr. Parsons told Jack that Linda Barrow had sent out an email to all parties, asking to schedule a committee meeting.

Baruch Hashem. Now, we just have to wait. And wait. And wait.

28 January 2016

Current mood: scared
Current music: Puscifer, "Grand Canyon"

I recently spoke to [my long distance partner] Kamyar. Blizzards have been raging along the East Coast. He sent me a photo of the snow outside his front door, its height dictated by a tape measurer: two feet. He said he'd spent all of Sunday shoveling out his driveway. I giggled, saying I'd love to watch him perform manual labor. I've only ever seen him dressed to the nines, his thick black hair immaculately styled. He even looks tidy in his sleep.

I informed Kamyar about Jack weeks ago—after he'd admitted to being attracted to me—but I hadn't had the chance to relay the newest developments. Kam's reaction was far less severe than Alex's, though he also bid me to be careful. When I asked if he minded, Kam said so long as I was happy, he was happy for me.

"It's so unfair," he lamented. "People fall in love, and what's the harm? It shouldn't matter that you're his student."

Well, perhaps in most cases, it *does* matter. But, not in mine. Not really.

The committee meets tomorrow.

I've been so on edge. I've had trouble sleeping. I've had no appetite; sometimes, I forget to eat until I feel weak or feverish. In the mirror, I watch my bones steadily become more prominent. The physical shift testifies to what's happening, although my affect must appear indifferent. As I've always hated my body, I hate dishonesty. Will I have to drag the lies as I drag this shapeless flesh-sack with each movement, day after day?

No. I'll get through the next few months, and once Jack and I are in the clear, I will fess up and beg forgiveness from the few people I've misled. I hope they'll understand.

Yesterday, I pulled my wedding dress from its box in my closet. I still love it, its wispy feel, the cream mesh and black lace, the sea-green satin and ivory polka dots. I wonder how I ever believed I'd marry Cody in that dress. That part of me seems so far gone, though it's only been about two years since we broke up.

I've set aside the dress to be worn at graduation. I don't like wondering when I'll put it on again.

I've been in college since the fall of 2007. My first class was Freshman Composition. Since then, the years have been characterized by a whirling jumble of external strife and self-destructive response. And while academia provided the accountability and structure to stay afloat and persist, I'm ready to move on. I'm bright, have great potential, and am driven (when I'm not crippled by self-doubt), but I'm also tired. I've outgrown my undergraduate status.

It has to be over soon—especially now, while I find myself smothered by fear and paranoia. Because I've fallen in love with the wrong person.

February

1 February 2016

Current mood: sleepy

Current music: Agnes Obel, "Fuel to Fire"

It's after eleven, and Mom's asleep. I arrived home too late to see her off to bed. When this happens, I always peek in on her. Sometimes, the vibrations of my steps rouse her, and we speak for a moment before I urge her back to sleep. Otherwise, I listen to her breathing for a moment and creep away, my anxiety quelled.

I can't sleep just yet. I've brought my laptop downstairs to huddle against the backdoor on the kitchen's crusty, peeling linoleum. Here, I smoke while I type, though Mom hates that I occasionally smoke inside. By my assessment, the smoke improves the smell in the house. Despite clearing out most of Dad's hoarded junk, the walls themselves seem to emit a swampy musk.

The committee met at one o'clock on Friday. At two-thirty, Susan called. She said I've been tentatively approved to take the alternative course with Dr. Blair in place of college algebra—with the condition that further documentation be provided. If a disability assessment shows that I do not, in fact, have dyscalculia, I'll be pulled from the course and a different conversation will begin. If the documentation supports the diagnosis, I'll remain in the course and graduate on time.

Baruch Hashem! My trembling guts can finally begin to relax!

I must also write about last night. Jack and I somehow arrived at the subject of betrayal. I divulged some specifics about my failed engagement with Cody: having already purchased the dress, getting a refund on our wedding venue, and how he'd started dating a friend within days of our breakup. We recently reconnected, and he's apologized profusely, but I still suffer twinges of bitterness and mourn certain aspects of our whirlwind romance.

I asked Jack if he'd been betrayed. Yes, he said. His former fiancée Teresa had confessed to cheating on him during an argument. However, at the time, this was of little concern to him.

They'd met and lived together during grad school. As their relationship progressed, Teresa's eating disorder worsened. She was dying right in front of him, he said. He wanted her to seek treatment, but she was combative and eventually moved out. He tried to stay in touch, but she died before things between them were resolved. She'd suffered cardiac arrest, which is unfortunately common for individuals with eating disorders.

"I didn't know I could fall in love again like that," Jack concluded. Then, he said, "You know, I want to take care of you."

"Jack, you've been taking care of me for six years." Because academically, he has been.

He laughed, "No. I want to take care of you in other ways now."

Clothes were peeled away. Our eyeglasses were carefully set aside. Jack's long bulk spread over me. As I climaxed, he cupped my mouth with his and drank up my brays. I tore at his shirt and my toes went numb.

We cuddled long enough for our sweat to evaporate into salt. It was getting late, and he had to be up early for class. He didn't want me to go, and I didn't want to leave.

5 February 2016

Current mood: in love

Current music: The Cure, "The Forest"

Last night, Jack sighed while I rocked and lifted my hips around him. "I still can't believe that it's you," he breathed.

Surreal—it's our word for this year.

It's hard to explain. In private, we are liberated. He's a confidant, a lover. In public, he's someone else: an authority, an instructor. I have trouble understanding that the differing statuses are embodied by the same actor.

When I see him on campus, I recognize him immediately. That's the environment wherein I'm most familiar with him. Elsewhere, I dissect his animations, the soft angles of his profile, and I ponder this person's identity. That man is Jack, rather than Dr. Blair. I know they're synonymous, but comprehending this fact is surprisingly difficult and requires a lot of cognitive flip-flopping.

On Mondays, we meet in his office to discuss coursework for both my internship and (now) Mathematical Sociology. The work is going well, but when he grasps my hand under the desk or sneaks kisses before I leave... How do I wrap my head around it? Violating the boundaries that define our statuses is a mind-fuck.

It's incredible to hear how he's admired me over the years and all of the little things he remembers from our interactions. And I'd just considered him a beloved teacher, and at most, a mentor to meet for coffee, as I've done with other professors.

This Monday, once the office door was closed, Jack reached across his desk, grabbed my hand, and whispered intensely, "YOU—you distract me so much! You distract me more than anyone has!"

I recoiled and apologized.

"No, no," he replied. "Don't be sorry—I like it! It's welcomed."

I can barely corral my thoughts long enough to get anything done for class—his coursework or otherwise. In British Lit, I sit with my head cradled over my textbook, bite my lip, and sigh. I try to listen and take notes, but inevitably drift away until I'm shuddering against my seat.

The third week of the semester has just ended, and it couldn't go by fast enough. It's becoming increasingly apparent that carrying on this secret relationship is one of the most rewarding, yet difficult things I've ever done. Yes, I'm unravelling. I'm scared and sick with love.

Before I left his house last night, Jack asked if I thought we could have made it the four months without doing anything.

I answered, "Maybe."

Smiling, he said, "I don't think so, either."

21 February 2016

Current mood: depressed

Current music: Nine Inch Nails, "The Day the World Went Away"

I dreamt Jack and I were found out. We'd been invited to a dinner party and were conversing with two other faculty members on the porch. Beyond us, the yard expressed a summer's lush green and glittered with fireflies. I'd found a place on a porch swing. As Jack lowered himself into a nearby chair, he slipped and crashed to the floorboards.

Rocketing to my feet, I cried out, "Are you okay, baby?"

The two professors gawked. My outburst was the announcement of a scandal.

I immediately awoke in terror.

Apart from this, I've been feeling out of sorts. On our off

days, Jack offers to ring me at bedtime. These calls mostly don't take place, and when I text him, I get no reply. I know he's busy, in poor health and tired by the end of each day. I'm unsure what expectations I can realistically have, but...

Ugh. Okay. I'm a worrywart. And Jack's health *is* worrisome, so my fears get the best of me. When he says he'll call and I don't hear from him, I balloon with anxiety and imagine a variety of disastrous scenarios.

Like, tonight. We'd arranged to hang out after Alex returned to [the city]. At six PM, I sent Jack a message to confirm. About thirty minutes later, he backtracked:

> Actually sweets—do you mind if we take a rain check till tomorrow... I'm starting to feel super shitty and need to lay down for a few.

My subsequent call and text messages went unanswered.

How do I approach this? The next time Jack says, "I'll call you later," should I reply, "That's okay. I'll just get in touch with you tomorrow?" That seems passive-aggressive.

Surely it's reasonable to be irritated when people don't do what they say they're going to do. Normally, I'm direct with partners, but... Well, I'm pretty hesitant to ask my professor and academic adviser to do anything.

Dr. Blair, it bothers me when you say you're going to contact me at the end of the day, and then fail to do so. However, given we're engaging in an unethical secret relationship, I don't feel I have the power to express my frustration. Rather, I'd prefer you make me no assurances than to disappoint me when you cannot uphold them because it makes me feel like an out-of-control crazy weirdo person. Thanks.

Yeah, perfect.

I feel terribly alone in this. I haven't been going to AA meetings. I can't see a counselor on campus (and can't afford to see one elsewhere). I'm afraid to visit most friends, as I don't trust myself not to slip. I already feel like too many people know. I knew this would be difficult, but I wasn't prepared for the extent to which it's alienated me from others and fueled my depression.

On Saturday, I met [my friend] Alice at [a bar and restaurant near my house]. We sipped soda waters and shared a cigarette while I talked. At first, she blamed my mood on my period. I countered, describing my paranoia-induced isolation. She then apologized for not recognizing my struggles sooner and said she'd be willing to listen whenever I felt the need to talk.

Alex, too, has offered to be a listener. Thankfully, his attitude toward Jack in recent weeks has softened from an anxious resistance to begrudging tolerance. But, I don't want to invite his previous sentiments to reemerge, so I try not to burden him with more than he needs to hear.

I just need time to go by. I just need to get the fuck through this.

22 February 2016

Current mood: anxious
Current music: Sóley, "Follow Me Down"

After class, I rang Jack and wandered the library until locating an empty chair in a secluded section of the basement.

He explained he'd gone to the ER twice this weekend. "As you know, being familiar with chronic pain, describing pain in words is often difficult... It was terrible. In my back, along my spine. I felt like I was being turned inside out, while simultaneously feeling like I'm on fire."

I experience mild chronic pain, mostly in my knees, shoulders, and neck. What Jack recounted was beyond me.

The results of his blood-work and the MRI were confusing

and "didn't add up," he said. A doctor eventually just shot him full of morphine and sent him home to sleep. I'm amazed he made it to campus today.

I felt awkward mentioning our communication mishaps—"we can discuss it later"—but he urged me to share.

"I didn't sleep well last night," I said. "I woke up in cold sweats. I just felt like something was off with you. I understand if you're insecure about having me around when you're ill, but I'd still like to be informed."

Jack said he hadn't had an "attack" like this in months, and it dredged up some traumatizing, even suicidal feelings. It alarmed him, in part, because of our relationship. As he's experiencing the bliss of being in love, he's still sick, and no one can tell him why. It's incredibly unfair.

I did my best to console him, and we agreed to see each other tomorrow.

He probably wonders how his health will affect us. When his symptoms first appeared, he'd been dating Tracy Hines, another faculty member. His illness had contributed to their separation. He's also said [his recent ex and colleague] Magda took it personally when he was too sick to hang out or be physically intimate. But, I know myself to be understanding and recognize Jack's illness has nothing to do with his feelings for me.

I'm scared, though. I hate the power behind my thoughts. I don't even realize I'm entertaining intrusive scenarios until my heart is racing, chest heaving. If anything were to happen to Jack—were he hospitalized or gravely ill—how would I find out? How would I react?

I imagine not hearing from him and becoming twisted with fear. Faking nonchalance, I'd ask Dr. Parsons if she's heard from JB. What details could she afford me? If he's in the hospital—where? If she tells me, I'd thank her and excuse myself. I'd tear down the halls, off campus, run all the way to my car and peel off. What then? Would I be stopped by hospital staff? Who would I say I am: his student or his partner?

What if the news was devastating—that he was in a coma or on life support *or worse*? Would I collapse in Dr. Parsons's office? Would I cry or scream?

Of course, I'm terrified of losing him. Across countless hours in the dark, splayed over his mattress, or intertwined on the sofa, we've pieced together the life we intend to share.

Last Thursday, he'd said it was really easy to love me. I'd laughed, taken aback. "That's definitely not been the consensus."

"Well, I see why being in a polyamorous relationship would be hard for other people," Jack remarked. "Being with you is such an intoxicating experience, so it makes sense people would want to keep you all to themselves."

Later in bed, I broke from his kiss, and breathed, "I cannot promise I will always be easy, but I can promise I'll never take you for granted."

"No," he replied, "you don't have to make any promises. *Life* isn't easy." He added more about us growing together—I don't remember his exact words, but I felt him and his message was conveyed.

March

1 March 2016

Current mood: sleepy
Current music: Placebo, "Blind"

Jack half-jokes about signing his 401(k) over to me, "just in case." While this speaks to his sense of commitment, it also freaks me out. Thankfully, his communication has improved on days when we're apart. Now, I'm mostly left with the usual, ever-present crushing fears about being found out. Awesome.

We were nearly caught in his office yesterday. At the very least, it was a close call.

Our weekly meeting was over. He'd grabbed me and ravenously claimed my mouth with his. Then, a knock at the door. The sound reverberated through me like thunder. I tore away from Jack and began collecting my things as he opened the door.

It was Magda. They had plans to walk to the art building to view a student's show. "We need to get going," she said delicately.

"Oh, I'm leaving anyway!" I declared, chasing the last of my papers into my bag.

Jack stepped through the doorway and turned to give me a high five, squeeze my arm, and—out of sight of Magda—mouthed, "*Love you.*"

Once they'd gone, I lingered there, trembling and gulping for air.

This weekend, Alex agreed to visit on short notice, so Jack had me over on Friday night. Within a couple of hours, he nodded off on the couch. I crept upstairs and amused myself by flipping through some books. In the garage, I smoked and made calls to Cody and [my best friend] Amber. Eventually, I brushed my teeth and crawled into Jack's bed. Lulled by the creak of the ceiling fan, I fell asleep.

In the morning, Jack stroked my head and said to sleep as long as I wanted. He'd left his house key on a table downstairs.

It was past ten when I finally awoke. Desperate for coffee, I quickly dressed, slipped his key on a ring, and walked home. Freshly showered and changed, I drove back to Jack's with my laptop and a basket of dirty clothes.

I'm grateful Jack has permitted me to use his washer and dryer. At home, stray animals have been wriggling into the basement through the crumbling rifts in the concrete foundation. Mom and I routinely hear knocks and bangs, as opossums climb into the basement's ceiling, their rotound little bodies colliding with the air ducts. Mom began taking her clothes to the laundromat months ago.

While my clothes spun, I washed dishes and wiped off the counters in Jack's kitchen. Then, I settled into the sofa with my laptop and began writing.

x

"Your mascara is running," he says. A finger curls over my cheek.

We have just made love. I don't tell him I'm terrified, that the tears were in fact echoes—*don't go, don't leave me*—before being absorbed by his sweater.

x

Erving Goffman proposed that we reinvent reality with every social interaction. Identities and facts about the self are constantly being reaffirmed or erased. So, what does it mean for the individual who behaves in secret? Who is one who hides?

x

He doesn't know that after leaving, I splay myself across the kitchen floor, where the daylight pools. For hours, I loop Mozart's *Requiem* in D minor and kiss the sun on the filmy linoleum. I lap at my lips and cough, but fail to conjure the essence of him.

x

She's become a lightbulb burning the last of its filament. Friends point out her embarrassing lack of presence. They ask when she last ate.

x

Jack returned around five o'clock. After shedding his jacket and joining me on the couch, he started to cry. It felt so natural coming home to me, he explained. Both beautiful and frightening because his illness eventually ruins everything. It finally dawned on me. "Are you afraid to love me the way you really want to because you're afraid you're going to die?"

"Yes," he sobbed.

There were no words. Just my small quivering hands stroking his back.

Before long, I had to go. Alex was on his way to my house, and I hurried to meet him.

We went to [a nearby bar and restaurant] for dinner. As Alex ordered a beer at the counter, I crafted a long message to Jack:

I love you and I'm not going anywhere. I want to be where you are. I'm scared too, but I'm not going to let silly ole' fear sabotage what's truly good about our relationship.

On Sunday, Alex headed back to [the city], and Jack invited me over. As soon as I sat down, he acknowledged my text message. "You said some really beautiful things."

"I meant everything."

"I know this," he said. "I can feel it."

Then, we made love on the living room floor.

5 March 2016

Current mood: relieved

Current music: Razed in Black, "Nevermeant_V2"

Per the conditions laid out by the committee in charge of my learning disability case, I had an assessment completed. According to the assessor's findings, I scored between average and high average in areas relating to language arts and writing (which is obviously very validating). Conversely, in the mathematics portions, I scored between low average and very low, "indicating these tasks are Very Difficult to Nearly Impossible to complete." Depending on the mathematical area in question, I have the same capacities as the average seven- to ten-year-old.

Well, fuck. *That* bad, huh?

I shouldn't be surprised. [My brother] Sam has said I'm so bad at math, it's like a parlor trick. He was kind enough to repeat this joke when I informed him of the assessment's results.

The report states I meet the criteria for dyscalculia and my impairment should be considered severe, "meaning that even with an array of accommodations and services, [I] may be incapable of completing [algebra] courses successfully." The assessor recommended the committee waive the "College Algebra requirement for graduation as any college-level math course may be nearly impossible for Ms. Phoenix to successfully complete." She also wrote, "Ms. Phoenix was a pleasure to work with and put forth a very strong effort throughout the evaluation...Despite her various struggles...she demonstrated perseverance and dedication to this assessment"—which was kind of her to add.

Wonderful news—sort of! I only need to obtain a couple of signatures and see that the registrar's office has cleared me to graduate—and obviously, to continue the alternative math course with Jack.

24 March 2016

Current mood: cheerful

Current music: Sisters of Mercy, "Dominion/Mother Russia"

I'm in Chicago for a sociology conference, sharing a hotel room with [my friend] Martel, his former mentor and the mentor's wife—darling people. I've come to the lobby so Martel can focus on his presentation. Last night, he admitted he could've polished his materials sooner, but couldn't be bothered. I appreciate his attitude; I take academics too seriously sometimes.

Jack is here, as well as Zach Cantor, a new professor in the department. Yesterday, they invited me to lunch with them, and I accepted, having no plans until Martel arrived in the evening.

We found a sushi restaurant nearby. From there, Jack invited me to his hotel room, where we fell into bed. He'd packed condoms, which surprised me—like, he'd planned for us to have sex here. I'd honestly not considered it.

Oof, I should stop writing now. Martel's panel starts in twenty minutes.

26 March 2016

Current mood: exhausted

Current music: Shostakovich, "Concerto for Violin and Orchestra #1 in A"

After his presentation, Martel slipped away to see some mates from grad school. Jack and I ditched the conference to tour the Chicago Art Institute and purchased tickets to see a special exhibit of Van Gogh's *Bedroom* paintings. It was extraordinary to view all three on display together and to compare the differences in perspective and color choice.

The exhibit was fucking packed, triggering Jack's social anxiety. At one point, he asked if we could stand against the wall while he caught his breath. Once we resumed our tour, I stayed nearby and offered small, soothing touches when his face hinted of strain.

At dinnertime, we reconnected with Zach and walked to a nearby Indian restaurant. They began discussing faculty-specific bollocks, so I remained a listener rather than a contributor during most of the meal.

Somehow, the alternative math course was brought up. Jack outlined the concepts I've been studying, then turned to me, saying, "I hope you've found this class to be exceptionally interesting!"

I choked and excused myself. I hustled to the restroom, where I burst with wild laughter. A little girl exited one of the stalls, and I stepped aside so she could wash her hands and glance warily at me in the mirror.

Later, I told Jack why I'd suddenly gotten up: because of what he'd done the previous Monday. I'd been skimming through some articles on his laptop, when he locked his office door and knelt down by the desk. His hand slipped up my dress and down my tights. As I squirmed under his touch, he calmly instructed me to order a book through interlibrary loan. Then, he moved to the opposite side of the desk, unbuckled his pants, and pulled out his erection. He spit onto his palm and began to masturbate. Finally, he ejaculated onto the carpet.

My eyes were frozen wide, hands pressed over my mouth to muffle nervous giggles.

So, yes. I suppose I am finding the alternative math class to be "exceptionally interesting."

April

13 April 2016

Current mood: confused

Current music: Philip Glass, "Violin Concerto #2"

About two weeks ago, Alex and I flew to Los Angeles, where I attended a writers' conference. While I fluttered around the convention center, Alex explored the city in a rental car. I'd also arranged to have dinner with a friend from home: Thea, who now lives and teaches there. Overall, it was a great trip—medicinal, really, given its effects on my mood. I was grateful to have a break from the *tsuris* at home and to spend some much needed quality time with Alex.

My sense of restoration didn't last long. On Thursday, Jack sent me a message explaining that people in the office have been in a shit mood, and he had an interview with a "big-time" drug dealer for his research, so we'd have to post-pone plans until the following evening.

I said that was fine, though I intended to swing by after my shift at the tutoring center to grab some leftover curry I'd cooked there on Monday.

He asked me to give him until seven PM. I got the impression he wanted space, so I added that I might just "take my lazy ass to the store."

A quarter after six, he sent a message:

> Hey—there is some weird shit going on at the house (Magda and I are fighting) so it's best to stay away.

I panicked slightly, praying she hadn't found something of mine in the house—like my quilt, which is laying in scraps on the floor of his spare room. I asked him about this, but he didn't respond until morning.

> Morning, love. Didn't see your earlier text. We were not fighting about the quilt or things like that… Fighting over selfishness and lack of empathy.

> *:(Oh wow. Ick! That sucks, honey. I'm sorry. Can I be there when you get home today?*

Usually, he'd be agreeable to this. He's constantly offering me his house as a sanctuary, a home away from home. Instead, he wrote,

> I'll call you—I'll be home late with job stuff.

> *Wow. All right, babe :/*

> It's not good stuff, babe. I'll try to see you later.

> In fact, it's terrible stuff. …But, anyway—I'm off to class. Talk soon.

> *Wtf, Jack?*

A thousand scenarios crashed through my head. Is he sick again? Are we found out? Is there something wrong with the house that he doesn't want me to see? *What the hell is going on?!* My curiosity took charge, and on my way to campus, I let myself into the townhouse to have a look around. The place was in order: no broken dishes, no furniture overturned, no evidence of fire.

Then, Susan called. There was a form for my academic adviser to sign. She needed it as soon as possible. Damn.

When there was a break between Jack's classes, I entered

his classroom and approached the podium. He received me with an enthusiastic grin. He signed the form and said he'd call in a little while. I told him not to worry about it, thanked him, and dipped out.

After some time, he sent another text message, to which I replied quickly.

I'll call you later, and we will be able to hang at the house.

I'm sorry about disturbing you between classes. Susan said she needed that sheet signed ASAP.

More back and forth. He asked if I was okay.

Yeah. I'm in a spot where I feel like I should give you space, but anxious to know what the "terrible" stuff is :/

I know I'm anxiety provoking. Sorry. Everything in time will be okay. I'll explain later—hard to do over text.

I'm just trying to protect you.

WHAT IN THE FUCK—I was driving when I read this second message. My chest took flight and my stomach clenched. At a stoplight, I managed to type a cool response:

And who asked you to do that? It certainly wasn't me.

I know, but you don't know the situation. I'll tell you later.

To eat up time, I dropped by Amber's and accompanied her and [my niece] to a thrift store. Jack sent a message around seven PM, inviting me over. It took another hour to wrap up with Amber, drive home, park my car, and walk to Jack's.

At first, he offered me food and drink. I declined.

"Well, I'll get right to it."

Please. For the love of Hashem.

First, he explained how he and Magda had argued because she wants to get back together. Jack insisted this isn't what he wants, referencing problems in their relationship, but she'd been dismissive and demanding.

Next, Jack said Eleanor [Dr. Parsons] requested to see him that morning. She started by confirming how he "likes to be the deviant" and "question the motives of the institution," but she's concerned he and I are too close. After the math fiasco, there's been "some talk" that he and I aren't actually working and are just "palling around."

Jack said this was bullshit; he treats me no differently than any other student, and I'm definitely completing coursework. "Well," Eleanor said, "I want you to write up a report detailing what's been done in the class." With that, their conversation ended.

Where the hell was this coming from?

Jack believes that because Magda feels slighted, she may be the source of "the talk" Eleanor mentioned, and suspects Magda may be monitoring his movements. He began to cry. He said he's committed to our relationship, but for now, we need to stop seeing each other romantically.

I hugged him. I didn't know what to say. He's the authority. He knows what's best.

The night carried on. We watched a little telly and chatted. I grew somber.

"You can say anything to me, you know," Jack offered, detecting my mood.

I said after all of this is over, we should just get married. "Fuck it," I declared frivolously. "My rabbi can officiate."

"So, *two* ceremonies, then," he replied. "I thought we could get married this summer at the pagan temple in Iceland."

"Are you *serious*?" I asked. I'd been joking around, yet he sounded measured, resolute.

"I've been thinking about it."

"ARE YOU FUCKING SERIOUS?"

He nodded, growing tearful again.

Holy shit. Oh my god!

Just to be sure, I asked if I should start looking for a dress, and he said yes. (*AHHH! Oh my god!*) He asked if he should wear a suit, and I told him to wear whatever the hell he wanted. I asked what color dress I should wear. He said something to match a grey suit—with a black silk tie and black shoes.

I asked about the weather in Iceland.

"If we go toward the middle of the summer, it'll be really nice," he said. "Chilly in the evenings, but with highs in the seventies."

I laughed, "So, I should bring a cardigan."

But, who would marry us?

"There *are* Jews in Iceland, you know," he teased. "I'm sure there's a rabbi in Reykjavík we could talk to, but I also thought we could have the high priest of the pagan temple officiate, and do something when we get back."

A small, informal reception? He liked the sound of this. The conversation eventually shifted to other topics, and the remainder of the evening was fairly unremarkable.

The following afternoon, Amber and I visited Naomi to mark her birthday. After we'd shared cake, Jack texted to inquire about my day. I responded, adding that if his proposal had been genuine, I was willing to marry him, one hundred percent. He wrote back saying he was serious.

I relayed all of this to Amber and Naomi, who shrieked with delight and offered to help me pick out a dress. Later, I called my mother to share the news.

But... There's a fly in the ointment, as Alex gently brought to my attention when we spoke that night. Yes, this is exciting, he affirmed; however, he cautioned me not to get carried away. "You've just got to get through the semester. He might be rushing into marriage because he's afraid he's going to die.

And if he improves or whatever, he might change his mind."

"And if he doesn't get better," I added, "he might retract everything because he's trying to shield me from his illness. I wouldn't put that past him."

"I'm sorry, babe. This is difficult."

"No, no," I insisted. "I need to hear this, and you're right."

Then yesterday, as if to validate Alex's warning, Jack confessed to feeling as though he's cheating me because he's a sick old man, and I deserve better.

I'm treading lightly. I'm confused as hell, and it's only gotten weirder.

He rang on Sunday evening, and we discussed the possibility of absconding to [the city] for a day. Jack suggested I call-in sick to work on Tuesday.

The following afternoon, I appeared for our usual Monday meeting. We were interrupted when Jack received a call to confirm a doctor's appointment for the next day. So, no skipping town. "Another time," I remarked.

"No," he persisted, "I'm determined to see you this week."

That evening, in the middle of British Lit, my phone buzzed. I crept from the classroom and exited the building, standing off to its side for privacy.

"Go ahead and call in sick and just come by the house in the morning," Jack encouraged. "Bring your laundry, do your homework—just make yourself at home." We would spend the afternoon together after his appointment.

Honestly, this didn't make sense. I pointed out that if I brought my laundry, I'd need to use my car to haul the baskets over, and wouldn't it look suspicious parked out front? Especially if he's concerned about Magda keeping an eye on him?

But, he said not to worry. So, I arrived in the morning and immediately started a load of laundry so the delicates would have time to hang-dry over the railing in the stairwell, over the tops of doors. For hours, I stewed over my *Wuthering Heights* research paper. When my head began to feel like it was packed with scrambled eggs, I closed the lid of my laptop and tidied up around the house.

It was nearly five o'clock when Jack finally came home and immediately scooped me up. We kissed and play-wrestled on the floor. He asked if there was anything I wanted to do. I suggested we head to bed.

Jack's face wrinkled with irritation. "We can't. That would violate our new terms. I thought I'd made these clear when we spoke on Friday."

What the hell? I was already in his house. We were kissing, rolling around on the rug. Why would it matter if we had sex?

I felt gaslighted. I thought our new boundaries were meant to curtail suspicion while our conduct is being scrutinized, and until the tension with Magda subsides. So, we shouldn't make love, but it's okay to have my car parked outside; have my clothes scattered all over his house; and be physically intimate—but not to have sex?

I don't understand.

19 April 2016

Current mood: hurt

Current music: Bauhaus, "Mask"

Very troubling news. As Jack put it, a person from my "inner circle of friends" has "betrayed" me. Apparently, an anonymous caller left a message with the sociology department. They asserted that Jack couldn't be trusted with female students—specifically those doing independent studies with him—and that he's a creep and is "currently being exploitative of a female student."

Jack described the situation during a call last week, after I'd questioned his behavior at the house and stated how I'd felt gaslighted. He said he hadn't divulged the full story before because he was trying to protect me and didn't want me to feel as though I had to instigate a "witch-hunt" among my beloved friends.

Given the caller's diction, I think it was [my friend] Thea. During our visit in LA, she hadn't reacted well when I disclosed my relationship with Jack. I can't imagine any of my other friends would report us. Many of them have had Jack as a professor and seem to support our relationship.

Jack said he'll now have to undergo sexual harassment training and have supervision when overseeing independent study courses with female students (which is ridiculous, but not awful considering how badly things *could* have gone). Still, even with this additional information, I sense there's more he isn't telling me.

So, no more private visits until after graduation. I guess doing my laundry at his house last Tuesday was a fluke.

Strangely enough, I feel pretty detached, emotionally blank. Jack noted he feels similarly: shutdown, yet angry. He said the thought of someone trying to hurt me fills him with rage.

I haven't said a word to Thea. I don't plan to.

I'm just so embarrassed. I entrusted the wrong person with my life's secret, and now Jack has to suffer for it.

May

1 May 2016

Current mood: hopeful

Current music: Bach, "Violin Concerto #2 in E major BWV 1042 2nd Mvmt Adagio"

Every year, [the university] hosts an event for students to showcase exceptional projects. This year, I signed up to give a poetry reading and a presentation on how I've used ethnomathematics to circumvent features of my learning disability in the making of my denim quilt.

I hoped to use my final paper in Sociological Math as the foundation for the presentation. Single-spaced and seven pages long, it's dense as fuck (because I'm a loquacious asshole). On Monday, Jack had me recite it to him, which took almost thirty minutes, so I definitely had to make cuts. We met again on Tuesday and Thursday. He slashed most of the essay to limit my narration to the allotted fifteen minutes.

During one of these meetings, I was reading aloud when he interrupted, "Hey, look up."

He was standing in the corner behind his desk. He'd loosened his pants, extracted his dick, and was jerking off in front of me—again.

"JACK."

"Shh," he cautioned. "Keep reading."

I hid my face in my paper.

"Go on."

I sucked my teeth, retraced my spot, and continued. When he came, he repeated, "Hey, look." Semen splattered across the wall and carpet.

I nearly tore my pages, biting them to contain an astonished outburst.

Jack obviously enjoys teasing the forbidden, but it freaks *me* out. Yes, we're lovers, but I'm *still* his student and prefer to focus on my studies in these meetings. I mean, kissing is fine, though this gets more heated than I'd like, when he envelops me, drinks me up. Time rolls by, and he won't let go... I suppose I can't blame him. We've not been in private together for a while. Until Friday night, actually.

Amber had a date planned with [a friend in a nearby city] and suggested I use her house to rendezvous with Jack. Since he usually feels sick after working all week, I thought he'd dismiss the idea. But, he said he'd keep me posted.

Everything hit me on Wednesday afternoon when [my ex-boyfriend] Pat rang to check in. I broke down, outlining my concerns for Jack; the anonymous caller; achieving two years of sobriety (on April 23rd) and what that signifies; and everything I'm putting off until after graduation, like finding a new job and buying a car. Pat was very sweet and supportive. He even offered to come by, and we continued our conversation in the living room with mugs of tea. At one point, he took me into his lap and held me. It was so relieving to finally cry and feel heard.

My presentations went very well. Mom took the day off so that she could attend. I wore a vintage red dress and black floral headscarf for the occasion.

At my poetry reading, [my English adviser] introduced me with such extensive praise that I grew *verklempt*. Then, I accepted the mic, and read poems thematic of romantic love as self-destruction.

Mom and I ate lunch in the cafeteria. From there, we headed to the sociology department, where [my friend] Troy was working. He was also scheduled to present and wore a three-piece grey suit. I teased him for looking so sharp—the freshest motherfucker to ever grace our dumpy little department—until he blushed and bellowed with laughter. A few minutes later, Jack showed up and met my mother.

Dr. Parsons stepped from her office, introduced herself to Mom, and remarked on how well I've done in the alternative math course. Then, she gave me a hug. This amazed me; not long ago, she'd questioned whether I was learning anything with Jack.

Magda also joined us and was kind and encouraging toward me. I was dumbstruck. I still don't know what to make of that.

I delivered my presentation with as much confidence as

I could muster. To end, I clicked to the last PowerPoint slide, which featured a picture of [my cat] Filburt, sitting next to some denim squares and quilting supplies—and asked if there were any questions.

An anthropology professor had several, and exclaimed how my research was "just fascinating!" I glowed with pride—a rare experience for me.

Later, Jack caught me in the hallway. I was still heading to Amber's this evening, I said.

"Oh, are we still doing that?"

"Yes, if you're feeling up to it."

He'd cancelled classes twice this week due to physical pain, so I was surprised when he smiled and said, "Well, I might have to change my plans."

Outside, Jack, Magda, and Troy walked ahead of us on the footpath. "So," I whispered to Mom, "what do you think of Jack?"

She remained tight-lipped until they'd climbed the stairs of the student union and waved goodbye. Once they disappeared inside, I badgered, "Come on—you're my mother! Your opinion means a lot to me."

"Well, I haven't had a chance to analyze him yet!"

I groaned. "First impressions!"

She said he was attentive, supportive, kind, and obviously loved teaching. "Oh, he's just a sweetheart," she sighed.

Satisfied, I looped my arm in hers and skipped onward to the parking lot.

Jack texted me at four o'clock to ask for Amber's address. I was already there, having helped Amber prepare for her date and seen her off. After a couple of hours, he arrived, looking handsome as fuck in an olive cap and a lightweight grey biker jacket. The moment the front door latched behind him, his arms and mouth overwhelmed me.

Having previously gotten Amber's blessing, we made love on the spare mattress in her sewing room. As he pulled on his pants and prepared to leave, I asked when he was scheduled to go to Iceland this summer.

"Around the end of June or early July," he said. Then, he smiled excitedly and asked, "When are *you* going to Iceland this summer? Around the end of June or early July?"

"You still want to do all of that—even the elopement?" The topic had eluded us for some weeks now.

"Yes, I do. It'll be just perfect. I've fallen in love with the country, and I think you will too."

I didn't say anymore, but my heart fluttered and a stupid grin stretched across my face.

10 May 2016

Current mood: apprehensive
Current music: Gary Numan, "My Last Day"

Today is Tuesday. I graduate on Saturday. Grades are in next Wednesday.

It'll all be over soon.

15 May 2016

Current mood: accomplished
Current music: Felix Mendelssohn, "String Quartet in A minor, Op. 13 #2"

I didn't sleep well the night before the ceremony (or the night before that—or the night before that). Still, I awoke ahead of my alarm. Alex had slept over, and I left him to snooze while I guzzled coffee downstairs.

I took a shower around ten AM. Towel. Lotion. Makeup. Underwear.

Then, *the dress*. Alex smiled reassuringly as I slipped it

on and raised its zipper. New shoes. A plain, black headscarf to wear under my cap. Two pairs of earrings: the silver crow skulls—an anniversary gift from Alex—and a pair of roughly cut amethyst earrings I made last summer.

Finally, I pulled on the robe and poked a couple of pins into the right breast. There were medals and cords as well. Alex helped me loop the tassel around the button on my cap.

"All right," I gulped. "Let's do this."

It was a gorgeous afternoon. The sun was warm, the skies open, and there was very little wind. We picked up [my brothers] Joel and Sam on our way to campus. Once we found parking, the four of us stood beside Alex's car to smoke.

"You look beautiful, sis," Sam remarked. "I'm gonna cry watching you graduate in that dress. Not if it'd been a wedding to that fucking Cody guy."

I laughed. "Oh, yes, you would have. You're all sensitive and shit."

Inside, students were starting the line-up process in the halls. I ran into [my close friend] Andy, who was graduating with her master's. We embraced and waited together to get our name cards. I showed mine to the man designated to pass out honors cords.

He congratulated me and gave me my cords: Cum Laude.

Andy asked for help fastening on her cap. I held it in place while she pinned it to her hair. "You are such a good human being," she murmured. "I'm so glad I'm not doing this alone."

We both began to tear up, and I told her to hush. But really, I was honored to share the experience with her.

Susan [from student services] found me in the hallway. She hugged me and said how happy she was that everything had worked out.

Goddamn. I'm crying now, remembering it all.

At exactly noon-thirty, faculty and administrative officials flowed into the arena in two queues and lined the walkway, clapping and congratulating the students who followed.

I saw Jack, who beamed at me. Other professors cheered and greeted me as I passed—and for once, I accepted the praise without feeling self-conscious and swelled with pride.

My parents were in the bleachers on the left side of the auditorium. Alex, Joel, and Sam were on the right. Naomi sat below them.

The ceremony was so...archaic. There was no way to overlook the fact that we were dressed like fucking wizards. The proceedings were kept short and sweet. I thought the President's speech was a bit disjointed. As he noted the importance of critical thinking, I looked to Naomi, who pretended to fall asleep with her mouth wide open. I strained to keep from cracking up. Eventually, we began walking. Master's and associate's students went first. When Andy was hooded, we shouted and whooped.

Then, the bachelor's students drifted toward the stage. Presumably, I was with them, but my memories are tainted in a blue haze. The whole event was ethereal. Although I'd referenced this day for years, I failed to fully grasp that I would experience it—even as it occurred.

"Callow Louise Phoenix. Sociology honors. Cum Laude."

I passed the podium and crossed the stage, thus graduating.

As I headed back to my seat, Jack stood and leaned into the walkway to embrace me. I kissed his cheek as our bodies met. He hugged me very tightly and said how proud he was. I thanked him graciously.

The students were recognized once more. All stood, hollered, and applauded. Once more, the professors lined up to congratulate us as our rows were led from the auditorium. Passing my mentor Charles, I grasped his arm affectionately and stopped to hug Grace Driscoll, a feminist professor whom I deeply admire.

The boys were waiting outside, and we headed for the house, where Dad insisted on taking pictures. Joel made faces until Dad barked with impatience.

"What would you like to do now?" I was asked. "Where would you like to eat?"

I suggested we just grab some burgers. Maybe other graduates throw parties at rented venues or have guests over to their neat, cleanly homes decorated with streamers and balloons, and have snacks and receive cash and cards as shitty pop music fills the background. But, I had no neat, cleanly home, and had made no plans. It was still unbelievable that it had happened at all.

Lunch was casual, unremarkable. We didn't talk about school or the ceremony. Actually, the topic of Joel's conception came up—where and how. Pretty standard subject matter for our family.

By seven o'clock, I was worn out, though still in good spirits. The family had dispersed, and Alex and I said our goodbyes with hugs and kisses. Then, fully prepared to celebrate our triumph, I headed for Jack's.

I still had on my dress, and Jack noted how gorgeous I looked. We collapsed into each other on the couch, remarking how the earlier excitement had drained us. "It's funny," he said. "We'd joked about being physically intimate today, but we're like a married couple who just hangs out on their wedding night because they're so exhausted after the long day."

I agreed, content just to spend the evening with him.

But, Jack broke my heart. He said he wouldn't have much time to hang out. That afternoon, he was informed that a colleague from another department was being granted early retirement after being diagnosed with terminal cancer. He was having drinks with friends, and Jack had been invited.

Oh.

I strained to bury my disappointment and make the most of our time. We talked and cuddled, but after about an hour, Jack slipped out of my arms and left.

I watched episodes of *Rocko's Modern Life* on his laptop

and began reading *The Romanovs: 1613–1918* by Simon Sebag Montefiore—a graduation gift from Jack. Hours passed. When he finally returned, I was dozing.

I asked after his colleague, and he said he was bummed, but was glad he'd seen him. Jack joined me on the couch, and I ended up falling asleep on his chest. He woke me within minutes, saying he didn't want me to stay over. He had to be up early to grade papers and didn't want to tip-toe around to avoid waking me.

This perturbed me. I'd routinely slept over before mid-April, and this had never come up. On the contrary, he'd said knowing I was there was a comfort to him.

Surely on *this* night, he'd let me stumble upstairs to sleep, and I'd wake to find him typing away on his laptop, or discover a note left on the coffee table, wishing me a good morning and stating he'd gone to the office—like so many times before. It was the very least he could do, after all we'd been through to get to this moment... Yet, it was not to be, and I can't begin to express how much this hurt me.

I didn't argue. I got up, gathered my things, and walked home. It took a long time for me to finally fall asleep there, alone, after the most important day of my life.

I did it, though. I graduated from college with two BAs. After eight years, I'm no longer a student. I know it's temporary, and I'll be looking at graduate schools soon, but... I don't know. It's going to be a different life now.

29 May 2016

Current mood: hopeful

Current music: Zeromancer, "Gone to Your Head"

I'm concerned about how I fit into Jack's life. Months ago,

we'd talked about moving in together. We'd discussed getting a little house, how we'd furnish it, and what colors we'd paint the rooms. We laughed about how, in merging our book collections, our house would become a library.

These conversations have halted, though he alludes to the subject in small ways. For example, he gifted me more books—some from his own shelves—and when I objected, he said, "I know, I know—but ultimately, all of this will be shared between us, so you don't need to worry about taking them now."

That's another thing: Jack hasn't mentioned our engagement plans in a while, and I don't feel bold enough to bring it up. Recently, I pointed out that he's invited me over less. I asked if it was due to his health, and he agreed. He said when he's feeling exceptionally unwell, he tends to isolate. I won't push it.

He's finally received some answers about his health. A new doctor diagnosed him with inflammation in his pancreas and liver, and a severe vitamin D deficiency. This explains his digestive issues, as well as some of the chronic pain and fatigue. His stress levels could account for the other issues: the sleeping problems, migraines, etc. He's started taking supplements, and I bought some cleansing teas and digestive enzymes to encourage him. His doctor also recommended a special diet to reduce the inflammation.

He'd welcomed me over on Friday afternoon to do my laundry. While he typed away on his laptop, I strung a beaded necklace and daydreamed. The afternoon seemed exemplary of what our life might be: us, sharing the same space as we pondered and toiled over our separate projects.

Shortly after he'd set aside his laptop, touching began, and he started biting my thigh—hard, until I gasped with pain. Then, he led me upstairs to bed.

Afterward, he collapsed beside me, chuckling, "Not bad for a sick old man."

Bruises have blossomed across my thigh where he bit me.

June

23 June 2016

Current mood: depressed

Current music: From Indian Lakes, "Runner" and "Search for More"

Jack had asked to see me on Saturday evening. By seven, I sent him a message, saying I wouldn't start watching another movie if he still wanted me to come by. Yes, we needed to talk, he replied. Sluggishly, I got dressed, walked to the townhouse, greeted Jack with a kiss, and curled up on my end of the sofa. He then launched into a monologue about how I'd upset him earlier in the day.

After our "good morning" messages, I'd asked what he was up to. He said he was out of town, visiting Magda and Zach. However, Jack has often *kvetched* about how moody Magda's been since they broke up and how Zach gets on his nerves.

If stress is aggravating his health issues, why not reduce contact with people who cause stress? I've never questioned his activities, but that morning, I suggested he might make better use of his Saturday by focusing on himself. Maybe pull out his painting supplies instead.

Jack interpreted this as controlling. I apologized and stated how I'm just concerned for his well-being.

We've been miscommunicating lately, he said, and maybe we needed some distance to sort ourselves out. He observed how we've been mirroring each other's dark moods, so we arranged to take a week or two apart to focus on self-care.

After returning home, I wrote a letter in further response to our conversation.

June 18, 2016

Dearest Jacky,

I should explain some things, since you said we have communication issues, and you're not wrong. I haven't been the most forthcoming. I'm unsure how to bring up my frustrations, so I just don't. It's not because I don't trust you; it's that I don't always know how to talk about my feelings due to our previous roles. Also, I'm self-conscious about my insecurities and emotional lows. So, I've kept these to myself.

I think I'm fucked up because I had some expectations about post-grad life. I thought this huge sense of relief—so vast it was to be spiritual in nature—would envelop us. I thought we'd be liberated. I thought we'd flip off the world and carry on as though we never had anything to hide. I thought we'd get drunk on idealism and elope in Iceland—because life's too fucking short anyway, and who gives a damn? Something like that.

Maybe my expectations weren't misplaced or misguided, but misinformed. I haven't had the chance to spend enough time around you and really come to build an understanding of how difficult your daily reality is, and how you have to arrange your time to placate your chronic illness. It doesn't always make sense for you to be spontaneous or carefree, or to plan ahead. And that's been hard for me.

I'm trying to be adaptive. I'm willing to work with you as you try to improve your health. I'm not sure how to be supportive as you make changes and learn to create boundaries at work and with your friends. Tonight, you said my messages came off as nagging, and this alarmed me. How can I be encouraging without being overbearing? I already think of myself as burdensome; I don't want you to think so too.

With this being said, I feel you're more willing to compromise for others—people who are not me. While our dates consistently get rescheduled or dismissed, you still set aside time for [friends] and colleagues. I try to be easygoing, but it hurts me not to get the same consideration of your time and planning capabilities as persons who are not your romantic partner. I might be wrong. If so, I'd like for you to show me.

Also… Jack, I understand now that we're not going to get married, and I'm not going to Iceland with you this summer. When we talked about it in April, it felt doable. Still, I wish you'd have told me when you changed your mind. You haven't breached the subject of late, not even when I've provided avenues. So, I stopped mentioning it. It really bothers me. You've known me through a failed engagement. It's not a subject I take lightly, and I thought you understood this about me.

I'm sorry it's been unnerving to be around me lately. Let me explain some aspects of my mental health so you're less inclined to worry when I have these low spells.

I've developed coping mechanisms to help with my depression and anxiety, and practice self-care. I like to sew and make jewelry. I like to journal, or process with close friends. I like to be preoccupied with films, music, or audiobooks. I like to take showers and put on clean clothes to feel warm and secure. I like to paint my nails, or lose myself in research.

It's rare now, but sometimes these activities aren't enough. When my body and brain are determined to be depressed, I give in, instead of fighting it. To fight it indicates that being depressed is wrong, which I don't believe is true. I just have to trust that it'll pass because it always does. It's not fun or easy, and I recognize I'm not fun or easy to be around when I'm depressed. And it's been exceptionally bad lately, but try not to worry. I always pull through.

I hope this letter is helpful. The tone shifted at points, and I hope you aren't upset with what I've written. As we discussed, we need to better our communication. So, I'll try not to hold back, even if I'm scared of hurting you or pushing you away. Those are never my intentions. I love you. You suffer enough abuse without me.

I hope we can meet and talk further when you're ready.

While he was at the office, I left the letter on his sofa to read when he got home. We met yesterday to briefly discuss its contents.

Yes, briefly. He had little to say except I was right about not being a priority, and he feels ashamed for how he's treated me. He knows he has to get his shit together. He understands that if we're going to be a strong couple, he needs to take care of himself.

"You were kind in your letter," he commented. "Your ability to write with compassion, even when explaining your frustrations... I can only imagine how you would sound if you were writing to someone you hated." Then, he asked if I had anything more to add.

Um, yeah. "When did you decide you weren't ready to marry me?" I asked. "What happened? Why didn't you tell me you'd begun to get cold feet?"

His response was un-fucking-believable.

"I didn't realize you'd taken it so seriously. I meant our plans to be on the playful side of serious."

I gaped at him. *WHAT?!* What does that even mean? *And how could you joke about something like that?!*

We'd looked at dates and airline ticket prices. He'd asked if my passport was current, if I owned a sturdy pair of boots for hiking. He'd described his research and explained how I could help him gather data and conduct interviews during our honeymoon stay. He'd shown me photos of and articles about the places he wanted to take me, including the newly constructed pagan temple, where he'd said he wanted to marry me.

WE'D MADE PLANS. That doesn't equate to being on the "playful side of serious" whatsoever! And yet, he appeared genuinely surprised by my commitment to the idea—to our *plans.* He shook his head, his expression limp with confusion.

I didn't pursue it. It required every speck of willpower in my being to remain calm, to resist smoldering into a lump of familiar disappointment and self-loathing.

Hahaha, here we go again! No one would ever actually *marry you, Cal! Haven't you figured that by now?!*

Jack apologized, recognizing how I might feel duped, as he probably presented himself a certain way and is now failing to live up. Although I didn't confirm it, he's right. I feel duped.

When I first told Alex about the engagement, he'd cautioned me not to invest too much certainty—and I'd taken this to heart. I didn't bring up the elopement with Jack; I let *him* bring it up, and even while we gushed and mapped out our trip, my thoughts remained prudent. *Just wait until after graduation. Then, see what he says.*

The subject last came up sometime last month, when we'd talked about what to pack for the trip. On his laptop, Jack had looked up a few sights in Reykjavík where he wanted to take me.

Then, nothing—until a couple of weeks ago when he mentioned his Icelandic research. I asked if he still wanted me to accompany him. He'd smiled apprehensively and said, "I think so."

"Should I bring a nice dress?" I asked gingerly.

"Maybe," he murmured. The hesitant smile held. "I don't know."

With this, I knew he was having second thoughts. As more time crept by and the final days of June were encroaching, I resigned myself to the reality that it wasn't going to happen.

After reading my letter, I'd expected Jack to contradict me, to say no. No, Cal. I still want to marry you. I'd like to reschedule for later in the summer, or next summer—a future summer. I love you, and I want you to be my wife, but not quite yet.

Instead, he said he hadn't meant it at all.

Bullshit. He's backpedaling—he just has to be! And *why*?! Is it his illness? Does he feel he's not good enough for me—what? What switch got flipped and when and why, and was it something I said or did?

But, can I *really* be so shocked? Like, really? No one has ever *seriously* wanted to marry me.

Well, Cody had been serious...until he wasn't anymore. Okay, fair enough. It was a doomed romance—an intense blaze that rapidly wasted its fuel and went out with a thread of smoke.

The dress was more suited for a graduation ceremony anyway. Though, the evening of my graduation hadn't exactly unfolded the way I'd been led to believe it would either.

I risked *so much* to be with Jack. Now, I'm unsure if my pains were worthwhile. I love him, but how do we proceed from here?

July

13 July 2016

Current mood: anxious
Current music: Beirut, "Prenzlauerberg"

On Saturday, June 25th, Jack sent me a frantic message saying his father had fallen and injured his hip. He sped down to Oklahoma and, to my knowledge, was still there when Alex and I left for our vacation in Tennessee the following Thursday. Through the first part of his absence, Jack stayed in touch. At the end of each day, he rang me from his hotel room to check in and give me updates on his father's condition.

It was during one of these phone calls that we returned to the topic of our engagement. Jack clarified that he'd considered the elopement as metaphoric—something we would strive toward—and not a literal arrangement.

That's right: apparently, ours was a *metaphoric* engagement.

"I feel like you're rushing into this faster than I'm comfortable with, and I can't keep up," he complained. "I don't know that I'm—at this time—capable of giving you what you want from me."

This had *really* pissed me off. Who'd said they wanted to take care of me, to share a home with me? Who'd given me a key and urged me to use their house as a second home, to cook meals, study, write, work out, and do my laundry there?

I brought this to Jack's attention, but I don't remember his reply. The conversation was a long one, and we repeated ourselves a lot. It left a bad taste in my mouth, though we ended the call by emphasizing our love for each other.

After some thought, I sent him an email suggesting we try to start over, reconfigure our expectations of and boundaries with each other. "Let's talk about what we can reasonably *do* for each other and who we can reasonably *be* for each other," I wrote. Why not? After all, we're still in love, and it's still exciting.

But, he never responded. Days passed. Alex and I left for our vacation. We stayed with a group of his friends in a large, country home outside of Nashville. On the Fourth of July, a huge party was thrown. It was a great time, but because I hadn't heard from Jack, I was distracted, pricked with worry. Eventually, I sent the following email and an exchange unfolded.

Jul 4, 2016 at 11:03 PM

subject: HEY ARE YOU ALIVE

Email me back and lemme know please. Have you gotten any texts or voicemail messages from me? I haven't gotten anything from you.

Sorry. I'm just worried :/

Jul 5, 2016 at 7:18 AM

Morning :) Hope you are well. My phone is all busted up (I haven't been receiving texts or calls nor have been able to send them… I've also been on the road (needed to get out of here) and have had limited internet access.

I'm going to a Verizon store today to try to get everything fixed —talk soon

Jul 5, 2016 at 9:52 AM

Okay. Will you be around when I get back into [town] tomorrow?

Thanks for the email.

Jul 5, 2016 at 7:50 PM

Hey, just letting you know that Alex and I arrived back safely. I'll probably head to [town] sometime tomorrow afternoon.

Hope you're doing okay. Miss you <3

Jul 6, 2016 at 6:17 AM

Hey: Glad to hear you and Alex are safe.

I won't be home for at least a few more days… I'll be traveling for medical stuff (more tests and treatment) and for family stuff.

Here is the big thing: it turns out that I'm more ill than I previously thought—I've passed out a couple of times over this previous week—and I've been having visions and auditory hallucinations, all triggered by over-exertion/dysfunction in my central nervous system—at least that's what the doctor says.

I can supposedly get better—but I need to get some major rest (and I'm in some clinical trials for new treatments), and I need to seriously alter my life patterns—which is why we unfortunately need to alter the nature of our relationship and return to being friends… We can't be boyfriend and girlfriend. I can't be in a physical relationship with you (or anyone) anymore, and I'm going to get worse before I get better... Even though I love you, I literally don't have the energy to hold a conversation, go out, make love, or be normal in any way for the foreseeable future. My situation causes me absolute misery, and I'm sick/frustrated of causing frustration and misery for you.

I apologize for this email. This is not a conversation I wanted to put into an email (but I have a little energy this morning to write). We can try to make time to talk on the phone later (if you wish).

I honor you every day for the time you have loved and cared for me, and I'm sorry that I can't be the person you deserve. I hope you understand. (Hopefully) talk soon, JB

Maybe I should have seen it coming, but seriously? What grown adult breaks up with someone through email? What an obnoxiously professorial thing to do.

Jul 7, 2016 at 1:13 AM

Jacky,

I'm sorry for the tone of this email; I've gone from numb to heartbroken to (currently) angry today.

Yes, angry! I'm sorry, but fuck you, dude. I risked eight years of academic labor and a future career to be with you. I lied to people I love to be with you. I was debilitated by the secrecy, the waiting and wondering, and the risks—to be with you. I poured myself and my being into being with you. I know you think you're doing me a favor, but you're not. You're being incredibly unfair.

You wrote that you can't be the person I need you to be. And who is that person? We now know our expectations of each other were misplaced due to miscommunication. Honestly, I think you're holding yourself to an imagined standard rather than one I've actually set.

I reckon you're disgusted and upset with yourself and believe breaking up will protect me. Has this relationship been difficult for me? Absolutely. Have I been frustrated and miserable? Sure, yes. But haven't I also expressed a willingness to work with you? Yes, I have.

If you want to break up, I will accept and respect your choice. However, I'm not going to just sit back and watch you disappear into a self-deprecating misery hole. If you want to be friends, then let me continue to love, support, and care for you. You shouldn't have to go through this alone. You shouldn't have to feel ashamed.

I'm sorry for being a stubborn asshole, but you're worth it to me. Call me soon, when you're feeling up to it. I miss you.

He never responded, and I didn't expect him to—at least, not right away. In the meantime, I sewed (and sewed and sewed).

To compile my quilt, I started by sewing four small squares of denim together (which I not-so cleverly called "four-squares"). For months now, I've carried a little cloth bag with needles, scissors, spools of black thread, a pincushion with pins, and denim squares. Whenever I had the chance, I sewed—during class, at the café with friends, etc. By March, I gathered up all of the four-squares and arranged them over the fleece I intended to use as the backside of the quilt.

I had enough to make a second quilt! Immediately, I thought of Jack—and if I really pushed myself, I could complete it in time for his birthday. I mapped out rows, numbered the four-squares, and brought a stack of them to stitch together during the ride to Tennessee and back. Later, I purchased a second length of fleece for this quilt—despite the breakup email.

Why? Because I'm a sentimental fool. Even if we'd never dated, he's still my favorite, most influential professor. What better way to express my gratitude?

By yesterday, I still hadn't heard from him and hadn't reached out. Naomi invited me to visit her at the tutoring center so she could see the quilt's progress. As I parked, I saw Jack's car in the lot and spontaneously decided to make a quick detour.

Jack wasn't in the office, but was somewhere on campus. I opted to wait, showing the quilt-in-progress to Connie [the administrative assistant] and Eleanor, and took a seat in the foyer.

After about thirty minutes, Connie sent Jack a text message to let him know I was there. He replied that he'd be busy for another hour. I said I'd come back.

As I stood to leave, Connie mentioned Jack had gone to Iceland recently.

Erm, what? My confusion was raw and impossible to conceal. "When?" I asked.

"Toward the end of June, until earlier this month," Connie answered.

Oh my fucking god. I tasted copper. I blinked to see straight.

Outside, I called Amber and smoked a couple of cigarettes before meeting Naomi. While she examined the quilt, I stomped between tables and bookshelves, grumbling over this revelation. Forty-five minutes later, I returned to the sociology department and continued to wait.

Jack eventually showed up. He seemed pleased to see me, though a touch nervous too. I followed him back to his office. He closed the door. I put my bags down.

"You motherfucker."

He nodded and said he'd been called this before and was deserving of it now. He asked how I'd been.

"Anxious. Frustrated."

He acknowledged being the source of these feelings.

"Hmm. So, what's up? What's been going on?"

"I've been so busy," he excused. Working, keeping doctors' appointments, isolating quite a bit, and not much more than that.

Uh huh—and? When he didn't mention it, I asked, "So, when did you go to ICELAND?"

Jack hesitated, pursed his lips, and nodded. He hadn't expected this—for me to know. "Recently," he said. He told me about the research he'd done there. The same research we'd talked about doing together, post-elopement.

"Did you even go to Oklahoma to see your parents?"

"Oh, yes," he said quietly, averting his eyes. "I saw them."

"How long were you in Iceland?"

"About ten days, I think."

"Well, I guess that explains why our communication was so hit-and-miss."

"That and because I broke my phone."

"How?"

He'd gotten bad news from the doctor and threw his

phone against a wall. He also broke a bookshelf, tore several books in half, and smashed dishes in his kitchen.

WHOA. For godssakes, why?

After hearing back from the doctor about the extent of his illness, he became enraged and lost it.

The timing of his breakup email was off-putting, unexpected. When did he send it?

During his pseudo-nervous breakdown, just after he'd broken everything.

Oh. This also seemed to explain a lot.

But, the timeline doesn't add up. He said he'd gone to Iceland for ten days, but was still in Oklahoma when Alex and I left for Tennessee, and was back in the States when he emailed me last Wednesday. I know I'm bad at math, but I can read a fucking calendar.

"How long had you been planning this?" I asked.

"Not long. I didn't think I was going to go. It was a last-minute, split decision."

"Why didn't you tell me you were going?"

Given my disappointment about everything regarding Iceland and the misunderstanding about our engagement, he didn't want to cause me "more bad feelings about it."

"So, you lied by omission, to protect me and my feelings?"

He nodded. "Yes."

I told him this was horseshit. I'm a big girl and can manage my own feelings. I want the truth, no matter how much it might hurt me. Nothing, I reminded him, hurts me more than being lied to by the people I love.

Our exchange lasted about an hour. For once, I didn't try to withhold or minimize my feelings, though I did apologize for showing up unannounced.

"I'm glad you did." He said he'd been telling himself to stop being a child and just call me.

"Well, I guess this saves you a phone call."

He smiled. "Yeah. Thank you."

I went to him, took his face in my hands, and kissed him deeply. As I pulled away, I sighed, "You're a pain in the ass, Jack."

I'd been so angry, so heartbroken. I was ready to slap him or spit in his face for lying to me. Upon confronting him, I was forced to remember that he's sickly and scared. Internally, he's a puppy. Who kicks a puppy? A bastard *putz*, that's who.

Before I left, I reiterated what I'd written in my email. "I said I respect your decision to break up, and I mean that. But, this disappearing garbage is unfair to me and others who want to be in your life. You know I'm really stubborn."

Jack laughed. "I'm sorry. I'm not laughing at you. I know how stubborn you are. But, I really do need to self-contain right now."

"I get that. Just don't disappear completely."

We hugged and kissed again. Then, I clasped his hands, insisting, "Don't you ever, *ever* do this bullshit lying-to-protect-me shit *ever* again."

"I promise! I promise. I won't do it again."

I made him pinky-swear, the asshole. Goddamnit.

30 July 2016

Current mood: irritated

Current music: Coheed and Cambria, "Here We Are Juggernaut" and "Far"

Summer is just beginning to wilt, and I've managed to accomplish fuck-all outside of pouring my savings—a little more than two grand—into buying a car and going to one job interview for a position at the public library (that I didn't get). No, this miserable bollocks with Jack—alongside post-graduate existential dread—has been all-consuming.

Jack, Jack, Jack... I've never dated a more difficult person. The gut-crushing, mind-fucking epic of the last eight months has left me shaken, confused, and embarrassed—duped. It's comforting that Alex, Amber, Alice, Naomi, and the other precious few who've followed the drama are equally surprised by how things have panned out.

I actually managed to complete Jack's quilt two days before his birthday.

Naomi was incredible. She demonstrated how to sew the denim topside to the fleece and helped me secure them with black yarn ties. Finally, we removed the safety pins that held everything in place, and the quilt was done!

I sent Jack a message straightaway. He reacted with excitement, and we made tentative plans for Thursday. But the following afternoon, he said he was too busy and couldn't take the day off.

I had to clarify:

You know I figured that I would just catch you for an hour or so after you finished up at the office, right?

Yeah, I know.

Alice was present during this text exchange. "Wait," she said, "he's known this whole time that you've been working on the quilt to finish by his birthday?"

"Yeah."

"Oh, fuck. I'm so sorry, Cal. That's messed up."

It is, isn't it? Ten minutes, even. I would've been satisfied with ten minutes.

Okay, he's not up to seeing me right now. This didn't necessarily mean that he shouldn't receive his gift on time. So, I stopped by the townhouse while Jack was at the office. I arranged the quilt over his sofa with a note wishing him a nice birthday and that I hope the quilt brings him comfort. Then, I grabbed a coffee mug and a bag of quinoa I'd left in his kitchen and went on my way.

I've heard *bupkis*. Not even a text message acknowledging the quilt, what he thought of it or a "thank you"—*nothing*.

I wonder if he thinks of me as this potentially volatile person who must be kept at arm's length, especially now that we're broken up, and that's why he says he's interested in making plans, but continues to use passive, noncommittal language. "Maybe," he repeats, "maybe." Even if he's sick and isn't sure of his schedule—cool. But, say that. Say it's not a good time, a good week, whatever.

It's so unnerving. Despite how critical I am of myself, I don't believe this is entirely about me. I strive to be a worthy romantic partner—to be gracious, forthcoming, humble, preemptive about conflict, and to accept accountability. I really, really try. I'm not perfect, but I do my best.

God, how did we get to this point? We were just rolling around his bed like loose beads, talking into the wee hours of the morning. We were snuggled up on his sofa with bowls of cereal in our laps, cooing at each other when we weren't cackling with laughter. What the hell changed? What did I do wrong? What turned him off?

This whole ordeal has been so demoralizing. I just have to suck it up, let him go, and move on.

August

Current mood: frustrated

Current music: Peter Murphy, "Cuts You Up"

This breakup is really fucking with me, and I'm terribly depressed. I've even thought about drinking, although I won't let myself consider it for very long, let alone act on those thoughts.

Classes start in a couple of weeks. [My former mentor]

Charles agreed to do an independent study with me. Our focus is grad school prep: editing work, compiling a portfolio, drafting cover letters, and the like. Re-enrolling will also allow me to resume employment as a tutor and access student amenities, like counseling and the health clinic. I'd love to see a counselor. With how vexed and fragmented I feel, professional guidance would be helpful.

September

12 September 2016

Current mood: grateful
Current music: Radiohead, "Daydreaming"

Jack and I have gotten back together. After a few weeks wherein we exchanged only sparse text messages, he proposed we do a research project together. If we managed to get an article published within the year, he said it would help him meet his quota and give me another publication to include on my CV for grad school.

It hasn't happened, and I didn't think it would after Jack informed me he'd be teaching an additional course this fall. Eleanor approached him just two weeks prior to the semester, saying she'd volunteered him to teach Race/Ethnic Relations, along with his four other classes. He protested, but she stuck to her decision, despite knowing about his ailing health, stress, and even his recent suicide attempt.

Earlier this summer, Jack said he'd broken his phone after receiving bad news from the doctor. Yet, the doctor had only further validated the diagnosis of stress-induced chronic fatigue.

Who flips out and smashes their phone over something

they already know? It didn't make sense.

I'd also begun to toss around the idea that he may have exploited me. Why? Consider the trajectory of our relationship: how things were blissful, yet strained, until graduation. Then, he seems withdrawn, and after a couple of conversations about miscommunication, he suddenly dumps me. Moreover, the gaslighting about our engagement and his intention to hide the Iceland trip from me?

What the hell was going on? Was fucking me part of some professor-student fetish? Is that why he didn't wait until *after* I'd graduated, and why he lost interest once I had?

I recalled something [my friend] Mikki mentioned, when I learned that Kayla's relationship with "Bob" was actually about Jack. As we'd talked over the situation, Mikki confirmed that while Kayla's behavior was ridiculous, "JB's definitely encouraging it. She's shown me text messages between the two of them, and he's not been appropriate with her. Like, as her professor, a lot of what he wrote wasn't appropriate."

I'd shrugged off Mikki's remarks. I highly respected Jack. I couldn't imagine he'd mislead Kayla, especially after what he'd said about her stalking behaviors.

Now, baffled by my own experiences, I wasn't sure what to believe. So, I rang Mikki and asked if she remembered anything Kayla had said about Jack or the text messages he'd sent her.

"Gosh," she sighed. "I really don't. It was years ago. I'm sorry I can't help." She asked why I was interested.

With a deep breath, I confessed, summarizing the heavenly highs and wretched lows, his health problems, the risks to my academic career, and the recent breakup.

"Well, you're not the same person as Kayla," Mikki offered, "and your situation with him sounds entirely different. It sounds like he really does love you."

Yeah, okay. Maybe I was worrying myself unnecessarily.

Following our conversation at his office in July, I reached

out. He invited me to visit the next morning. I arrived prepared, having rehearsed statements and memorized questions. As soon as we settled into the sofa, I dove in, first expressing how his explanation of events didn't add up. I was beginning to feel used, which confused me because I didn't see him as a malicious person.

"Look, I'm really bothered here," I emphasized. "I'm wondering if I shouldn't start to feel exploited."

Jack's eyes widened into plates. I went on. He listened, but ultimately disagreed. He in no way intended to make me feel used. He reiterated how he's viewed me as a peer for a long time.

What about the timeline? I opened my weekly planner and asked him to point out which days he spent in Oklahoma, when he left for Iceland, and when he got back.

He grew flustered, flipping the pages. While he knew his return date, he couldn't indicate the exact day he flew to Iceland. He mentioned his lapses in memory were concerning his doctor.

Though I sound like a *schnook*, I don't think he was lying. He seemed genuinely upset when he couldn't remember the specifics of his trip.

Next, I tried to clarify what led to the breakup email.

"So, okay," he began. "This is another example of how I've been dishonest with you, and I'm sorry." He hadn't flipped out and broken his phone because he'd gotten a call from his doctor. Rather, he'd tried to kill himself.

Jack started to cry, yet spoke with calm control. He'd been in so much pain, felt so desperate. Succumbing, he looped a belt around his neck and threw the buckle over the top of a door in an attempt to hang himself. The belt broke, *baruch Hashem*.

He considered another method. To halt the suicidal thoughts, he responded with rage: kicking in a bookshelf, tearing textbooks in half, smashing dishes, and throwing his phone against a wall.

Reflecting on his behavior, he decided he had no business being in a relationship. So, the following morning, he sent the breakup email.

Wow, okay. Oh my god. I crawled into his lap. His face nestled into my shoulder, and I stroked his back until his tears were spent.

He still loves me immensely and wants to be with me, but he can't justify it until he's gotten a better grip on his circumstances. "My sincere hope is that we can pick up where we've left off again, in the future," he concluded, braving a smile.

After this conversation—but before his invitation to do research together—I began seeing Marie, a counselor on campus. I told her the relationship started after graduation and had lasted only about six weeks. I also referred to him with a pseudonym and didn't specify the department to which he belongs.

I described how I worried endlessly about Jack. I struggled to give him space and only messaged him once a week to check in. While I waited for a response, I boiled with anxiety. If I didn't hear back after a couple of days, I'd drive to campus and look for his car. If it was there, I knew he was okay, and my anxiety was temporally quelled. When it wasn't, I panicked.

Driving by and checking for his car was the only way I knew how to quash my fears over his well-being without contributing to his stress levels with overbearing text messages or phone calls. But, I also felt insane, like a stereotypical "crazy" ex-partner.

Marie was great. She said I had every right to feel as I did, given Jack's suicide attempt. Since he wanted to be friends, he was responsible for getting back to me. She suggested I ask what being a friend means to him, so I'd have a better idea of how to approach our interactions.

She scheduled a session for the following Monday, and I

texted Jack as I exited her office. I stated how I was reaching out on the advice of a counselor, and could we meet to talk?

Jack responded within a few minutes. Come by in the morning, he said. He wanted to talk anyway, about some research we could do together.

Just before ten AM, I almost ran to his house. Jack had left the front door cracked, and as I walked in, he surprised me with a kiss. We settled into our usual places on the couch, and I outlined my session with Marie and the extent of my anxiety.

He apologized and said he would try to respond more quickly; I had good reason to worry about him, and he appreciated my love and concern.

As we spoke, he scooted closer to me. He touched my thigh and held my hand. We ended up entangled on the living room floor.

At our next session, Marie was pleased Jack had agreed to work on improving his communication but also advised that he and I meet again to clarify our roles. A sexual relationship was possible, but we should set terms. She also proposed that Jack and I establish a time to meet every week, if we really were going to work on research.

Armed with this advice, I called Jack. He said Tuesday evenings were best for him.

As I mentioned earlier, we've never done any research. We've developed a comforting routine, however. We catch up, leaving just enough time to joke around and make love before I'm asked to go home so he can grade assignments, write lectures, or go to bed. Two or three hours every Tuesday isn't much, yet it's what he can offer. Given his outrageous workload this semester, I'm grateful to have that.

Though, this last Tuesday, we didn't joke around or make love. Seemingly out of nowhere, Jack became furious. He grabbed a pencil from his coffee table and began breaking it into pieces while he stomped around the living room and loudly insisted that our relationship was exploitative of me. He admitted to pushing me away as a means to protect me—sounds familiar, huh?

We made up, more or less, over the phone yesterday, confirming that we're still committed to each other. Ultimately, I think he's sick, terribly stressed out, and tired of disappointing me. I'm treading carefully and keeping my own pains to myself to avoid burdening him further.

I'll see him tomorrow. It'll be okay. *He* will be okay. We love each other. We've been through so much already—what's one more semester?

21 September 2016

Current mood: impatient

Current music: At the Drive-In, "Non-Zero Possibility"

Last night, Jack finally showed me the contents of his art school portfolios. I gingerly picked through the pieces, studied them carefully. There were so many! At one time, he was fairly prolific.

As I studied the paintings and sketches, he lifted weights on the opposite side of the garage. Here and there, he stopped between reps to rub my shoulders and leave sweaty kisses on my forehead.

During one such pause, Jack hesitated as he walked toward me, staring distantly as if something had just struck him.

"You know, I haven't showed this work to anyone," he said. "You're the first person to see it."

My heart swelled with a deep sense of privilege. After he finished exercising and the portfolio was packed up, our bodies met on the couch upstairs.

October

15 October 2016

Current mood: anxious

Current music: Gregory Alan Isakov, "Dandelion Wine" and "The Stable Song"

I started a personal essay concerned with new developments in my relationships with both Jack *and* Alex. I've included it here, since I can't conceive of a way to describe the last few weeks without using these pages for reference anyway.

x

It's all the more unbearable because I've memorized Alex. Nearly a decade in, and I can taste his moods, even when there's a phone and many miles between us. He doesn't have to speak a word, and he often doesn't. This particular subject he tip-toes as if he were creeping between headstones. But, I know he's dissatisfied.

"It just seems like…"

"Like sex between two people who've been together for eight years?"

He laughs, "Right, yeah. I see your point. Still, I don't feel like we have much passion anymore."

After a thoughtful pause, I say, "You know, maybe we don't have passion, but we do have fun. We laugh a lot. We know what works for us, and there's a lot of security in that. I love you, and it's a beautiful kind of connection because it's taken a long time to develop. Maybe we don't have passion, but we have plenty of intimacy."

"I love you too," he says. "You'll always be my baby."

Still, he isn't entirely content. Sentiments alone cannot feed a wanton hunger, and he is human after all.

x

More than once, we'd chewed on the prospect of him seeking other sexual partners.

"Let's say I even meet someone who's interested," Alex would suggest. "As soon as I tell them I have a girlfriend, they'll drop me."

"That's not true," I'd say. "Not if you meet other polyamorous women."

"I'm not poly', though."

"No, but you're in a poly' *situation*."

"Yeah, but how do I meet them? And don't most of them around here know you? Wouldn't that be weird, if I met someone who knows you?"

I'd shrug. "No. Not if they're cool."

x

Jack's workload intensifies. Our communication seizes, begging a trickle. We arrange to meet on Tuesday evenings for a couple of hours, which is all that he can afford us.

"It's criminal how much work they're expecting me to do," he agonizes. "I'm putting in probably a hundred hours every week."

I listen, helpless and bruised. I offer to

assist in any way I can, but we both know I lack the expertise to craft lectures or sift through the stacks of papers he drags from work to home and back to work.

"It's a temporary arrangement," I point out. "It won't be like this forever, and you've survived worse than this." Though, I don't know if I'm saying this more for his benefit or mine.

x

Two months from our eight-year anniversary, I sit beside Alex in bed with his laptop cradled on my knees. Together, we look over his profile on a dating website.

"*Hi! I'm a silly, quiet dude looking for someone to hang out with casually. Things to know up front: I'm currently in a long-term, open relationship with a polyamorous woman. Honesty and openness are important to us. She is and will remain my primary partner.*"

"Looks good," I say. "I'm glad you emphasize our relationship. It'll filter out anyone who doesn't already have some understanding of non-monogamy."

I direct his attention to another subject heading. "This says to list six things you could never do without. You only have four: coffee, computers, nature, and cute animals."

"Oh, yeah. I wasn't sure of what else to put. You know me better than anyone—what else?"

"Cheese," I blurt. "You fucking love cheese." I type it into the list for him. "What else?" Then, "Oh, I know." I add *Bob Ross* to the end. For the last few months, we'd integrated *The Joy of Painting* into our bedtime routine, falling asleep to a different episode every night.

He laughs. "Can't get enough of that show."

"You might add something about how you've started cross-stitching somewhere on here."

"Really? I haven't been doing it for very long."

"So? You say that you like creative people and art. And you are a creative and artistic person."

He concedes, and I insert it into the description he's already developed. "All right," I say. "That should do it."

x

A week passes, and Alex is driving us to a burger joint for lunch. At a stoplight, he says, "Someone messaged me."

Although my chest lunges, I nonchalantly take a drag from my cigarette. "Oh, yeah? How's that going?"

"It's good—casual. We're just getting to know each other, but she seems cool."

"Well, that's exciting."

He asks if I'm okay, and I am, really. "Just keep me informed," I say.

x

While Amber sings [my niece] a lullaby, I heat two mugs of water in the microwave for chamomile tea. Then, we descend to her basement to chain smoke while we process.

"I think it's just the uncertainty. This is

the first time Alex has *ever* tried to date someone else while we've been together. And really, it's fine. I'm not a jealous or possessive person. I'm just a little territorial of our time and the space we share."

Amber nods. "Right, and this will benefit your relationship in the long run. He'll be able to have his needs met and he might start to understand what it's like for you with Jack and your other partners."

"I guess I do worry about that—how to remain objective and try to console him if anything goes wrong."

"But, you can do that. You do it for all of us," she says, meaning herself and my other close friends.

"Yeah, and Alex is my best friend. Eight years is a long time. I know I mean the world to him and that I'm his first consideration. I guess… It's just the change. Change always makes me feel out of control."

"*Pfft*." Amber lifts her mug in agreement. "I know that's right. Even good change freaks me out. After years of miserable shit, I'm suspicious of anything good."

x

They have their first date on a Tuesday afternoon, meeting at a diner during her lunch break. I send him a text message in the evening to check in: *How did it go?*

Alex writes back that it went well. They even kissed goodbye.

Yay! Rock on, I return, indifferent, except for a cautious ache in my head.

x

Jack cancels our evening plans. He's too tired and has to have a long conversation with his ex, Magda.

The weight of my disappointment provokes tears. Seated on Amber's sofa, I clench a pillow to my stomach and take measured breaths.

Amber paces. "Goddamn it," she grumbles. "He can't put it off? He cannot tell her that he has plans?"

"No," I sob. "The office becomes unbearable when she's in a bad mood. He has to put out the fire. She takes priority because she's directly connected to his source of labor—where he also derives his sense of value."

"Hmm, still. It pisses me off. Don't *you* always add to his sense of self? Haven't *you* helped to improve his self-esteem?"

"Yeah, but I'm more understanding than other people. And all I can do, while he's going through all of this shit, is to stay that way, even though it fucking kills me."

"Doesn't he know how much it's killing you to never see him?"

"No." I exhale slowly. "But, he's worth it. I just have to be patient."

Amber plops down beside me and lays a comforting hand on my knee. "I'm sorry, honey."

x

I scramble to make other plans, leaving Amber's house to meet Will and Carly at a café. I watch them tip back beers. Will's cheeks plump with salad. I have no money to eat-out, so I pinch my hunger with cigarettes. Lately, I haven't felt like eating anyway.

When my phone announces a call from Alex, I excuse myself. Will nods, unbothered by the interruption.

"What's going on?" I ask the receiver.

"Do you know someone named Lindsey?"

"No," I tell him. "Why? What's wrong?"

"Well, she says she knows you and you intimidate her, and now she's not sure if she wants to do this with me."

Alex's anxiety is profound, and it shakes me. I know how difficult it is for him to foster relationships with new people.

Apparently, Lindsey and I were in the same literature course three years ago. She told Alex I was unruly and often argued with other students. She thought I was attractive, but my attitude seemed aggressive.

"She worries that seeing me will invite drama because of how you are."

"Alex, I'm really sorry. I don't know what to say. I don't remember her *at all*—I was *wasted* all through that class. I used to sneak a bottle in and nip when no one was looking. Tell her I'm sorry if I ever made her feel uncomfortable. Tell her I quit drinking—that I went to rehab! I'm a different person now."

"Okay, thank you. I'm sorry. I just didn't know what to do."

"No, no. It's okay. Did you tell her it was

my idea that you did this?"

"No, but I probably should."

We wrap up, and I sit back down. I ask Carly to look up Lindsey's Facebook profile on her phone.

"Is this her?" She shows me a photo of a young woman with an oval face and mid-length blonde hair.

I shake my head. "That's her, but I don't remember her."

x

That night, I wear my shame around the bedroom. Because booze is no longer an option and I have no food in my stomach to purge, I stretch my nudity before the mirror. My ribs poke through, and I marvel at them, unsure of the significance behind their visibility. White-pink and plentiful, old scars appear in the abrasive glow of the overhead light.

Parallel to my right breast, I pull a pen knife over and away from my flesh until new, tight dashes appear, followed by tiny orbs of blood. I read these cuts; they're comforting in their lack of abstraction, in the control I'm able to exercise over their placement, depth, and number.

Humming with some relief, I slip on an old T-shirt, turn off the light, and call Alex, wondering if he salvaged Lindsey's interest.

"I told her how you've worked to better yourself and that you encourage me to be a better person too. She knows you're my best friend. She says she gets mental health stuff; she went through a period of her life when she wasn't okay, but she's gotten over it."

"So, you were able to fix it?" I ask.

"I think so, but she wants to sleep on it."

"That's fair."

"Are *you* okay?"

"I just feel bad," I say. "I'm embarrassed about the person I was when I was drinking, and it's really shitty that my old behavior can affect the people I care about. Like, I can handle people thinking negatively about me, but it sucks that those impressions can impact you. Especially after all of the work I've done."

"Yeah, but we know who you really are and how much you've changed." When I don't respond right away, he adds, "I'm sorry you didn't see Jack today. I know how much that sucks for you."

"Thanks," I mutter. "It's awful."

x

The following morning, Alice drops by. In an attempt to distract me from the implosive weight in my chest, she invites me to sit in on her theater and film class. I concede and slip off my pajamas. Alice notes a wound beside my right breast. "Is that a bug bite?"

"No. It's… You scrape away the first couple layers of skin, like a rug burn. When you cut over the top, it hurts really, really bad."

Her face tightens. "Cal, I'm worried about your cutting."

I hook my arms into a tank top. "It's the most reasonable vice I have anymore."

We walk to campus together. Jack drives by,

slowing to ensure that we see him.

My chest releases, and I throw up my hands in a show of relief. "And there you go!" I declare. "Now that I've *seen* him and *see* that he's okay, I'm fine."

"Our lives are so absurd," Alice laughs.

x

Alex and I share a cigarette in the garage. He sits beside me on an old tool box. I talk with my hands, gesturing broadly.

"In the past," I explain, "when things are complicated or strained in my other relationships, it's easier to manage because I've still had security through you."

"Right. I've always been the stable one."

"Yeah, you're my rock. You've always kept me grounded. Now, we're in this situation that invites all of this uncertainty. And shit's still up in the air with Jack. I worry about him constantly."

I offer him a drag. He plucks the cigarette from my fingers. "Yeah, but you don't have to worry about me," he assures. "I still love you, and I'm not going anywhere. I'm doing everything I can to make sure you're okay."

"I know. You've been great, and I want you to do this. I want you to be happy; you deserve to have your needs met."

"I appreciate it. Thanks for helping me to get through that hump with her."

"Sure, of course." The cigarette smoke curls into the ceiling. I watch it absently and scratch at a flake of dry skin on my cheek. "Things still good between you two?" I ask.

"Yeah, we're good. I'm really surprised I'm connecting to someone so well."

"I'm not."

Alex looks at me, touched, and lays his hand on my thigh. "Thanks, baby."

Tears sting, brought on by his tenderness. I look away so he won't notice and snuff out the cigarette in a nearby dish.

x

Suspended through Tuesday morning, I finally send Jack a message to clarify our plans: *Am I going to see your big sweet face tonight?*

An hour and a half passes. I'm at the café with Alice and our friend Joanna—waiting. My skin itches.

Finally, Jack responds: "Hey beautiful, I've been in meetings all day. And I'm in another meeting till nine tonight. May we reschedule?"

Both Alice and Joanna embrace me. I cry as I type a reply: *Sure, honey. We'll figure it out!*

Joanna gives me two tissues from a little pack in her purse.

"I'm so sorry, baby," Alice says. "I wish there was more we could do. I wish we could tell him how much this affects you."

"I know," I sniffle into my hands. "But, there's nothing."

x

Later, the usual group of Tuesday night regulars converges on the café's patio: Huascar,

Carly, and Nicole. I'm glad for the distraction of their tale-bearing, even while I perch in my chair, knees to clavicles, and yearn to collapse inward until only a dot remains. Already, I feel like a speck, but my body refuses this impression, remaining stubbornly huge and amorphous.

Huascar and I pass a cigarette back and forth. For a moment, I stare at his glass of beer. *Does that look good—would I drink that? Feh. No. No, I'm okay.*

Will pushes his way onto the patio, greets us, and finds a spot against the railing beside me.

"It's good to see you, Cal," he says. "Although, I'm sorry you're here."

He doesn't specify *because it's a Tuesday night, and you're not with Jack*. It's implied.

Nicole and Carly agree with sympathetic nods.

Jack's gravity on my sense of placement and overall merit must be so obvious—maybe palpable—to those around me. This realization probes me with guilt. Even if the pull of my dented, anxious heart prevents me from sharing in it, I still want everyone else to have a good time.

x

The following Tuesday leaves me bereft once more, after Jack says he's had last minute work dumped on him. I'm at Alice's house. We're lounging in the screened porch when I hear from him.

My phone drops into my lap, and I stare beyond the objects in my visual range until they become pixilated fog. *Feel something,* I command myself, but nothing stands out except the doughy slope of my backside, anchoring me to the lawn chair, into place.

"What did he say?" Alice asks, though she already knows.

With effort, I rediscover my phone in the seat cushion and pass it to her.

"Ugh. I'm sorry, bunny," she says, handing it back.

I whimper, "I don't know what to say. What do I say?"

"Ask him if he's eaten anything."

The message appears on the tiny screen: *Have you eaten? Can I bring you anything?*

With a beep, there's a brisk response: "I haven't eaten, but I will. Thanks." Moments later, "I know we need to talk," he writes, "but I don't have an available minute right now."

I know what this means. I can taste the inevitable disappointment: a rusted, swampy film at the back of my tongue.

x

In the morning, I show up to one of Jack's classes and take a seat in the back row between Alice and Naomi, who—unlike me—are actually enrolled in the course. Irritation paints a gloomy picture of Jack's face. We try not to look at each other for the next hour. When the lecture concludes, students rise with a chorus of rustling pages and scraping chairs, and filter into the hallway. I stay put.

Jack collects his papers and attempts a

smile. "Hey," he sighs.

"Hey."

He is a frantic husk. He reminds me how I know better than most how stressed out he is, how thinly stretched. "I know we need to talk, but I just haven't had any time," he repeats.

"What do we need to talk about, Jack?" But before he can answer, I do so on his behalf. "We're not doing Tuesdays anymore, are we?"

"No. It's just too much for me right now."

The rest of the interaction is a blurred performance. We hug weakly. He says he sees me around and I look happy, and that's enough for him. But I'm not happy, I insist; I'm miserable. He shrugs, stung, but exasperated, because he's too stressed to care. And he's late for a meeting.

Wait—I just have to know: is this relationship something we are putting on hold to explore later, when everything smoothes out, clears up, dies down, releases?

That's the hope—that this can be allowed to blossom in some future time that is not now.

Is that something you want?

I don't know; I cannot care right now. I'm sorry. I have to go.

The door breaks from the frame, and he disappears beyond it.

My jacket lifts from the back of a chair and folds me into its sleeves. My purse strap loops over my shoulder. My feet speak to ankles, who speak to my knees, who prompt my body forward. I leave the room, leave the third floor, touch the stairway, descend like a stone until the second floor opens before me—and he fucking walks by, sees me in the stairwell, but doesn't react, trotting quickly, wedged heels of his boots scraping, and he is gone around the corner, so I continue to step, step, step, attempt not to stumble, floating really, as this cannot be real, please no.

x

Outside, a concrete bench keeps me upright beside Joanna and Alice. I don't remember texting Alice, but she'd come right away. We three smoke, but I don't remember where the cigarettes came from or how they were lit.

"Cal, you work today, don't you? Are you going to go to work?"

Semi-hysterical laughter spills forth. I cannot fathom. I cannot be.

Alice says I'm in shock. Then, she is carrying one of my arms.

It's cold and grey, yet I'm amazingly immune. Buildings scoot by, and I'm partially fused to Alice, being ushered forward and pushed somehow vertically between the sidewalk and the sky, which threatens to descend and consume, if it isn't already.

x

Finally washed free of the day's oily drag, I speak blankly through the dark into the phone. Alex says it's Jack's loss, and I hate this response. It dismisses *my* loss. It implies everything I've mustered over the last year was a waste of emotions, time, and soul. That the exchanges Jack and I shared were, in all actuality, punchlines.

"I don't know," I meekly disagree. "I guess I don't see it that way."

"Well, you still have me," he says, but he is someone else.

x

I stop by the department, where there is coffee, free to students. The administrative assistant is standing in the doorway to Jack's office. I perk up at the gentle rumble of his voice. I hadn't expected him to be in, but now that I know he is, I anxiously wait. I blow over the coffee's surface while the cup stings my palms.

The phone rings, and she runs by me, sighing.

I tread down the hall and creep into Jack's view.

He brightens, greeting me, but there isn't time; he's typing up a recommendation letter that is due in minutes.

I circle the desk to hug him. His embrace is unyielding, yet we're both too tense to melt into each other while the door is open and there's so much to be done.

"I'm sorry for imposing myself yesterday," I say into his shoulder.

"It's okay. I understand why you felt you had to be there."

We release each other, and I gravitate back toward the door.

"Hey, you know, as long as you're alive, you're going to get through this."

He smiles. "I'm not sure that I'm alive right now, but thank you."

I teeter, reflecting the same wear in his smile. "I love you," I mouth, soundlessly—desperately.

"You too," he returns, kissing his fingers before waving to me.

I leave, and it's the most tranquil afternoon I've sensed in weeks.

x

There. Hopefully, that brings this journal up to speed.

25 October 2016

Current mood: anxious

Current music: Radiohead, "How to Disappear Completely" and "Motion City Soundtrack"

Yesterday, I saw a new counselor, who suggested I try to speak to Jack again. It didn't need to be a long conversation, she advised, but one had to take place to address my anxieties. I've been afraid to pressure Jack into seeing me again, given the monolithic amount of strain he's under. Nevertheless, I agreed that until we spoke, I wouldn't get the closure I needed to start shifting my focus back to myself—my own needs and ambitions—and my other relationships.

I wasn't planning to talk to him today. I'd only stopped by the department for a cup of coffee and noticed Jack's door was open and [another professor] was standing inside. I politely waited in the hall. After [the professor] left, I skidded inside and shut the door. I trembled and labored to catch my breath.

"I'm so sorry," I began. "I know it's hard for you to see

me because it forces you to be vulnerable at a time when you need to be robotic to get shit done, but..." I explained how I felt strangled, unsure how to exist with so much uncertainty. I wanted to give him space, but it was killing me not to be informed.

Jack radiated frustration. He didn't know what to tell me, reiterating that I know better than anyone how much he's drowning. He said he's emotionally vacant, and though he could see that I was upset, he couldn't offer me anything.

My knees continued to shake. "I need to sit down."

"I'm going to keep working," he grumbled. After a long, tense pause, he said, "You look imprisoned by your feelings, Cal. If you need me to tell you to fuck off so that you can be free of this imprisonment..."

"But, do you want to tell me to fuck off?"

"No—"

"Then, I can't! How could I, if it's not truly what you want?"

The conversation was all over the place. Unfortunately, I can only isolate bits and pieces.

He asked how I was, though I obviously wasn't well. I shared the consuming fears about his physical and mental health, and that I worried he may continue to be weirdly distant once the semester ended and his workload decreased.

He asked about Alex. I shook my head, starting to cry. He frowned. "What, did he run off with that other woman or something?"

"No, we've agreed to take a break until I can get my shit together and sort out what's going on between you and me."

"Oh my god, okay." Jack stood. "Come here. Come over here."

We hugged, and he kissed me.

Jack apologized for his anger and explained how it was a masking emotion, obscuring his sadness and pain. He said he's been "exploding on everyone," and even blew up in one of his Intro classes after a student pulled out their phone during a lecture. "I probably dropped the F-bomb thirty times," he admitted.

Most importantly, I didn't have to worry about him attempting suicide again. "The thought hasn't even entered my mind," he assured me. I cannot accurately express what massive relief this brought me.

Still, he couldn't give me a definite answer about our relationship. He just kept saying he didn't know, and doesn't foresee his workload subsiding. He wants to continue seeing me, but he's unsure how to achieve this.

I said I'd wait. He has all of me, and I'll wait.

When it became clear I had to leave, we stood. We hugged again, and he kissed me with urgency. His hand fell to my breast and curled around until he found my nipple. The other slipped between my legs.

I asked if he'd be interested in getting dinner around Thanksgiving break. He said he would like that and would be in touch.

"Good luck," he called, once the door was open and people could hear us, as if we'd only deliberated where to find the best doughnuts in town or some shit—anything besides what was actually said.

So, I have no idea what's going to happen between us. But, Jack said he's not suicidal. He's overworked, but he's been proactive: seeing a counselor, working out, and eating well. He's not going to bottom out. He won't die.

28 October 2016

Current mood: groggy

Current music: The Irrepressibles, "In This Shirt"

Over the last couple of days—as I try to make sense of things with Jack—I've found myself contemplating my relationship with Kamyar. In flashes, I've noted similarities in their personalities and mannerisms. Otherwise, I think they're nothing alike.

Kamyar lives two thousand miles away. He frequently works twelve-hour days; he commutes. We speak less now than ever before; lately, we manage a phone call only once or twice a month (although these conversations can last hours). Yet, I feel closer to him than I do to Jack, who lives a few blocks from me, who I see—or saw—once a week.

But, Kam and I have been at this long-distance love for ten years. We've cultivated context and time. When talking to Kamyar, I feel secure. I view little evidence of his daily life, but his reports add up, based on whom I know him to be. I don't always feel this way about Jack, given how often I leave our interactions with more questions than explanations.

I used to think Kamyar was mysterious. Compared to Jack, that's fucking laughable. I don't know what this means, only that it troubles me.

Last night, I couldn't sleep, so I sat up in bed and wrote Kam an email. I shared some of these ideas, though I mostly just relayed how much I miss him. I sent the email after one AM, and he's already responded.

If all goes well, we'll see each other in February, while Alex and I are in Washington DC for next year's AWP Conference. I hope it comes together. I cannot survive the present without something fueling me forward.

November

5 November 2016

Current mood: broken

Current music: Lera Lynn, "My Least Favorite Life"

After the conversation in Jack's office last week, I'd felt calmer, more hopeful. Then Tuesday came, and I collapsed in bed, sobbing ferociously. Mom found me, placed a comforting hand on my back and was surprised by the prominence of my spine, bulging against skin—and she began crying too.

"You've got to let go of this man. It's destroying you," she begged. "If I could take your pain away, I would."

This was too much: my precious, warrior mother, so disturbed by my anguish. Too many people are being impacted by what a loathsome disaster I've become. And there's nothing they can say. It's up to Jack to tell me something—anything—to specify what he wants of me, who I am to him.

Instead, he's said, "I don't know, I can't say." These utterances are followed by secret, wild kisses and caresses in his office, and the promise to see me at Thanksgiving or after the semester—ah, but we'll reexamine this relationship at a later time, in the future, eventually.

What the fuck am I supposed to infer from that? I *need* certainty. I don't understand why he can't give that to me, regardless of the amount of stress he's experiencing. God, does this make me sound too insistent?

I sent these messages on Tuesday, post-weeping spell:

Really hate to tell you any of this. It's embarrassing, but it's me, and how I react to uncertainty. I can't stop crying—literally, a day hasn't passed in the last five weeks in which I haven't broken down in tears. I can't get anything accomplished—nothing for grad school.

I feel emotionally abandoned and really confused and even angry. I'm pretty scared of myself, honestly. I was so much better when we were able to see each other. Now? Now, I'm just a total wreck.

Ya know what's ironic… You actually thought pushing me away was going to be the best thing for me. You said you were afraid that, if we tried to see a relationship through, something explosive might happen, and you'd be scared of what that would do to me.

I don't know what to do. You're the only person who can [give] me any direction on this. I'm so sorry. I'm just so confused.

He never replied, of course.

The following day, I had a counseling session scheduled. This new counselor doesn't know what to do with me. She's mostly quiet, as if she's shaking her head internally, at as much of a loss as I am.

"What do you need from him in order to start letting go of the relationship?" she asked.

"I need him to clearly tell me it's over, if it is. And to tell me why—if it's something I did, or if it really *is* his health or that he's got too much on his plate."

She shrugged. "It sounds like you need to try to talk to him again."

Oy, how many times have I done so already? I stared blankly at her, at the blue-speckled carpet, and picked at my cuticles until our time was up.

From there, I trudged to the sociology department. Jack's door was open, but he wasn't in. I elected to check the room where his last class had just ended. Maybe he'd stayed behind to chat with students.

He was there—and so was Alice! They appeared sullen, deep in conversation. I wavered at the window, but my hunger for some kind of resolution—any definite answer!—was overwhelming. I also thought having Alice there was positive. Maybe she could mediate, if necessary.

I walked in. Alice looked up, her eyes dull and sad. Jack turned, saw me, and was immediately exacerbated.

"Hey, look!" I greeted. "Two of my favorite people!"

"Cal, could you please leave us? We're talking about some

really good stuff here."

"Fine. I'll go wait in your office."

"I'm not going back to my office."

"I'll go wait at the house."

"Cal..." Jack was grim. "I don't know why this keeps happening. I don't know what you want from me."

"I need to know if this relationship is on hold or is it over?"

Then, the bastard gaslighted me. "I've already told you three times now that this is over," he declared. "There's no more relationship between us."

I was aghast. He'd never stated he wanted the relationship to end at all! To lie so boldly—and to do so in front of Alice, as if he wanted to make me look totally unstable. It was infuriating.

"No, Jack!" I countered. "No, you have *not* told me that! All you've said is that you don't know!"

"Okay, fine. So, I'm telling you *now* that it's *over*."

"Indefinitely?"

"Yes."

I plopped down on one of the desks. "Fine. Please tell me why—after everything that's happened between us. Is it your workload, your health? Is it the vulnerability of being in a relationship?"

"It's... It's all of those aspects and more," he fumbled. "It's unhealthy for you. It's just not practical. I just want to be your friend."

I asked why he hadn't messaged me back the day before.

"I didn't respond because there have to be boundaries," he replied.

Amazed, I shook my head. The *chutzpah*! For him to speak of boundaries is fucking laughable.

More was said, but I was so anxious and shocked, I can't recall much. In the middle of the exchange, I became suddenly fixated on the idea that I'd worn the wrong cardigan (blue) with my dress (also blue), as if I could have shifted the conversation in my favor if I'd worn a black cardigan instead. Ludicrous, I know.

Before long, I migrated toward the exit and apologized in earnest for interrupting them. "This isn't me," I swore. "This isn't representative of who I am. I don't like to be invasive or pushy. But, I'm at my wit's end; I didn't know how else to get the answers from you that I needed."

I walked out. I went to the tutoring center, found my desk, and began waiting on students. Thirty minutes later, Alice rang. When I met her outside of the student union, she was surprised by how calm I seemed. And I *was* calm—because I'd finally gotten what I needed: a proper answer.

Why hadn't he told me sooner? Like, why try to protect me from a breakup? He's broken up with me before (only to decide he wanted "to do research" together)! He probably thought I'd eventually give up and move on, like a stray cat he stopped feeding. Still, I'd said I'd wait for him. Why had it required a witness for him to officially end things between us?

If he hadn't wanted to be with me, why did he continue to kiss and touch me? Fuck!

Alice and I agreed to meet at her house so she could fill me in without the risk of being overheard. But before I headed that way, I went home and gathered up everything Jack had ever loaned or gifted me. This amounted to a huge stack of books.

I returned to campus, hiked to the social sciences building, marched into the department, and dropped the books on Connie's desk, accidentally startling her.

"What's wrong?" she gasped. "What happened?"

"I'm fine," I dismissed. In truth, I was livid and well, panicked. Here I was, making it completely obvious something had happened between me and Jack. But, I don't know if I care anymore. I graduated five months ago. What would [the university] do, and why would they bother? Anyway, it's over now. I'm done being his dirty little secret.

Hands trembling, I dug into my purse for my keys. I fumbled Jack's key from the ring and left it on top of the books.

"These are Jack's," I specified. "I don't need them anymore. Will you see that he gets them back?"

"WHAT'S HAPPENED?" Connie's eyes were saucers.

I said nothing. I just waved goodbye.

At Alice's, we retreated to her screened porch with cigarettes and cans of soda water. She described how she'd pulled Jack aside after class to talk about her grade. At first, he tried to blow her off, but she emphasized the difficulty in focusing on her schoolwork while she dedicates so much time to caring for her family. "And CAL IS MY FAMILY," she'd added.

This got his attention. He asked Alice to wait until the rest of the class left so they could speak privately.

She informed Jack that I've been wondering aloud about whether he's exploited me, and how she's talked me out of reporting him. She could see he loved me. But, the unknown—his well-being, the status of our relationship—was tearing me apart. She detailed how poorly I've been: losing weight, cutting myself, and beating my legs until they were spotted with bruises.

Jack's responses were flat, indifferent. By Alice's retelling, it didn't sound as though he was interested in how I was doing or if it even mattered to him.

"I've been trying to end things for a while now," he'd said, adding how he couldn't understand how I'd failed to recognize that.

He hadn't been direct enough with me, Alice pointed out, and it certainly didn't help matters for him to be physically affectionate with me.

"Well, she always starts it," Jack stated.

What. The. Fuck. This is simply untrue. He'd first kissed me last Tuesday in his office, and when we started having sex again this summer, it was only after he initiated it. Furthermore, who gives a shit? There's *always* been a power imbalance. If he didn't want me to touch or kiss him, he's the one with the power to stop it—and he never has. He's *always* sought me out. I can't believe he'd say that!

All right. I have my stupid, *fakakta* answer. Does it make any sense? Has any of this made any sense?

No, but I believe you cannot make sense of insensible people. And Jack has acted insensibly toward me. Chronic illness aside, I think he's a deeply wounded person. I think he's unskilled at keeping friends and having relationships that require real emotional work or compromise. I wonder if loving me made him feel exposed.

Because I'm a pathetic *schnook*, I'd be willing to see Jack during winter break and listen as he decompresses from this insanely stressful semester. But to rekindle a relationship? No fucking way.

I just need to focus on repairing myself. I'm sick of crying everyday—*every single day*. The all-consuming anxiety, the distraction. Missing shifts at work. Hurting myself in empty attempts to objectify my pain, confusion, and worry.

I'd like to get some sleep. Start rebuilding intimacy with Alex. Recommit myself to my immediate goals. I haven't touched any materials for grad school in a long time.

I just want to feel like myself again, but at this point, I don't know what that would take. Everything has come second to Jack for so long.

THE EXPLOSIVE SOMETHING

"What can be more fantastic and unexpected than reality? In fact, what can be more improbable than reality?"

-Fyodor Dostoevsky

"He seemed
For dignity composed and high exploit.
But all was false and hollow; though his tongue
Dropt manna, and could make the worse appear
The better reason."

-Jack Milton, *Paradise Lost*

"If people were always kind and obedient to those who are cruel and unjust, the wicked people would have it all their own way; they would never feel afraid, and so they would never alter, but would grow worse and worse. When we are struck at without a reason, we should strike back again very hard; I am sure we should - so hard as to teach the person who struck us never to do it again."

—Charlotte Brontë

November (cont.)

11 November 2016

Current mood: distressed

Current music: Chelsea Wolfe, "The Color of Blood" and "The Abyss"

On Saturday, Alex, our friend Amy, and I saw Ira Glass speak at [a performing arts center]. We had a wonderful time. We applauded and cackled gleefully, as if Glass's jokes were meant just for us. It was a restorative experience.

The following day, my former classmate Zahra made a Facebook post about attending the event. I commented, and she replied that she'd spotted me in the balcony seats above. Jack once said he'd briefly dated Zahra, after he and [his partner] Tracy Hines had split up. I'd asked what their relationship was like.

"Oh," he said flippantly, "she was *crazy*."

Weird. She'd only ever struck me as energetic and passionate.

I'd asked Jack what he meant. "She was just nuts," he claimed. They dated for a few months after she'd graduated, but he ended things when she'd suddenly freaked out, fearing she'd contracted herpes from a previous boyfriend. I asked Jack if they'd had sex, and he said no, "everything but intercourse."

Remembering this, I reached out to Zahra in a private message. I figured it would help to process my breakup if I had the benefit of someone else's impressions. Female solidarity and all that.

She responded that evening, and we arranged to speak first thing in the morning. By the time she rang, I was already up and dressed. I'd just bought a pack of cigarettes at the gas station and was on foot, heading toward campus.

Firstly, Zahra wouldn't refer to their interactions as dating, as all they'd done was hang out at each other's respective homes, watch movies, flip through books, and talk. They may have kissed, but that was as far as it went. Ultimately, she wasn't willing to start a relationship while she was still his student and he had power over her.

Hearing this, I stopped walking. My blood froze. "Wait, what? You were still in class with him?"

"Yeah, although I can't remember which one. And it was fine—hanging out. I just, you know, I worked really hard to get the grades I got. I wouldn't want someone to think I got good grades because I was fucking around with the professor."

Zahra continued, stating she thought Jack was a fun, thoughtful person and didn't hold any ill will against him. She simply wasn't looking for anything substantial, whereas he was, so they opted to be friends and respect their faculty-student roles.

However, she'd been creeped out on one occasion. A friend dropped by her apartment to grab something while Jack was there. He'd hid in the hallway, motionless and silent, until her friend left. Zahra thought this was shady, like he was afraid of being seen with her.

Zahra also described asking about a leadership program on campus. That day, she was wearing a necklace Jack had bought her during a trip [abroad]. The woman assisting her turned out to be Tracy Hines. She complimented the necklace. Zahra explained how a friend had acquired it in [Europe]. To which Tracy replied, "Oh, how funny! My significant other just returned from [Europe]. You might know him..." She was, of course, talking about Jack.

At this part of Zahra's narration, my brain exploded. Totally. Fucking. Exploded.

I saw white. I struggled to hold the phone, which suddenly weighed fifty pounds. Knees swaying—*oh my god I'm going to pass out*—I leaned into a wall. I gulped for air.

If he'd cheat on Tracy... Magda. Oh my god, Magda. Had he—no. No, surely not.

And yet... Maybe. It would make sense.

While I scrambled on my end, Zahra went on, saying although this exchange had bothered her, she gave Jack the benefit of the doubt. When they'd started hanging out, he told Zahra he'd just gotten out of a long-term relationship—and his house *was* sparsely furnished, as if someone had recently vacated. Tracy referred to Jack as her significant other, but did it really mean anything? Maybe she said it out of habit.

Eventually, Zahra asked what Jack had said about her. I admitted her impressions of him were more forgiving than the way he'd described her, how he had called her "crazy."

She laughed. "I'm definitely not crazy, and I most certainly was never crazy with him. What a weird thing to say!"

I asked about the herpes scare. Zahra was shocked and hurt by this. It was totally made up. She couldn't understand how, years later, Jack would say anything like that.

Zahra asked if I remembered Kayla, adding, "I heard they were going out a while back."

I shared what I knew of their situation: how Jack said Kayla was being "stalk-y" toward him, and how Mikki confirmed they'd been texting, carrying on some bizarre, sexually-charged...something.

Before ending the call, Zahra and I agreed that while Kayla was an odd duck, she was bright and sweet, though perhaps a little naïve. Neither of us believed she'd stalk anyone—not unless she was being led on. Not unless she believed such extreme measures were justifiable.

Certainly, I know what it's like to have no alternative but to appear unannounced to get Jack's attention. Still, I always walked away feeling like I hadn't gotten the whole truth. I suddenly have a lot of empathy for what Kayla must have gone through.

Nevertheless, I was resistant. Jack loved me. I'd felt transcendent with him. My friends noted how it emitted between us like electricity. It had to have been real. There's no way he—he, of all people!—would have faked it or intentionally strung me along. Not this man, whom I've known for so many years and wholly trusted.

My role model. My mentor. My lover. My heart.

No. No, no, no, no, no... I couldn't believe it. It still seems so unbelievable.

But, I *had* to see it now.

How often did Jack see Magda? I knew, despite breaking up, they remained buddies. Through the spring semester, she'd stopped by to watch TV. After their program wrapped up and she'd gone, Jack invited me over, always around seven-thirty. Other times, he'd cancel our plans to rush over to Magda's and help her with something emergent, or because they'd quarreled and had to patch things up. Why had they continued to have so many arguments if the relationship was over?

Once during the summer, I'd driven by his townhouse on my way to the store. Magda's car was parked outside and was still there, hours later, after I'd left home again to go to Amber's. I thought this was peculiar, so when Jack and I started dating again, I'd asked if he and Magda had been intimate.

"No," he answered. "She has put her head on my shoulder in a comforting gesture, but that's been the extent of our intimacy." And I'd believed him.

Jack was always so paranoid about being in public together, even when we were surrounded by strangers while wandering landmarks in Chicago, and later, after I'd graduated. He wasn't trying to protect me or my academic reputation. No, he just didn't want Magda to find out!

I had to be sure. I had to check something.

After my call with Zahra, I finally sent a message to [my friend] Thea. I wasn't mad at her, I explained; I was just trying to figure things out. I asked if she'd made an anonymous call to the sociology department in April, proclaiming that Dr. Blair was exploiting a female student.

Thea wrote back, saying no, she'd done no such thing.

My moment of epiphany wasn't delicate or evanescent as it's sometimes expressed in literature and other artistic media. No, it was far more brutal—beyond the tired clichés about a light coming on or a slap in the face. This was an eruption, violent and unanticipated, with the pulverizing force of a mudslide or tsunami. Like my very soul, after having been slowly twisted into a contorted wad over the last eleven months, suddenly snapping loose to flap wildly and shred my sense of reality into ribbons.

Saying he'd always been attracted to me—one of his star pupils. Saying he hadn't loved anyone as deeply as he loved me. Saying he wanted to take care of me. Contemplating how we would live together, combining our books and furniture. Entrusting me with a key to his home, the password to his computer. Talking about signing his 401(k) and insurance benefits over to me. Talking about taking me to meet his parents and see where he'd grown up. Talking about writing, making art, and doing research together. Discussing plans to marry.

Telling me I knew him better than anyone. Telling me things he said he'd never told anyone. Showing me artwork he'd never shown anyone. Crying in front of me, with me, and in my arms.

The abrupt loss of interest after I'd graduated. Failing to make solid plans or canceling them outright. Stonewalling communication. Holding me emotionally hostage.

Telling me I was trying to make him into someone he wasn't, when I tried to express how his behavior made me feel. Accusing me of rushing things, imposing myself on his space—after he'd given me a key, a toothbrush, bought us groceries to share, and encouraged me to use his home as a sanctuary.

Telling me he hadn't been serious about marriage—that it

was meant to be symbolic, a metaphor. Appearing confused because I'd taken our plans literally. Then, traveling to Iceland anyway, and intending to hide it.

Shifting the conversations toward his physical health, his suicidality. Blaming these issues for everything that didn't seem right between us. Rarely did I have an opportunity to raise my own concerns as everything about his circumstances was so imperative.

Always emphasizing the harm that would come to me if administration learned of our relationship—the threat to *my* academic future, *my* reputation. Saying it would "stigmatize" me, follow me into graduate school "like a scarlet letter."

I was inflated with terror all semester and into the start of the summer. And yet, once I began to question the validity of his warnings, I was still too scared to say a word.

Two weeks ago, I sat with that counselor, rippling with anxious dread, in part because I was worried about Jack, but also felt confused and abandoned, and...

"Why can't you let this go?" the counselor had asked.

Because I'm afraid I was right, and he has *exploited me.*

He'd lied to me. I was not special. I was not the first.

Me. Zahra. Kayla.

Was I just one more cog in his conquest machine? Just another young woman to fall under the scope of his fetish—his student? *His fucking students!*

More than one. Others. Plural. Me plus.

There could be someone else. He's cancelled most of our recent plans with last minute excuses. Later, I would drive or walk by as I headed home from campus or the café, and notice his lights were on—often late at night, when he'd normally be asleep. And I just assumed he was still up, working...

Oh, god. Who could it be? What if it's another student?

I have to do something. Someone else might get hurt.

I called Alex, Bevel, Kamyar, and Amber. I deliberated with Alice and Will.

All were deeply unsure and echoed the same hesitation: the risks to my academic career. To bring attention to Jack, I'd have to throw myself under the bus. My sociology degree could be revoked. I might have to re-enroll, retake a slew of classes, and delay my graduate school plans. Was I *really* willing to make that sacrifice?

Yes, actually—*yes.*

What lessons have been beaten into my brain over the last decade? Personal troubles are public issues. The things that happen to you don't belong to you. No social action occurs in a vacuum. An object in motion stays in motion unless acted upon by an outside force.

"It's not just about me," I told them. "It's about protecting other students—other *women.*"

There was no question about it. I couldn't live with myself if I didn't speak up. I had an ethical responsibility to report him. And if my suspicions were accurate, there was no time for hesitation.

I needed a plan.

A few times this semester, Alice has brought me along to her film and theater class, which is led by Grace Driscoll. I'd admitted to Grace that Jack and I were dating and touched on some of our issues. Grace hadn't liked what she heard, but was supportive nonetheless.

Because we trust her, Alice suggested I first ask Grace for guidance. She gave me her phone number, and I called right away.

I briefed Grace on what I'd learned after talking to Zahra. Grace huffed angrily. She declared the situation was fucked up, and Jack sounded like a predator. Hold tight for further instructions, she advised.

As promised, Grace rang back the following morning and provided the phone number of a trustworthy [human resources representative]. I jotted the number on my hand and stepped outside of the library with my phone. I don't remember how the conversation began, but it ended with the HR rep instructing me to meet with Linda Barrow, the ADA coordinator, who also acts as the Title Nine coordinator.

Ugh. This was not what I wanted to hear. Dr. Barrow was known for failing to take Title Nine complaints seriously. Too, as my learning disability case was being processed, her exchanges with Jack had conveyed an awful impression.

I didn't like the idea of going to anyone before speaking directly to the department head, Dr. Eleanor Parsons. Rather than catch wind of my complaint via some vague, through-the-grapevine bullshit, I thought she should hear from me directly. Plus, Jack required immediate accountability at the departmental level, if he had really moved on to another student.

After the call with the HR rep, I went to see Connie. She quietly asked if I was all right. She'd been worried about me since I turned up with Jack's books and the house key. "I've never seen you like that," she observed. "You were so frantic!"

"Did he say anything when you gave them back to him?" I asked.

"No. He didn't tell me anything; he just took them."

I nodded, mulling nervously, and poured a cup of coffee from the pot beside her desk.

Without specifying the reason, I asked Connie if I could schedule a meeting with Eleanor, adding that I'd like her to sit in as well (so I wasn't alone).

We settled for Thursday (the 10th) at noon.

"Jack will be out of the office," Connie offered gingerly. Our eyes met, and I looked away.

Then, I heard Jack's voice in the hallway and hastily left. As I retreated, I stole a glance over my shoulder and saw him leaving the stairwell with a student athlete. When he saw me, he smiled and waved a couple of fingers.

I glared back, lips pursed, and got the fuck out of there.

For the next two days, my anxiety was a constant battering. I rattled inside of my clothes, shivering with fear. To distract myself, I met with friends at the café to watch the election coverage. I couldn't focus, could barely react when I awoke on Wednesday and learned that motherfucking Donald Trump was elected president, *oy gevalt*!

Yesterday morning, I cried as I drank my coffee and got dressed. My head splintered. My *kishkas* churned. I can honestly say I've never been more afraid in my life.

As I trudged to campus, I blathered to myself in an attempt to organize my thoughts, but it was pointless. So much has happened since last December.

I deserted my desk in the tutoring center to trace circles outside and smoke like a grubby engine. I checked the time again and again, stacking the minutes. I'd written Jack an email, and just before I began walking to the sociology department, I pressed "send."

Nov 10, 2016 at 11:51 AM

subject: Turning you in

Jack,

After last Wednesday, I was prepared to disregard what's happened between us—to chalk it up to you being overworked, overstressed, suffering low self-esteem, and lacking the self-awareness to be a good partner. Then, after talking to a former student of yours, I changed my mind. She was someone you said you'd dated briefly after you and Tracy split up. She also told me nothing you'd said about your relationship with her was true. She was intimidated by the power imbalance and unwilling to fuck you while you had authority over her.

I think you similarly pursued me because you get off on the dominant-obedient dichotomy. This would explain why you seemed to lose interest in our relationship after I graduated. I also believe you are conflict avoidant, reckless, and have nonexistent boundaries.

Finally, you are a loathsome fucking liar and emotionally abusive. You strung me along when you talked about eloping with me in Iceland. You lied about your relationship with my classmate and called her crazy. You lied when you said I was the first student you've ever gotten involved with. I think you lied about Kayla as well. And with all of this in mind, I suspect you dated Magda longer than you indicated to me.

The worst part is I can no longer believe anything that passed between us was genuine. I can't believe that you loved me. I can't believe I'm really as beautiful or brilliant as you said. I can't believe I mattered to you. After all of this, I'm having difficulty believing that I matter at all.

I feel very much like the quilt I gave you—the quilt I worked my ass off to finish in time for your birthday. The quilt you said was a piece of artwork and should be exhibited—which I saw crumpled up in the back of your fucking closet the last time I was in your house. Like you should treat a piece of art, huh?

How can someone who preaches social justice treat a person with my background the way you've treated me—or any of us? We students are vulnerable, stressed by the pressures of supporting ourselves in school, completing our studies, and preparing for the next chapters of our lives. And me: I live an impoverished lifestyle, am recovering from alcoholism, and always work to try to better myself, despite devastating hardships and my inherent desire to self-harm or self-sabotage. You knew all of this about me, and you made me believe you loved me, wanted to take care of me. Then, you gas-lighted me, suggesting you'd never expressed these sentiments and acted confused when I referenced them. How fucking heartless are you?

I should have listened when you freaked out in September and said what was occurring between us was exploitative. At the time, I thought the root of this talk was your pitiful self-esteem. Now, I understand it was a crisis of conscience.

So, I've decided to report you. I don't trust that administration will address your sexual misconduct with any fruitful outcome, but I do hope speaking with Eleanor and Connie will provide you with the accountability you so badly need.

I wouldn't wish the last year of my life on anyone. I became a different person to facilitate my involvement with you. I betrayed myself, only to be betrayed by you. Now, when I look back on the end of my undergraduate career, I feel sick to my stomach; I feel like trash. Given this, I

> feel I have a responsibility to share my experiences if it means discouraging you from engaging in this kind of abuse with other students. This should not have happened—to me or anyone else. It surely shouldn't fucking happen again.

I stumbled into the foyer. Upon seeing me, Zach leaned into the doorway of his office and conjured a gentle, parental tone. "Hi, Cal. How are you?"

"Not good."

"It's going to be okay," he assured, which further alarmed me. *What does he know?*

Connie beckoned me into Eleanor's office. The door closed, and before uttering a single complete word, I started weeping. Connie held my hand. Both she and Eleanor encouraged me to relax and take my time. They were very patient, very kind.

"I'm so terrified and embarrassed," I finally managed, "but I'll just start at the beginning and try to be as linear as possible." Then, I told them *everything*.

I first provided background: how I'd taken classes with Dr. Blair on and off for years, and when I declared a second bachelor's in sociology, he offered to be my adviser. Throughout all this time, he'd maintained professionalism—until December of last year, when he hit on me.

At this, Eleanor's face darkened; her expression of curious concern turned to disgust. Connie stiffened in her seat.

I admitted feeling flattered, though confused. I explained how we began meeting at his home to discuss my homework during winter break, then to hang out casually, and how, "to make a long story short, we began a sexual relationship."

I recounted asking Jack how we should proceed, and how he convinced me to keep it a secret because if anyone found out, it would call my achievements into question, delay my graduation, and put my sociology credits at risk of being revoked.

"Cal," Eleanor interrupted softly. "That's just *not* true."

I gawked at her. "You mean… I'm not in trouble?"

"No, that's not how this kind of situation works." My grades were mine; no one could retroactively withdrawal my course accomplishments. She said as a student, I wouldn't be punished because my professor was acting inappropriately. He was the responsible party. If there was to be disciplinary action, it would be ascribed to *him*.

"But…" I croaked, disbelieving. "Are you sure?"

Eleanor nodded. She was sure.

So… HE LIED ABOUT THE RISKS, and I've been so scared and paranoid and trapped—FOR NOTHING!? ALL THIS TIME!?

I buried my face between my knees. Eleanor handed me tissues from a box on her desk.

"I promise I did the work!" I cried. "I did all of the assignments for him, and I worked my ass off. That math class—it was really hard!"

"Shh, of course you did the work," Eleanor soothed. "I *know* you did. I saw your presentation. I saw how much you put into that class."

When I got to the part about the anonymous caller, Connie was astonished. It had never happened. Eleanor, too, said this was the first time she was hearing anything about it. Furthermore, there'd never been a conversation between her and Jack about us being "too close." She'd never asked him to provide a summary of what we'd done in the math course.

He'd made it all up.

When I referenced Jack's suicide attempt, Eleanor was stunned. No, he hadn't confided in her about any such thing. "Did you see any marks on his neck?" she asked.

No, not that I remembered seeing.

"Surely, it would have left marks."

So, he lied about that too? Had even cried in my fucking arms—*AND IT WASN'T TRUE?!* Oh my god. It's too despicable!

Finally, I relayed everything Zahra had shared about her

experiences with Jack, and about the obscurities regarding his conduct with Kayla.

Shaking her head, Eleanor said she now regretted never saying anything to Kayla. She remembered Jack mentioning that Kayla was displaying some stalking behaviors toward him, but he hadn't seemed bothered—just annoyed, really.

"I could kick myself for not pulling Kayla aside to check on her," Eleanor lamented.

I told her she couldn't blame herself. Why question him if he appeared to have the matter under control? She trusted him. We had all trusted him.

I also brought up Jack's workload. "Is there any possible way that he's working as much as he says? A hundred hours per week?"

"No. Not even close."

I explained how angry he'd been when she'd dropped a fifth class on him only two weeks before the semester began.

"No, we'd discussed that at length. He *volunteered* to help co-teach that course with me."

My sobbing resumed. If he wasn't as busy as he'd said, then he couldn't have been as stressed out either, so he couldn't possibly be as sick as he'd described... *Oh my god, oh no.*

Finally, I asked about Magda. "Do you know when they broke up—at the beginning of last semester or later? Was there overlap? I *have* to know."

Connie and Eleanor exchanged looks. Cautiously, Connie admitted she knew a little about their relationship; however, Magda had shared these things with her in confidence.

"But, was there overlap?"

She looked down at the floor and tightened her lips.

No. Please no.

"Oh, god!" I moaned. "There *was*, wasn't there? He cheated on her—that poor woman!" I broke down again. "Someone has to tell her! She deserves to know!"

Again, they traded glances. Discomfort bloomed between

them, but they said nothing.

What happens now?

Before all else, Eleanor asked me to cease all contact with Jack.

"I have nothing more to say to him," I said. "I don't expect him to reply to my last email. He's been ignoring me lately. He didn't even text me back last week when I told him I was afraid of what I might do to myself because of how confused and hurt I was."

Eleanor angrily sucked her teeth. This was not the person she'd known and worked alongside for all these years—the professor who always seemed willing to bend over backward to support his students.

She requested all correspondence between us—any documentation regarding his conduct. I stammered in response. I don't have a smartphone; my mobile forces me to delete text messages once it reaches a certain capacity. The last messages between us begin in September, and there's nothing noteworthy in them. I have a few emails and the notes he'd written to me. I have this diary.

Eleanor wants all of it.

She also instructed me to see the sexual assault prevention coordinator (SAPC) and maybe file a report through her. I agreed to do so on Monday.

Overall, they seemed stunned and appalled by what I had to say. It felt both validating and depressing to see their reactions—like, *oh god, everything really was that outrageous and awful.* And they were so kind and supportive. I'd expected disbelief and punishment. Yet, this hadn't happened; moreover, no one blamed me or questioned my academic fortitude. It wasn't anything like Jack had described.

Before I left, Connie and Eleanor pressed me to keep seeing a counselor and to take care of myself. They reminded me I was the victim in this situation, and I didn't need to make excuses for Jack anymore. "It's okay to allow yourself to be angry now," Eleanor advised.

15 November 2016

Current mood: anxious

Current music: RAKTA, "Intenção"

Monday was a shit-show. As I wept and repeated my story to the SAPC—which took about an hour—she gawked silently. Then, she sincerely apologized. My situation required filing a Title Nine complaint against Jack, and the one person who could do that with me was Linda Barrow.

It was my turn to gawk. *Um, so if you can't take Title Nine reports as the sexual assault prevention coordinator, what do you do exactly? Pass out handouts? Give little speeches at fraternities?*

I didn't ask. I muttered, "Thanks anyway," and limped away.

[My close friend] Andy walked me to the administrative suite to make the appointment with Dr. Barrow. She offered to accompany me, but I declined. I'd inconvenienced Andy—and my other close friends—with my troubles enough already.

The meeting was very uncomfortable. Dr. Barrow started by dryly outlining Title Nine protocol. As she spoke, I chewed my lip and tugged at the lacy skin around my fingernails. Then, she leaned back in her chair with a notepad, and again, I recounted events.

I've repeatedly heard that Linda is rigid, hard to read, and demanding. And perhaps this is true; she definitely came across as phlegmatic. However, by the end of my testimony, she was noticeably bristled and said Jack sounded emotionally abusive. She even phoned the local women's center to explore what counseling services they offered and urged me to visit them.

Linda also asked me, in addition to all of the stuff I gave Eleanor, to write her a general outline of what's occurred. I have no fucking idea how to start. How do I possibly summarize the *tsuris* of the last eleven months?

I'm exhausted, desperate for the pain to halt. I am sick: tense, nauseous, cramped, sore, twitchy, and deeply damaged.

Oh god, why has this happened? How did Jack end up being someone else? My god, I don't know him at all.

19 November 2016

Current mood: solemn

Current music: The Mars Volta, "Roulette Dares (The Haunt of)"

Before my meetings on Monday, I reached out to Magda. If Jack cheated on her and I was an unwitting participant, she has a right to know anything she wants—and I'd rather she heard from me than through some haphazard gossip in the department. She hasn't responded, and I'm unsure if she's even seen my message.

Alice hasn't returned to Sociology of Art since she'd spoke to Jack after class—the conversation I'd interrupted. She says the thought of sharing a room with him makes her nauseous.

She broke down and begged my forgiveness for dismissing my fears of exploitation and convincing me not to report Jack sooner. "I really *did* think he loved you," she mourned. "I was wrong. I thought I could see it, but he was pretending, and I just didn't know!"

"You gave me the best advice you could, based on the information you had," I said.

I don't blame her. No one had seen this coming.

To save her from attending Jack's class, Alice asked to meet with Eleanor and discuss her options. Alice requested that I tag along. Eleanor was just as gentle with her as she'd been with me. It was decided she would complete her assignments for Sociology of Art, but would turn them over to Eleanor instead of Jack.

Because Alice is so behind on her homework, I offered

to help. She's been an invaluable friend to me. Composing chapter reviews is the least I can do, even if the textbook I'm using is Jack's old copy, with his professorial scrawl and underlining of passages featured throughout the chapters—ugh.

21 November 2016

Current mood: crying
Current music: Massive Attack, "Saturday Come Slow"

The cold has swept in. My extremities constantly burn with chill, so I crave the refuge of Jack's townhouse, which was always warm and comfortable, when I rarely felt warm or wholly comfortable elsewhere.

Even in bed, under all of my blankets, I'm freezing. That bastard had promised to take care of me. He'd promised me a home, *an actual home*—an escape from this musty, decrepit house, its corners still packed halfway to the ceiling with Dad's hoarded boxes and junk electronics. This house, which Mom and I share with moths, beetles, spiders, and freeloader opossums and feral cats who've infiltrated the basement.

I can't entertain any memories of him now. It especially revolts and frightens me to experience the occasional stab of yearning, but it's like muscle memory, and I can't control it. My body has become foreign to me—a snare. Loving Jack had been magic; I'd idealized him.

Well, *of course* it had felt fantastical—*BECAUSE IT WASN'T FUCKING REAL.*

More tears. How haven't I run out of tears?

26 November 2016

Current mood: upset
Current music: VNV Nation, "Rubicon"

Alice says Jack raped me.

Amber isn't sure. When I asked what she thought, she responded with the same question: "Do *you* think you were raped?"

"I don't know," I groaned. "Maybe? I don't know was else to call it."

I know he manipulated and abused me. I would've never consented to even a goddamn hug if I'd known what I know now. But as Alice says, it wasn't just that I was oblivious; he lied about everything. That makes my consent uninformed—or worse, coerced. And sex without consent, or coerced sex, is rape, isn't it?

I think she's right. I mean, wouldn't that explain why I've been a disaster in a meat-sack? Crying, shaking—the embodiment of crisis. If it wasn't rape, then why I am reacting like a rape victim?

Decmber

1 December 2016

Current mood: overwhelmed

Current music: RAKTA, "Ganex E Black Mob"

This weekend, I received a text message from [a friend]. She said Phoebe Kosel, an anthropology professor, had mentioned I was going through a really difficult time and to send her love. [My friend] asked what had happened and said she was available if I needed anything. I thanked her without elaborating.

Yesterday morning, I stopped by the department for some coffee and to check in with Connie. Phoebe passed the entrance, in conversation with a student. Upon seeing me, she greeted sweetly, "Hey! How are you?"

Outside of her office, I dangled against the wall until the other student left. Then, I dipped inside.

I told her [my friend] had messaged me and asked Phoebe how she'd heard.

"Through an unofficial source," she said.

Ah, hell. People are already tale-bearing. "How much do you know?"

"Pretty sure I know everything." She kept her voice low, warning, "We don't want Anna to hear." After a bit, she said, "We should probably talk downstairs, since Anna's in her office."

I assumed Phoebe was referring to the new professor, whose office is next to hers, and switching locations was meant to protect my anonymity. So, I followed Phoebe outside, where we stood in view of the parking lot below the hill. She said Magda was coming to campus and it wouldn't be good if she saw us talking.

"Did she see my message?"

"Yeah, she's seen it."

"Is she okay?"

"No—ah, no."

Fuck. Obviously, she wouldn't be okay. Stupid question.

Phoebe spoke quickly and boisterously, and was completely unforgiving of Jack. She described an incident I knew of: a fight between her and Jack during a faculty meeting. In Jack's version, Phoebe had lied about some pretty significant information. When he confronted her, she erupted and beat her fists on the table. She'd stood up, demanded they take the fight outside, and *threw a chair at him*. Then, she burst into tears, and Eleanor ordered Jack to leave so they could console Phoebe.

When I relayed this, Phoebe threw her head back with laughter. She said she'd had a back injury at the time and could barely carry groceries. How the hell could she have thrown a chair at him? Moreover, his version was backward. She'd called *him* out for lying, finding discrepancies in what *he* was saying. She'd hit her fist on the table—once, in frustration—and did say they should take their disagreement "outside" because it was disrupting the meeting. Jack responded by walking out of the room and filing a complaint with Dean Witterman. Phoebe was required to take an anger management course and write a letter of apology to Jack. She said it was "absolutely mortifying," and she'd felt completely gas-lighted because, as Jack's account circulated, she began to question her own recollections.

So, yes. Phoebe believes I've been victimized, as has Magda.

Then, she spotted Magda's car cruising through the parking lot and directed us to the other side of the building.

I asked when they'd broken up, since I still didn't know for sure.

"Last week, after she saw your message."

"Wha—they've been together *THIS WHOLE TIME*?"

"Yep. They broke up before Thanksgiving break."

"*Oh my god*—I'm going to throw up. I'm gonna fucking puke." I bent over, clutching my stomach to halt the sudden pulse of bile. "Oh my god. I had no idea—*no idea*. He'd told me they broke up in January!"

"Nope, and there's another person I know he's been with too."

I shot back up. "*Who?* A student or another faculty member?"

"I can't say."

"Since *when* with this other person?"

"I think January or around then. Before spring."

"But, that's when I got with him. And it wasn't me? Someone else?"

"Yep."

I hunched over again. "Oh my god, I *have* to get tested. I've been having unprotected sex with him this whole time. He had me thinking I was his only partner."

"Yeah, you and Magda both should really get tested."

With this, Phoebe had to go. She knew Magda would want to see her. She told me to hang in there, and we parted ways.

Now completely distraught, I staggered to the student health clinic to make an appointment to have blood drawn and a pelvic exam—the whole nine yards.

As I stood at the window and told the administrative assistant what tests I wanted, I began to cry uncontrollably. She called over her shoulder toward the counselors' offices that someone was in crisis.

"Oh, no. I'll be fine." Although, I clearly wasn't.

She told me to have a seat. Shortly after, Heather—my new counselor—summoned me into her office. After about thirty minutes, I'd relaxed enough to resume my shift at the tutoring center.

No students were waiting, so I logged into the computer and checked my Facebook account. There was a message from [my friend] Naomi:

> Hey. I wanted to tell you that a bit of a broohaha went on at the end of JB's class today, and it sounded serious.
>
> *What happened?*
>
> About 5 min before the end of class, a woman with short hair came in and sat in the back row. As soon as class was done, she went up to him and said something about his office. I was on my way out the door... Then she started speaking more adamantly, but I couldn't hear what she was saying. And he replied, "No, I'm not doing this with you right now." She got louder and insisted that he had to.
>
> He kept saying his office was open, and that she and whoever else they were talking about could go in. But he insisted he had

to talk to students at the moment.

I exited as this woman said other things I couldn't understand, and she stormed out the other side of the lecture hall, and he called out, "That's right, I'm a bastard!" I caught one last glimpse of her as she looped around the hall to where I was standing, passed me, walking in a fury, then went down the stairs.

I thought of you. I wondered if you had been in his office...

I've had no contact with him.

Ok. I hope you're ok. Whatever was going on with him, it seemed pretty serious. Hopefully, he's experiencing some consequences for his behavior.

I imagine the woman was Magda. I know she came to campus today. JB hasn't stepped foot in the department since I talked to Eleanor. That's why he's not holding office hours. Ha. What does that tell you?

Later, I ran into [my friend] Troy outside of the library. He's still working in the sociology department this semester, and told me Magda had approached him that afternoon.

"She thought you knew about her and JB the whole time," he reported, "and now that he's broken up with you, you're pissed, and that's why you messaged her."

"No!" I objected. "He told me they broke up during the first week of the spring semester. I had no idea they've been together this entire time!"

Troy nodded. "I told her that. I mean, with the way you've been talking about it, I thought they were broken up too. She's been on sabbatical, so she hasn't been around for me to see anything between her and JB in the office that would make me question what you were saying."

Magda also asked about my romantic lifestyle, and whether

I justified the relationship with Jack because I'm polyamorous. But, Troy had explained how polyamory requires informed consent from all involved parties.

Though he couldn't say if his insight had any effect, I was still grateful he'd defended me. We wrapped up our conversation, hugged, and returned to our respective work desks.

Late that night, I was sitting up in bed when Troy rang.

"Hey, Magda just sent me a message on Facebook asking for your phone number. I didn't want to give it to her without asking you first."

"Yeah, totally," I said. "Give it to her. Let her know I'm still up, if she wants to call now."

Within five minutes, my phone rang again. I'd thrown myself into a robe, pocketed my cigarettes, and descended to the kitchen. I probably sounded petrified when I answered. But, so did Magda.

At first, she expressed anxiety about her sexual health, stating all she wanted to know was if my other partners and I were clear of STIs. I shared how I'd made an appointment to get tested earlier in the day. She'd gotten in with her doctor just that afternoon. She was kind enough to offer to disclose her results with me, since it'll be a while before I get my own.

Once this was resolved, Magda remained on the line, requesting details about my relationship with Jack. We compared timelines, discussed his questionable behaviors. We just tried to make sense of it all.

I learned she was, in fact, the woman Naomi saw that afternoon. Magda said Jack has avoided her all week. To get his attention, she'd appeared in his last class of the day. (Pfft, how familiar!) After his lecture concluded, she asked to speak privately in his office. He tried to brush her off, saying he had to meet with students, right there and then, because he's no longer holding office hours. Magda persisted. Jack fumed. They began yelling, and she called him a predator.

Whoa.

From there, Magda described going to Anna's office and demanding to know what she and Jack were up to—if Anna knew she and Jack were a couple, though she had to have known.

This is where Magda lost me, and I needed her to expound.

Okay, so... Before Magda saw my message, she'd already begun to worry Jack was cheating on her with Anna McNeil.

Anna? The same person Phoebe had referenced before steering our conversation outside? As it turns out, yes.

Anna was hired last year, and apparently, she and Jack have been spending a notable amount of time together. Another professor informed Magda that she'd seen Jack's car in Anna's driveway very late one night. Magda asked him about it, but Jack denied being unfaithful and said he and Anna were just buddies and had a lot in common. (Fucking gag me.)

My message was a blow. After reading it, Magda immediately rang Connie to verify what I'd written about making a report. Connie confirmed I'd met with her and Eleanor, but couldn't provide details. When Magda asked if she believed me, Connie said that even if I'd lied about half of what I'd accused Jack of doing, the other half was too fucked up and illuminating to disregard—not in those exact words, but of the same sentiment.

Finally, Jack agreed to see Magda at his house. They had a massive argument because if I was telling the truth, then he was certainly lying about Anna too.

Over Thanksgiving break, Magda couldn't get through to him. She knew Anna was attending the Standing Rock oil pipeline protests in North Dakota during the holiday. And as Magda slipped into Jack's class that afternoon, he was showing Power Point slides of photos taken at Standing Rock.

Both Alice and Naomi said he'd cancelled class on Monday, which would have extended his holiday weekend... Holy shit. *Holy fucking shit!*

When Magda confronted Anna about sleeping with Jack,

she denied it. Though she appeared baffled by the accusation, Magda thought she was lying.

Yeah, well. Probably. I don't know Anna, but if I know anything about Jack, he most likely gave her the same string of bullshit he'd given me: that he and Magda were broken up, but she was clingy and afraid of being alone, blah blah blah—rubbish.

Magda also asked Anna if she knew of the complaint filed against Jack. Not exactly, Anna replied. Jack had told her a student was spreading slanderous emails around to faculty about him. Ha! He wouldn't admit an official complaint has been filed; he's just painting himself as a victim of some thwarted, bat-shit student to elicit Anna's sympathies.

Our conversation was all over the place, and left me dazed. But when Magda brought up Iceland, I completely fell apart.

We were trying to fathom how neither of us had suspected anything, since we'd spent so much time in his home. We both had house keys, for godssakes! I'd *occupied* that house. Earrings beside the sink. My laundry, books, bedding, and clothes tossed in designated piles around his bedroom. My quilt, mapped in pieces on the floor of his spare room. Unfamiliar food in the kitchen—my dishware. How had Magda not noticed?

"I never went upstairs or went to the kitchen," she explained. "If I needed anything, he always offered to get it for me. Whenever I would get there, he'd bring me a glass of water from the kitchen, so I never really went in there."

Hadn't she ever *smelled* anything strange? I pointed out how Jack encouraged me to smoke in his garage when it was especially cold outside. He assured me the lingering, smoky odor didn't bother him, but had Magda detected it or seen my cigarette butts in his trash?

"Well, *actually*," she recalled, "there was one time I remarked on a weird smell after we'd pulled into the garage and gotten out of the car. He blamed it on his neighbors."

She also brought up all of the gifts she'd given him over

the years that are sprinkled throughout his house. Specifically, Magda mentioned buying Jack a present while they were in Iceland together—a folk stylized figurine of a cat—and how he'd displayed it on one of his bookshelves. "But, I guess there was no way for you to know that those were things I gave him," she concluded.

"*What?*" I gasped. My knees swayed and my hands gripped the tile countertop for balance. "You... You went to Iceland with him?"

"Yeah!" She described how they both used money from teaching awards they'd received that spring to fund their trip. He'd flown into Reykjavík ahead of her, and she joined him about four days later.

I choked back a sob.

"Why? What's wrong?"

I divulged our elopement plans. How he'd gone to Iceland without notifying me, intending to have kept it a secret—but not before he gaslighted me, saying he didn't understand why I'd taken our plans so seriously.

Magda was furious. "That is so fucked up!" she shouted. "How does someone do that to another person? How heartless!"

Apparently, *they* watched videos of sites in Reykjavík. They visited the pagan temple. They did research together. They hiked the fucking glacier.

The news sliced through me. My hands slipped from the counter and my knees met the floor.

This accounted for everything: why Jack was unreachable during the last half of that week. He stopped texting or calling me once Magda arrived. And breaking up with me as soon as they returned? If Connie hadn't mentioned it, I may have never known.

Anyway, he told me he'd bought the cat figurine for himself.

4 December 2016

Current mood: sick

Current music: Lebanon Hanover, "Gallowdance"

Magda and I talked again last night, comparing our versions of events in more detail until nearly two o'clock in the morning. Afterward, I was too agitated to sleep, so I baked some oatmeal chocolate chip cookies, ate a couple while watching part of a movie, brushed my teeth, washed my face, and eventually went to bed around four.

Shortly after, I jolted upright, completely soaked. I'd cried out—I remember—because Alex responded that I was okay and was safe with him. I began to cry because I was shaking, wet, and cold. Alex urged me to get up and change into dry clothes. I did so, then snuggled into his back to get warm again.

I don't remember the dream, but I know Jack was the antagonist.

I've had nightmares for the last five nights. This weekend, I had one in which Jack lunged at me, and I tried over and over to deter him. I kept picking up different weapons—a stake, a steel blade—but nothing would penetrate his chest or throat, so he continued to weigh me into the ground. It was a horrifying dream. I awoke in a state of complete helplessness. I've felt that way most of the year.

6 December 2016

Current mood: angry

Current music: Gary Numan, "Rip"

Last Thursday, Alice drove me to the women's center where we met with a therapist named Sonya. As I discussed my reasons for accessing services, my phone rang. It was Linda Barrow.

She'd finished investigating my complaint and had concluded, based on the evidence I provided, my relationship with Dr. Blair had been consensual. Therefore, my claim about having been coerced was unfounded.

What? I haven't given her my victim impact statement yet. Instead of writing an outline, I decided to compose a different report that focused on Jack's more specific abuses and how these have affected me.

Repeatedly, I said I didn't understand. I respectfully disagreed with her findings. What about the inherent power imbalance? What about fabricating risks to my academic career to coerce me into silence? Why was I sitting with a therapist at the women's center—per her recommendation—requesting treatment for rape trauma syndrome if what had occurred between me and Dr. Blair was consensual?

It was fucking absurd.

Linda sounded frazzled, though not angry. She asked again, as she had during our first meeting: did he proposition me in exchange for good grades?

"No, never."

So, the sexual relationship wasn't part of a *quid pro quo* arrangement?

"No, I would have told you," I insisted. "We *never* talked about the grades I should expect from him. He kept assigning me homework, and I always did it and turned it in to him—throughout all of it. The way he coerced me was *different*. He just kept saying that if anyone discovered us, it would ruin everything I'd worked for. He said my sociology degree could be revoked."

Linda wanted a different answer. She could do more with a different answer, but I wasn't going to lie. Surely, the facts were devastating enough.

Linda paused, then sighed. Her decision stuck. The complaint was being closed.

In tearful frustration, I continued to protest.

Eventually, she inserted, "Cal, I don't want you to think I don't have compassion for what you're going through." She apologized for how this has impacted me, emphasized her concern for my well-being. Finally, she wished me the best and hoped counseling would help me heal. She sounded genuinely sorry, I must admit.

As usual, I spent the weekend in [the city] at Alex's. I tried not to think about it. I jogged. I went to *shul* and joined [my friend] Stephen for Shabbos dinner. As soon as I got back to town and entered my house, I saw the official letter from Linda. Mom had set it aside for me.

December 2, 2016

Dear Ms. Phoenix,

This letter is in follow-up to our November 14, 2016 meeting. You provided Dr. Eleanor Parsons, Department Chair in Sociology, with copies of your diary and some handwritten notes. Dr. Parsons provided these documents to me on November 14, 2016, after you and I had met. During our meeting, I gave you a copy of the Non-Discrimination Policy and went over the policy with you.

During our November 14, 2016 meeting and subsequently during our December 1, 2016 telephone conversation you told me that Dr. Jack Blair, Professor of Sociology, did not condition grades or assistance in the class on you entering a relationship with him or engaging in sexual acts with him. You told me that you felt coerced and exploited because:

- Dr. Blair told you that he had never entered into a relationship with a student before, but he believed you were more mature than most students and would be able to emotionally handle a relationship.

- Dr. Blair led you to believe that he was no longer in a relationship with his colleague, Dr. Magda Clark, Professor in Anthropology even though he continued his relationship with Dr. Clark.
- Dr. Blair advised you not to inform anyone that the two of you were sexually involved because it would cast aspersion on your academic record.
- Dr. Blair had told you one of your friends had anonymously contacted Dr. Parsons and reported that Dr. Blair was exploiting you. You told me that this caused you to lose trust in your friends because you did not know who called Dr. Parsons and you began avoiding your friends. You said you met with Dr. Parsons and she denied receiving such a report about you and Dr. Blair.
- Dr. Blair became distant and failed to reply to your attempts to contact him after you graduated even though he had led you to believe that he would marry you.

You wrote in your journal entry on January 16, 2016, "It was my idea to kiss him. I don't believe he would've touched me if I hadn't presented it as an option, made the first move." You also told me on November 14, 2016 and wrote in your December 2015 entries that Dr. Blair helped you complete an independent study course that would count for the Race/Ethnic Relations requirement and a math substitution course so you would be able to meet the requirements to graduate in May 2016.

To assess your complaint of sexual harassment and decide how to resolve your complaint, I reviewed the definitions of dating violence, domestic violence, relationship violence, sexual harassment, and sexual violence in the Non-Discrimination Policy and examined the information you provided and reviewed my interview notes.

Based on the information provided to me, I have decided to close your complaint with a finding that your complaint does not warrant further review under the Non-Discrimination Policy because the actions you described, if true, do not constitute sexual harassment, sexual violence, dating violence, domestic violence, or relationship violence as defined in the Non-Discrimination Policy. Specifically, you acknowledged that you initiated the intimate contact, and you did not provide evidence that Dr. Blair threatened to deny you educational opportunities or to take a negative action against you based on remaining in a sexual relationship with him. Even though Dr. Blair told you your academic integrity would be questioned if anyone found out about your relationship with him, you acknowledged that you felt that Dr. Blair had provided you favors (e.g., grades, course substitutions) and that you were concerned that your academic integrity/success may be questioned if anyone knew about your relationship with Dr. Blair. You journaled in April 2016 that Dr. Blair had proposed marriage and in June 2016 you journaled, "Jack, I understand now that we're not going to get married, and I'm not going to Iceland with you this summer." Finally, you did not provide sufficient evidence to support that you experienced a hostile environment while you were taking classes under Dr. Blair.

I have referred your complaint to Dr. Anna Witterman, Dean of Arts and Sciences, for her review. I have asked Dean Witterman to contact you for any information she may need to complete her review of your complaint. I have provided Dean Witterman with your telephone number.

I took the letter over to Alice's, though there's nothing more to do except to *kvetch* aimlessly. The matter was officially dealt with, closed—*fin*.

Back home and ready for bed, I knew sleep would elude me, so I took my laptop downstairs and smoked a couple of cigarettes while crafting a response. A fruitless task, but for the sake of being heard and getting to bed with a clearer head, I went about it.

Dec 6, 2016 at 12:49 AM

subject: Reaction to Follow-Up

Dr. Barrow,

I received your follow-up letter today. The contents were upsetting, and I'm really confused. I feel as though the information you were able to derive from the diary entries and emails I provided weren't used to facilitate my case, but rather to build a case *against* me. I feel you took things out of context and presented some materials in a way that blamed me for how Dr. Blair has treated me.

In my January 13th entry, I did say Dr. Blair issued me grades I didn't feel I deserved. What you don't understand is that I put a lot of pressure on myself. I'm afraid of failure, or of being perceived as lazy or "half-assing" my work. In many of my past classes with Dr. Blair, I'd felt inadequate as a student because I was distracted by difficult personal circumstances. Throughout my undergraduate career, when I didn't earn anything above a B, it was due to outside conflicts that affected my prioritization of school. In no way was I suggesting that Dr. Blair provided me grades as a method of showing favor or in exchange for anything. I simply didn't have confidence in my work.

If I'd felt Dr. Blair was showing me special regard in this way, I would have reported this. I always did the work assigned to me, and I always tried to do my best. But, perhaps I'm the one who is wrong, given what I now understand about his character and the limitless depths to which he is willing to sink to manipulate someone. It's very possible Dr. Blair issued me good grades because he was trying to gain my trust. I don't know. I don't know that I want to know. It sickens me to think this could be the case.

Nothing else you pointed out in your letter sits well with me, as it's completely dismissive of the fact that, throughout our entire relationship, Dr. Blair continued to have more power than I did. I absolutely feel he used my ignorance of the administrative landscape to his advantage.

I realize the current policies don't regard what I experienced as abuse, but even you yourself recommended I reach out to additional counseling services to treat my trauma-based symptoms. I have done this. I'm doing everything I can to get through this experience safely. But, I'm not going to be okay if something isn't done to prevent a situation like this from occurring again with another student. I cannot live with that.

I'll go ahead and attach my victim impact report to this email, since I didn't have a chance to get it to you sooner.

This afternoon, she replied. Based on the content of her email, she must have read my impact statement, which is good, although I don't know how influential it can be at this point.

Dec 6, 2016 at 12:13 PM

re: Reaction to Follow-Up

Cal,

I have referred your concerns to Dean Witterman and I believe she will follow-up with you. Your suggestion about a policy regarding dating relationships where there is a power differential is being taken seriously. I understand that there is a proposal to create such a policy in a Faculty Senate committee at this time.

> I want you to know that I understand how devastating this has been for you. Even though the case has moved to Dean Witterman, I want you to know that [the university] is taking your concerns seriously. If you have not interacted with Dean Witterman, I believe you will find her to be a good listener and concerned for the academic success of students. In addition, I want you to know that I am concerned for your welfare and I understand that the road to recovery will be long and arduous for you. I wish you the best in your recovery and your future career successes.

I'm still mad, but I'm not directing my anger at Linda Barrow. I don't think it would be fair. It's...all of it, really. The big picture and how my individual experience fits into broader realities. The fact any of this is happening, when all I did was try my best in school and was ultimately victimized by a beloved professor.

I'm angry that everything I've believed for the last eleven months was manufactured. I'm angry because I don't know myself right now, and it's disturbing, makes me feel trapped and itch to peel off my own flesh.

Pondering it all, I do have empathy for Linda. I doubt [administration] has been made aware of a case like this. Even if Linda wanted to pursue things further, I can only provide proof of a sexual relationship. There's no documentation of his coercion, and it wouldn't matter if there was. All of the policies are aimed at addressing "violence."

Semantics has robbed me of justice.

Damn, he was fucking slick. He's probably been getting away with this for a long time.

He just got sloppy. He raped the wrong student.

8 December 2016

Current mood: tired
Current music: Klaus Nomi, "The Cold Song"

Since emailing Linda Barrow, I've also provided copies of my victim impact statement to my counselor Heather, and Eleanor, who'd expressed interest in reading it. Here's an abridged version, highlighting some of the more significant details:

November 21, 2016

When Dr. Blair and I originally began a sexual relationship in late January of 2016, I'd asked him about [the university]'s stance on student-professor relationships. He'd told me there was no policy for or against it, but they were generally frowned upon. When I asked how we should conduct ourselves after becoming intimate, he suggested it would be best to keep it a secret.

It's true that I consented to sexual relations with Dr. Blair. However, I made this decision based on the information he provided to me. I was told his interest in me was unprecedented. He convinced me I was an exceptional person to him, and if it had not been for this, he wouldn't have pursued me while I was still his student.

I now understand these explanations were lies, and he has a pattern of sexually pursuing his students while they were subject to his evaluative discretion. Importantly, Dr. Blair also said he was in the process of dissolving a romantic relationship with his colleague, Dr. Magda Clark. Unfortunately, Dr. Blair did not end his relationship with Dr. Clark at the time he'd specified.

This means I consented to a sexual relationship with Dr. Blair under false pretenses. I was misled and manipulated into providing consent that was *coerced* because I was wildly deceived. As a result, I *feel raped*, because if I'd been aware of the reality of Dr. Blair's past behaviors with students and the extent of his involvement with Dr. Clark, I would have *never* given my consent. Indeed, counselors have pointed out that my responses are consistent with rape-induced trauma.

I've come to equate sex and romantic attention with deception and abuse. When I watch television shows or movies, or read anything that contains these elements, I panic internally—I shut down. Giving or receiving hugs from trusted persons is suddenly difficult for me. I don't want to be touched; even accidental bumps or brushes with people makes me jumpy. I've become hyperaware of my proximity to others, leaning away or moving when people feel too close. I've become unusually distrusting of others—even people I know very well.

My ability to sleep regularly has been severely compromised. I have trouble falling asleep.

Then, I usually wake up several times in the night; sometimes, I awake in a panic or in cold sweats. I've also begun to regard sleep with apprehension, as I've been experiencing a lot of violent nightmares that feature Dr. Blair.

Too, I'm frequently overcome by bouts of weeping, which is out of character for me. Sometimes, these crying episodes seemingly come out of nowhere. I've embarrassed myself by crying at work, in restaurants, or in Shabbos services. This is particularly hard to cope with.

I've also had trouble maintaining focus on tasks, managing my time, or self-care in general. I've had difficulty fulfilling my job duties at the tutoring center, which require patience and attention to detail. I'm constantly exhausted, yet on edge. I've become ambivalent about most things, including both responsibilities and pleasurable hobbies. Nothing appeals to me, whether through necessity or enjoyment. I'm grateful to get to the end of every day, while terrified of what the following day might bring. I end up making meticulous step-by-step mental maps of my activities. For example, before I leave work, I have to know exactly where I'm going, how long I will be there, and what to do when I leave. I'm also apprehensive about being alone for too long, out of the need for distraction and the security to my person.

After what's happened, moving ahead with my academic career is suddenly a very frightening prospect for me. I cannot stomach the reality that I can, again, be under the scrutiny of another male professor, or be enrolled in workshops or share residency spaces with strangers, especially men. Thus, I've decided to abandon my plans to attend graduate school.

I used to view Dr. Blair as a role model—someone I should aspire to emulate. I'd trusted him implicitly. So, to have been taken advantage of and abused by him has shattered my sense of reality. My self-esteem has been crushed. I don't know my merit, my skills, or my value as a person any longer.

In an attempt to objectify my hurt and confusion, I've engaged in self-harm. Though this is done without suicidal intention, it's worth noting that I have considered suicide in recent weeks. I don't want to die, but suicide has come to mind as an extreme method of escaping these uncertain, painful circumstances.

I strongly suggest that administrative consequences be passed down to Dr. Blair to deter him from engaging in future abuses. What has happened to me is completely unacceptable. He has betrayed his role as a protective mentor, and in doing so, has denied the ethical responsibilities dictated by his position.

While I don't feel Dr. Blair should continue to teach, I acknowledge this opinion may not be shared by administrative staff. At the very least, I don't think Dr. Blair should continue to have unrestricted contact with students. He shouldn't be allowed to advise students or maintain regular office hours from behind a closed door.

I'm urgently advocating for policy changes to be made. Students are a vulnerable population, given their lack of power and inability to access authoritative control or justice. Romantic and sexual exchanges between students and their professors should not be permitted. It's very disturbing to me that this university has failed to protect us by providing a policy *against* student-professor relationships. This needs to be addressed, in order to save further students from ending up in situations similar (or worse) to mine, and to ensure that if incidents were to occur, there would be established avenues for rectification.

Yesterday, I gave a copy of my statement to Dean Witterman and sat there, chewing my lips into threads, as she read it. After she'd finished, I gave my account once again, beginning from my first class with Jack in 2009 and up until my recent conversations with Zahra and Magda were relayed. The meeting lasted nearly two hours.

Most notably, Dean Witterman agreed that sexual relationships between faculty and students are exploitative due to the power imbalance, which greatly relieved me. She also echoed something Linda had mentioned about the Faculty Senate proposing policy changes. She promised to keep me informed.

Dean Witterman has upcoming meetings scheduled with both Jack and Magda. I asked if anyone has reached out to Anna to check on her, but I don't remember Dean Witterman's answer. I imagine they're trying to keep everything specific to my complaint. Still, as a woman on behalf of another, I worry about Anna. I'd speak to her myself, but I don't think it's my place to get involved any further. Hopefully, the commotion in the department will inspire her to distance herself from him.

9 December 2016

Current mood: anxious
Current music: AFI, "...but home is nowhere"

An entire year has passed since Jack first flirted with me in his office. One year, and now the thought of him wracks my bones, blood, tissues—down to my very cells.

Don't think, don't think—distract yourself, do something, keep moving, don't think about it. Over and over. On repeat.

Winter break begins soon, and I'll be out of work until mid-January. I have counseling sessions scheduled. I have an appointment at the student health clinic on Monday. Magda's results were all negative, *baruch Hashem*. Knowing this is a huge relief, but I'm still getting myself checked out to be on the safe side.

Both of my counselors have said I must be grieving the loss of the relationship. I don't know if I agree. What's to grieve? He lied about everything. I couldn't have truly loved him because *I don't know who he is*. My love for him was the product of manipulation—and grooming, as Heather pointed out. There's no love to mourn because there was no real love to start. I was being misled, abused. Period. End of story.

I've taken the same approach to my memories of him as I did with alcohol. I can't glamorize alcohol. Did I have fun sometimes? Sure, but those moments are completely overshadowed by the fact that I was poisoning myself, and if I didn't stop, I was going to die. The fun was fleeting; the constant was a sluggish crawl toward suicide. Now, the thought of drinking is repulsive and scary, an invitation to death. I was very lucky to have survived my alcoholism.

It's similar with Jack. Was it passionate and blissful? Sure, but it wasn't rooted in reality. I can't glamorize a coerced fiction. When he now comes to mind, I equate these thoughts to exploitation because that was the truth. Our sexuality—passionate? No. I was being *raped*, completely unaware of what he was imposing onto my body and psychology. He strategically lured me into those "passionate" exchanges.

Nothing to mourn there.

What I do mourn is the loss of time and focus on myself. I mourn the unfulfilled goals, the financial and creative losses. I mourn for those who've also been hurt by what's happened to me. I mourn being the bearer of bad news.

God, it sucks. Why couldn't he just be the person he'd led us all to believe he was?

Sonya did confront me with a tough question: how has this experience made me feel as a woman? I didn't know what to say. My experience has made me incredibly aware of my womanhood, in terms of being victimized by a man. Otherwise, I've felt disconnected from my body and distrusting of my intuition.

The suicidal thoughts are probably the worst part. My mood shifts, depending on what's happened, what I've heard and who I've talked to. Still, I wouldn't want to give that *ganif* the satisfaction of dying over him. He doesn't deserve that power.

10 December 2016

Current mood: apprehensive
Current music: Beirut, "East Harlem"

Yesterday, as I was preparing to go to *shul*, Magda messaged me after her meeting with Dean Witterman. She's expressed anxiety about the conflict with Jack and Anna affecting her job. So, when Dean Witterman asked her to cease contact with me, Magda wrote to say we shouldn't talk anymore.

I was disappointed, even a little crushed. I've grown to love and care for Magda. She's really wonderful—the complete opposite of the way Jack described her.

Selfishly, I also began to panic because this means I've lost another pair of departmental eyes and ears. Both Dean Witterman and Eleanor have stated, due to confidentiality, they cannot reveal what's going to happen to Jack as a result of my complaint. However, the recommendation to file a civil suit was dependent on this—on the ramifications Jack will face and whether I deemed them satisfactory. I reckon one way the school is trying to avoid a law suit is to request the people involved stay away from each other, thus disrupting the exchange of information.

So, I freaked out. Should I wait? Should I talk to a lawyer now? A lawyer could request an account of Jack's consequences. Maybe I should file a suit anyway and start creating a paper-trail? Argh! I don't know!

I cried throughout service. During the rabbi's sermon, I sent Grace a text message, asking for her input. She replied that from what she's heard, [the university] is taking my complaint very seriously.

Phew. Okay.

Grace rang this morning and said all we can really do is wait. She encouraged me to permit myself to relax and practice self-care while administration interprets the current policies in relation to what Jack has done. She understands how the uncertainty is difficult. We set a date to meet and discuss my next steps, which won't be until late January, when the spring semester begins. We'll have to see each other anyway, since I've enrolled in an independent study with her.

A few friends have asked why I intend to stay on campus. Surely, it must be so triggering. Surely, I'd do anything to get the fuck away from that place.

To be honest, it doesn't bother me. I'm familiar with Jack's routines, and I've looked up his schedule for next semester so I can avoid running into him. Plus, I have friends there; were anything to happen, I could find support immediately.

Not to mention, I simply can't afford to lose my student status just yet. I'm dependent on the university's counseling services so that I can continue processing all of this garbage in my sessions with Heather. Outside of the student clinic, I have no access to healthcare, no insurance. I have no other job prospects lined up. Staying enrolled would allow me—as with last semester—to remain employed in the tutoring center. Moreover, how would I hold [the university] accountable to creating consequences for Jack or implementing policy changes if I just disappear?

I shouldn't have to vacate the places where I feel safe. I've done nothing wrong. If Jack doesn't like it, he can catch fire. He can shit blood.

I just need to take big, deep breaths, pick up the scattered parts of myself, remember that I'm loved and valuable to others, and remind myself of the things I enjoy and find beautiful.

When I'm feeling especially overwhelmed, I like to make to-do lists. I've written one to reference at times when I feel lost or stuck.

x

Quilt: will have to dismantle the original quilt to remove the squares from Jack's pants. Request denim donations from friends as motivation to start over.

Clean and tidy my bedroom: sweep, mop, dust (bookshelves, ceiling fan—get those cobwebs in the corners of the ceiling). Review contents of the closet—what's going on in there?

Modify clothes: switch out buttons and sew some black lace or trim onto some shit. Cut up old band T-shirts and turn them into tank or tunic tops. Maybe experiment with stencils and fabric paint.

Reorganize books and literary magazines: there are piles all around your room and it's a mess. The bookshelves are already alphabetized, so it should be easy enough to file the rest away.

Thrift: shoes, hoodies, and maybe leggings. Cardigans, always. Watch your spending. No items exceeding five dollars.

Watch some interesting new movies: art films with subtitles, ambient soundtracks, and characters suffering ennui—that pretentious high-brow shit you like. Maybe the movies will inspire you to write something, but if not, that's okay.

Keep running/walking: you've been doing so great! Keep it up!

Start strength training again: the gym will be open during most of winter break. Try to get in there twice a week to lift weights. It'll be good to tone and strengthen, in addition to the jogging. Look into exercises you can do at home. Develop a plan for yourself. Try to make it fun, and remember you don't have to be perfect.

Cook at home with Alex: you're making a broccoli and three-cheese casserole tonight—nice! Copy down recipes you have saved on your computer into your recipe books. Bake some challah or soda bread. Make soup. All that shit.

Submit: if the spirit moves, check calls for submissions and see what's going on out there.

Read: audiobooks, until your concentration returns.

Write: if something comes to mind, jot it down. Regardless of everything that's happened, you're still a writer, and no one can ever take this from you.

x

Having this typed up is helpful. I even feel a little empowered—god forbid! Though, I don't know. I flip-flop constantly. One moment, I'm thinking, *yeah, I can totally get through this*, and the next, I've begun to cry and I just want the pain to stop, and *oy vez mir!*—because if the last year had been different, I wouldn't have to work so hard to ground myself, to be functionally okay.

16 December 2016

Current mood: restless

Current music: Chelsea Wolfe, "Feral Love"

I usually allow myself to sleep in on Friday and Saturday, but I think I'm going to limit myself to Friday mornings without an alarm. If I don't stick to some semblance of a routine during winter break, my already fragile mental health will completely bottom out.

I cried this morning when I saw the temperature and weather forecast—too cold to go running with my current shoes. (I'll need to buy new ones with more insulation if I'm going to keep this up.) Crying over the weather seems like an overreaction, but it signifies how generally overwhelmed I continue to feel. It's frustrating to be unable to complete an activity that brings a sense of accomplishment due to elements outside of my control. I already feel so powerless.

My appetite has gradually returned, which is unsettling after lacking one for so long. It doesn't help that my body image is so fucking distorted. Mirrors bewilder me more than usual. I lean into them or take steps back. I twist and pivot my body, tug mounds of flesh: tilt, lift, drop. I pinch my face, unsure and disconnected.

My body isn't mine anymore. I'm a walking, talking product of someone else's sinister imposition. I've been reduced to a brittle shell, a desecrated husk.

18 December 2016

Current mood: relieved

Current music: Daughter, "New Ways"

Since the realities of Jack's abuses fully sank in, anything related to sex has filled me with nervous dread. Anytime I feel even the slightest pinch of desire, I've immediately repressed it. But for the last few days, I've been pricked with urges.

Last night, I couldn't shake it. I paused our show—we're rewatching *Deadwood*—rolled over in bed, and Alex spooned me. I admitted feeling conflicted because I wanted to make love, but was really scared and didn't know if I was ready. He stroked my head and said it was okay to feel this way.

While making dinner, we kissed deeply for the first time since our anniversary in November (which was the only, even remotely sexual thing we did that day). My body reacted with sudden, painful cramps. I peeled away and sat in the bathroom with my head in my hands. *Why is this so hard, why can't I detach?*

Later, I bravely curled into him, and we started kissing again. I suggested he touch me and we'd see how I responded; I'd tell him to stop if I panicked. So, he gently slipped his hand between my thighs.

How long has it been? Three, four months?

I was surprised that it felt good and nothing hurt. I didn't think of Jack; I was very aware that my partner was Alex, my *b'sherter.*

I wanted to try. Alex was apprehensive—"Are you sure, are you sure?"—but said he'd go slowly.

I came quickly. Then, I buried my face in his arm and cried, but it was okay. Alex rocked me until my sobs subsided and I could continue. By the time we finished, we only had a few minutes to cuddle before he had to get ready for work.

I'm really grateful this has happened, but I don't want to push myself. There's no switch in my head. Having sex with Alex doesn't mean I've healed. Though, this was a relief, a sign that I'm getting better and maybe someday, I'll be okay.

He's been saintly in light of everything—so immensely supportive, patient, and gentle. I'm glad he has his other girlfriend Lindsey, so there's no pressure on me to be the sole source of his sexual reprieve.

Tonight, he's going into work early for inventory, which sucks. I still have trouble being alone. It's when the nastiest of intrusive thoughts creep in, when I hurt myself, and when I weep most fiercely.

28 December 2016

Current mood: anxious
Current music: RAKTA, "A Busca Do Círculo"

Jack resigned. He fucking resigned! That wretched *momzer*!

Or, he was asked to resign, which—as I understand—could mean nothing will be documented in his permanent file. And because my complaint was dismissed—again, as I understand—there's no record of it either. He just walks away!

I don't know what happened for sure, and no one who knows can tell me. The news first reached me via Grace, who said she'd just heard that Jack had quit "effective immediately." Shortly after, Magda also sent me a message saying faculty within the department had received an email from Dean Witterman about Jack's resignation.

Sure enough, Dean Witterman had also emailed me.

Dec 20, 2016 at 11:40 AM

Ms. Phoenix,

I write today to inform you Dr. Jack Blair submitted his resignation from [the university]. If you have questions, please do not hesitate to contact me.

I wrote back that night.

Dec 21, 2016 at 2:07 AM

Dean Witterman,

I do have some questions/concerns. I hope Dr. Blair's resignation will not relieve the urgency behind the Faculty Senate's decision to make policy changes regarding student-professor relationships. I strongly feel these are still necessary.

To be honest, a couple of other students have approached me, saying they too have been harassed by faculty, or overheard professors bragging about their inappropriate conduct with students. So, it's apparent I'm not the only student on campus experiencing such difficulties. Additionally, when I asked these students if they'd be willing to speak with Linda Barrow, they stated they didn't feel comfortable doing so. It's concerning that students don't feel safe enough to report their experiences to administrative persons. I hope to see these problems addressed.

Also, if you can tell me, I'd like to know if Dr. Blair independently submitted his resignation, or if he was provided this option over the termination of his position. I'm gravely concerned about the potential for Dr. Blair to leave [the university], only to find work at another college where he can continue to perpetuate abuse. As he is resigning, will there be any record of my complaint that hiring universities will be able to access? I feel other institutions deserve the ability to make informed hiring considerations before taking on a predator like Dr. Blair.

Again, thank you for keeping me in the loop. I'm grateful. And I'd appreciate any more insight you can give me.

On Wednesday morning, she replied.

Dec 21, 2016 at 11:25 AM

Dear Cal,

I cannot give you any further information about this situation because it is a personnel matter.

We are continuing to work on updating our policies and agree this is important. [The university] remains committed to creating the best learning environment for our students.

Best wishes for the New Year.

Well, can't blame me for trying. It never hurts to ask.

Also, everything I'd written about students approaching me with their own stories of creepy, gross professor bullshit? COMPLETELY TRUE. *Oy, gevalt!*

I was just beginning to relax into winter break and embrace the task of rebuilding myself—then, this *drek* about him resigning! I was waiting to see how [the university] handled Jack before I determined whether I should inquire about a law suit. Whelp. That plan got chucked in the bin.

I went ahead and made some phone calls. With the upcoming holidays, I wasn't expecting anyone to get back to me right away. I ended up being very lucky.

After a recent session, my counselor Heather sent me the contact information for an organization that works to prevent sexual violence on college campuses. They might have advice or ideas on legal resources, she'd proposed. So, I rang them and left a message with an assistant.

Later that afternoon, the organization's founder, Christie, personally returned my call. She took the time to speak to me while driving, and even stayed on the line as she stopped to order lunch. Her willingness to hear me, the way she handled my questions, the insight she provided, and how she validated my feelings—my god. She was really amazing.

These are the highlights from our conversation:

- Christie was both surprised and disgusted when I told her [the university] had no policies to regulate student-professor relationships, outside of what's covered by Title Nine.
- [The university] is already under federal investigation for mishandling Title Nine complaints.
- She was shocked to hear Linda Barrow acts as both the ADA *and* Title Nine coordinator. Christie said those roles should be fulfilled by separate individuals. I mentioned it was probably due to budget cuts and administrative restructuring, and she agreed with this assessment.
- Christie was especially bothered to hear that Dr. Barrow records, investigates, and makes the final decisions on Title Nine complaints. This is highly irregular, Christie said. Generally, in order to deter bias, someone records the complaints and a second party investigates them. This way, there's more impartiality between the receiving and pursuit of information—a type of checks and balances.
- Christie also seemed confused why the Dean and the Vice President of Academic Affairs were informed of my case. (I haven't mentioned this before, but Linda emailed me earlier this month to ask for my permission to show my diary entries and emails to the VP of AA, who'd requested to view them. I said this would be fine and I was available to meet with

the VP if [they] wished, but I never heard back.) When I asked why this was strange, Christie said something about how this didn't follow protocol or the usual chain of communication, especially because these meetings and requests for my documentation occurred *after* Linda had already closed the complaint.

- Christie's not a lawyer and couldn't say whether I should pursue a lawsuit against Jack or [the university]. She warned a law suit against the school could end up taking years. I'd have to put my life and recovery on hold, and in the end, it would be my word against his. Furthermore, unless I found a lawyer to work for me *pro bono*, it'd be horribly expensive, and I'd probably lose anyway, given a lack of evidence and [the university]'s lack of policies.
- Still, it wouldn't hurt to talk to a lawyer about a civil suit against Jack, or anything else regarding how the school potentially mishandled my complaint—just in case.
- Christie said I should be "very, very proud for speaking up" and having the courage to do so. It's wonderful Jack's left (or lost) his position. Students and faculty are safer now. Christie was also impressed to hear the Faculty Senate is proposing policy changes. Ultimately, these would be the most desirable outcomes for a law suit anyway: for Jack to lose his job and for [the university] to respond with new policies. And I'd been the catalyst for both already. As far as she's concerned, my work on the matter is done, and I couldn't have asked for a better outcome.

After our conversation, I felt weightless, almost serene. The storm of worries was tempered. Christie has no idea how much that thirty-minute phone call meant to me. I'm truly beholden to her.

Next, I rang a lawyer's office. Grace had offered me his phone number in case I felt compelled—by anxiety, no doubt—to explore legal counsel before the spring semester begins. Although it was late afternoon by the time I called, the lawyer was available.

He listened while I shared a condensed version of events. I ended with Jack's resignation, but added my concern about his ability to continue working in higher education or with other vulnerable populations.

In response, the lawyer sighed with regret and said he was very sorry for what I'd experienced. Unfortunately, he couldn't take my case because he was leaving the country for Xmas and would be gone for some months. However, he gave me the name and phone number of a lawyer in [the city] whom he trusted "like a sister." He promised to call ahead to make a referral. I thanked him and later left a message with this other lawyer's office.

As I was driving yesterday, the firm's legal assistant, Sasha, returned my call. I quickly pulled over. We spoke for about forty-five minutes. In the end, Sasha wasn't sure the firm would take my case, due to how difficult it would be to prove Dr. Blair coerced me, and because the school has no policies prohibiting student-professor relationships.

So, I may not have legal recourse. Still, Sasha's going to present my case and get back to me with the firm's decision.

I'm accustomed to waiting and uncertainty, but I'll never wear it well. That dress appears as bruised, battered thighs and trembling bones and purple slashes and eating too many cookies—when I'm not starving myself—and binge-watching television for distraction and crying, crying, crying...

You know what I could use? A lobotomy. I mentioned this

to someone, though I can't remember who. They said I'll be a stronger person for getting through this, and that my memories are necessary to conquer my pain. To which I replied, "Haven't I gone through enough?" How much pain must I endure to demonstrate how strong I can be? Everything I am is the consequence of adapting to life's prosaic grind. I'm always in flux. I'm always escaping something.

Oh, for it to be quiet for a time... For it to be boring! To have nothing new to report—that would be incredible. I've had enough destructive excitement for at least the next decade to come.

January

1 January 2017

Current mood: cranky

Current music: The Last Dance, "Nightmares"

Sometime last month, I went to my appointment at the student health clinic. The whole episode was absolutely humiliating. I couldn't stop crying, couldn't calm down.

The student worker and nurse practitioner kept asking what was wrong, unsure how to console me. Eventually, I cracked, explaining I was there because a professor had sexually exploited me, and I just recently found out he'd also been sleeping with multiple other women, and now I feel raped—*SINCE YOU ASKED.*

My hysterics made quite a racket. Another NP was brought into the room: Rachel, who's been my primary provider over the years. She offered me a hug, and I flew into her arms, sobbing. My appointment was rescheduled for the following week.

I've been experiencing intense dissociation from my body, especially my sexual and reproductive parts. Recently at bedtime, [my cat] Filburt was batting at the hem of my blankets so he could slip beneath and lay beside me. As he walked over me, he stepped on one of my nipples, and it shocked me so much that I cried out—because I'd actually forgotten about the existence of my breasts.

Worse yet, when I started my period that month, it frightened me. I didn't know what was happening and was momentarily horrified by the blood I discovered while taking a piss. That's how fucked up I've been: reacting with confused terror to the mundane aspects of my womanhood.

I later described this to Heather, and she said it made a lot of sense that I'd psychologically disconnect from the places on my body where Jack hurt me. It wasn't uncommon for victims of assault or rape to "forget" their own bodies. This was immensely helpful to hear—that this was a verified symptom, and I wasn't crazy.

I reappeared at the clinic to have blood drawn and the pelvic exam completed. And—surprise, surprise!—it was a fucking nightmare. Dotty, a nurse with whom I've developed a good relationship, accompanied the NP. During the procedures, she held my hand and tried to distract me.

I was already shaking, but when the speculum was inserted, I burst into tears and involuntarily howled, "HOW COULD HE DO THIS TO ME?!"

Dotty cooed and rubbed my arm. The NP proceeded as quickly as she could, and once she and Dotty left the room, I sat in my paper gown and wept bitterly for a long time before I found the strength to stand and put my clothes back on.

Although I considered the exam necessary, it inflamed my sense of violation. Jack had been so reckless with my body—and to think he could have given me an STI, when he'd already infected every aspect of my being. In the end, the tests all came back negative, *baruch Hashem*.

This morning, I compiled a list of safe foods I plan to eat exclusively, for a while at least. It's a coping strategy, not a diet. And by "safe," I mean foods I can consume without feeling shame. Foods that actually comfort and motivate me, rather than feel like a passive form of self-destruction.

I've also covered this topic with Heather. She said it's normal for individuals who've experienced excessive stress or anxiety to lose weight because they're not eating or have no appetite. It's common for those persons, once they begin eating again, to have a preference for foods high in salt, fat, and sugar. These tastes stimulate the brain's reward circuit and provide calming effects. It's also a way for the body to literally protect itself from a taxing environment, as foods high in fat and sugar cause weight gain. It's an instinctual cycle—an ordinary stress response.

Like most things, I approach eating in extremes. If I'm not careful, I can get locked into one extreme—not eating or overeating—and further stress myself out. So, Heather suggested I aim for moderation.

Here's the list of safe foods:

- coffee and tea with almond or soymilk (duh)
- all fruits and vegetables (also, duh)
- brown rice and potatoes
- lentils and beans
- cheese
- chocolate chips (serving size portion)
- bag salad kits (with predetermined condiments)
- homemade soups, curries, casseroles, and all that
- nuts, seeds, and peanut butter
- yogurt, kefir, and eggs

- oatmeal (serving size portion)
- fresh smoothies
- hummus and salsa
- all herbs and spices
- and condiments, such as jams, salad dressing, cooking sauces, etc.

Not bad, right? With the holidays and previous engagements—such as a Chanukah party on Thursday—I've slipped. But, implementing change is a process. Aiming for perfection only guarantees failure.

I've just crawled out from under the rubble. I'm sick. I'm miserable. I am a damaged thing. I cannot let that bastard win. Taking care of myself is the best way I can get back at him.

Oof. What am I going on about?

I know I'm hyperfocused on food because I crave control. Historically, my size has been my most unhealthy preoccupation. I've always internalized conflict and taken it out on my body. While I'd rather not perpetuate this, making healthy decisions can be a double-edged sword. I always end up holding myself to some arbitrary ideal, only to punish myself when I perceive failure. I need to learn to be more self-forgiving.

I also recognize that these are temporary fixations—distractions. The reality is that I'll inevitably cycle out of the eating plan and exercise routine, as I switch to other activities and coping techniques. As [an outpatient counselor] once said, if the coping skill we're using isn't working, try another. If you end up using some for a while, only to never use them again, that's fine too. There's no single, fixed way to keep yourself okay.

Honestly, as long as I go to bed sober every night, then I'm going to be fine, regardless of whatever else happened in the day. That's the rule.

The counselor also told us that if you *have* to entertain one of your addictions, choose the less destructive one and try to be smart about it. The example she gave was compulsive shopping. As an alcoholic, she won't drink, so when things are particularly bad, she'll go shopping. However, she takes little money along and keeps receipts, so she can return truly frivolous purchases later, after her mood has improved.

So, if I have to restrict my eating or cut myself to get through the horror and hurt until more time has passed and I have a better grip on my trauma? Fine—as long as I don't drink. I don't deserve that anyway. I deserve to remain sober.

A couple of people have said they're surprised I haven't relapsed over all of this. A couple more admitted they're surprised I haven't tried to kill myself.

Yeah, well. You and me both, I guess.

18 January 2017

Current mood: blah

Current music: Joy Division, "No Love Lost"

Last month, I unfolded my first quilt. The rows were only half-finished. Squares from the jeans Jack had given me were scattered throughout.

I deconstructed almost the entire quilt to remove those squares. It was a tedious project, seam-ripping countless stitches with a razor blade, undoing countless hours of work. After the quilt was disassembled, I organized the squares into stacks, with Jack's denim set aside.

Alex suggested we set them on fire in the backyard. I laughed. Sure. Why not?

Denim is surprisingly flammable. We touched a corner of one square to the flame produced by my lighter—and it went up immediately. I dropped this fiery piece onto the rest of the squares, which were quickly engulfed. Within minutes, nothing was left but a few charred threads and a black stain on the ground.

There's something poetic in this, I suppose. Besides a couple of books I'd overlooked—and I'd never burn books—the denim squares from his jeans were the only physical reminders left. Eventually, I'll take up the quilt again. I'll have to almost completely start over. I guess there's something poetic in that too.

24 January 2017

Current mood: thoughtful

Current music: Iron and Wine, "Faded from the Winter"

One piece of advice I've heard from Heather, Alex, and Naomi is to stay immersed in my spiritual practice. They've all pressed me to keep attending Shabbos services, even if I don't feel like it, don't want to leave the house or be around people, and just end up sitting in the back crying while I attempt to *daven* or sing along. They've all asked, "Have you considered talking to your rabbi about what's been going on?"

I hadn't, though I agreed it was probably a good idea. Anything to help. Every day, I'm white-knuckling sanity.

So, I sought out Rabbi Alpert, and we made arrangements to have coffee. Admittedly, I was nervous—another male authority figure—but I hoped meeting in public would help ease my apprehensions.

After buying our coffee, we found some comfortable chairs in a corner of the café. I started off by giving him a summary of what happened and how it's affected me, and asked if there were any prayers or anything scriptural I could refer to for reassurance.

Rabbi Alpert sighed and rubbed his face. I've been eliciting this reaction a lot lately.

He urged me to read Psalms and recite any passages I find inspiring. He also gave me permission to say Kaddish to myself, though traditionally, it's meant to be read aloud in a *minyan* and only when someone related to the mourner has died. Still, he agreed with my counselor; I'm grieving and given this, grieving prayers were appropriate.

Oy, that word again: *grieving*. It irks me. I don't think of myself as grieving. If anything, I'm grieving the death of Jack's disguise—that which I fell in love with.

How do I grieve in the face of truth? It's left me broken and trembling—but I was already broken and trembling. I was being abused without realizing it. So, while I accept I'm experiencing aspects of loss, I also feel liberated because of what I know now. Thank god for Zahra, Magda, Eleanor, Connie, Phoebe, and everyone else who's gifted me with truths after so many months of Jack's treachery. I can't imagine where I'd be without them.

I haven't told anyone this, but in instances of great, chest-panging anxiety, I closed my eyes and silently mouthed the Sh'ma to calm myself. Or, when pummeled by intrusive thoughts while driving, jogging or cooking, I've meditated over these words until the anxiety dulls: *oseh shalom bim ramov, hu ya'aseh shalom aleinu, v'al kol Yisrael, v'imru amen*. Deep breath. Repeat.

I've taken Rabbi Alpert's advice and recited Kaddish to myself. Now, when those wicked heart-constricting sensations descend from nowhere, I think, *Yit'gadal 'yit'kadash sh'mei raba...* Usually, by the time I get to *y'hei sh'lama raba min sh'maya*, the tension is mostly gone.

I reread Ecclesiastes—my favorite book in the Tanakh—and Psalms and Proverbs for passages that stand out. How's this, for starters? Psalms 22:2–3 says, "My G-d, my G-d, why have You abandoned me; why so far from delivering me from my anguished roaring? My G-d, I cry by night—You answer not; by night, and have no respite."

Considering my anger, I rather liked these verses from Psalms 58:4–9: "The wicked are defiant from birth; the liars go astray from birth. Their venom is like that of a snake... O G-d, smash their teeth in their mouth...let them melt, let them vanish like water."

What ferocity! When I imagine King David writing these lines, he's furious, scribbling and clenching his jaw so tightly, he spits blood. But, he was a murderous fuck too, so whatever.

There are numerous passages equating deception to wickedness. It's no wonder we have so much commentary associated with lying in Judaism. For example, Proverbs 15:4 says, "A healing tongue is a tree of life, but a devious one makes for a broken spirit." Although, if my memory serves right, there are a few exceptions to lying. We can lie to save the life of another person and—I think—to preserve the livelihood of a fellow Jew.

I didn't expect reading the Tanakh was going to console me, but it has. Though I consider myself an atheist and don't believe in the existence of Hashem as an omnipotent deity, I'm really proud to be Jewish. To be of the peoples who've carried our sacred writings and exalted them through some of the most devastating collective trials, across millennia. To be a Jew has required and still requires so much bravery and resolve.

I'd like to think these traits were passed on to me by my relatives, who had to be so courageous to abandon everything and everyone they knew to come to and survive in America. What's worse—I wonder—losing your tribe, your language, and your god, or losing your life to the pogroms? My family chose the former, which is the only reason I exist today.

And even if Jack has made it immensely challenging to recognize parts of myself independent of our shared interests and beliefs, and his controlling influence... He could never corrupt my Jewishness. That exists completely outside of him, despite his efforts to relate to it. So, *baruch Hashem* for this. And to hell with Jack. May he speak to lizards. May he grow like an onion, with his head in the ground and his ass in the air.

February

2 February 2017

Current mood: anxious

Current music: Gregory Alan Isakov, "That Sea, the Gambler"

Last month, Phoebe informed me of a fucking mess of an article in [the university]'s student newspaper that described the hostile exchange between Jack and Magda in the classroom. Their argument was taken completely out of context and painted Magda's actions as unwarranted and erratic. The reporter also quoted a student witness who stated that as they tried to leave the room, Jack grabbed them. He declared that he wanted to be honest with them, and said there were allegations against him for being sexually inappropriate with a female student. But, he wanted the witness to know it wasn't true.

I read the article several times. I could see the reporter's intent wasn't to focus on the conflict between Jack and Magda, but to use it as a vehicle to cover the sexual misconduct allegations. He'd done a poor job of emphasizing the point and flooded the article with unnecessary witness accounts that made Jack look better than Magda. After having Jack as a professor all semester, of course his students sided with him. They probably didn't know who Magda was, let alone her relationship to him.

It was upsetting. Magda didn't deserve to be portrayed as doing anything wrong. That scene could have been avoided if Jack had just agreed to talk to her in his office, as she'd requested.

I looked up the reporter on Facebook and couldn't believe it. I recognized him; he'd tried to add me as a Facebook friend a few weeks ago, but since I didn't know him, I dismissed his request. He obviously knew something.

I called the newspaper's office on campus. No answer. I double-checked the reporter's Facebook account. There was a phone number. I dialed it. He answered.

"Craig?"

"Yes?"

"I'm... I read your article this morning, and I'm someone who can provide you with a lot more context."

"Ah. I think I know who I'm talking to."

"Right."

He was running an errand and said he would ring me back as soon as he was in a more private place to talk.

Between calls, I wandered around the first floor of the house—carefully, to not wake Alex—and considered how to approach the conversation: 1) I couldn't speak to Craig on the record until I'd heard back from Sasha about a potential lawsuit; 2) I wanted to know what he already knew before giving him any details; and 3) was he following the story for shock value or was he legitimately trying to inform readers about abuses of power on campus?

When Craig called back, I immediately inquired after what he knew and how he'd heard, and he began unloading.

For all of this to make sense, I have to backtrack.

When I first discussed my fears about Jack having moved on to someone else—before I knew about Anna McNeil—Alice had told me about her classmate Irene from Sociology of Art. Irene often stayed after class to talk to Jack. He seemed especially friendly with her. So, after I made my reports, Alice invited Irene out for coffee to discuss her concerns. Irene replied that she appreciated the offer, but she thought she already knew what Alice was alluding to.

According to Magda, Irene had been present during the fight between her and Jack. As Magda left, she lightly touched Irene on the shoulder and warned her to be careful because Jack was a predator. Irene was totally freaked out and tried to exit the room. But, Jack cornered her, saying they needed to talk.

Just as she indicated to Craig for his article—she'd been quoted anonymously—Jack told Irene there were allegations against him for sexually exploiting one of his female students, but it wasn't true. Irene shook him off and bolted for the department. She met with Eleanor, who verified the complaint against Jack.

Magda had singled out Irene for good reason. In one of our earlier conversations, Magda said he'd begun to talk about Irene in the *same ways* he'd described *me* in the past: frequently bringing me up and praising my work, ideas, and personality in private conversations with her and other faculty. After getting my initial message, Magda suspected he might be involved with Irene as well.

In her messages to Alice, Irene assured her nothing had happened and she'd been startled by Magda's warning and by what Jack told her. He'd never made her uncomfortable, but now that she knew there was a complaint against him, she was going to be careful. Alice wrote she was happy to hear she was okay, and if she wanted to know anything else, she was welcome to contact me.

Shortly after, Irene sent me a friend request on Facebook, and we began to talk. I didn't reveal any details about my case except to say I was being treated for post-traumatic stress, and to clarify why we were concerned about her.

As we spoke, it quickly became clear that our fears were justified. Irene said she and Jack had been working on an independent research project together—for a year and a half!

I was horrified. I knew nothing of Irene until Alice mentioned her. Jack had *never* talked about her, *never* told me he was doing research with another student. In fact, when I'd asked if he had other independent study students, he'd said no. He'd stated this before I graduated and again during the fall semester.

So, he straight-up fucking lied. Why? Why lie about directing an independent study if his intentions weren't unsavory? I think about what Magda said, how he talked about Irene and how this reflected his previous praises of me, and it makes me nauseous. And Irene is so young. She's not even old enough to drink!

But, she's okay, *baruch Hashem.*

Returning to my phone call with Craig... He'd initially heard about the allegations from two friends who'd approached him in confidence. The first person was Irene—small world—and the second was a nursing student worker, who'd described my distress at the clinic. She hadn't disclosed my name, but there aren't exactly a lot of other tattooed, headscarf-wearing goth students on campus, so... Well done.

Craig received the more intimate details, including my name, from [a mutual friend of ours]. This didn't bother me. I figured if [my friend] had told Craig about my situation, then she must trust him.

Craig had been hesitant to contact me because he understood it might compromise the Title Nine investigation. When I stated that Linda Barrow had concluded my relationship to Dr. Blair was consensual and closed the case, he expressed anger on my behalf.

Incredibly, he also told me about another student who'd been involved with Jack. Craig mentioned his friend Mike, with whom I'm also acquainted. As he'd relayed to Craig, Mike had a close friend who'd slept with Jack. After Mike graduated, he met Jack for lunch and brought this up to him. Jack apparently laughed it off, telling him this was one of the perks of getting your master's: once you start teaching, you can fuck your students.

An appalling story, but I'd believe it. I'm not close to Mike, but we've spoken candidly over the years. He's a fairly sensitive person. I don't think he'd make up this kind of shit, especially because he'd looked up to Jack. This additional revelation was aggravating as fuck.

Throughout my conversation with Craig, I paced and chain-smoked in the garage. I probed him for the reason behind his interest, and he cited a couple of other incidents in recent years: a sexual harassment law suit against a faculty member (who is still employed there) and an on-campus rape. In both situations, he felt [the university] mishandled the way they communicated with the student body, and as a result, many students felt unsafe. He stated social institutions need to be held accountable for creating safe environments and taking abuses seriously.

Satisfied with this explanation, I agreed to go on the record, pending the decision of the law firm in [the city]. We also discussed his article. To balance the tone and amend his poor representation of Magda, Craig hoped to revise and re-release the article with added witness testimony—and he did, a few days after our phone call.

A few weeks later, Sasha finally got back to me. She apologized for the delay; the holidays had thrown off everyone's schedule and it'd taken a while to get the firm organized. Ultimately, they declined to take my case.

"It would be too hard to prove discovery," she said. "Do you understand what that means?"

Yes. I have no concrete proof of coercion. The threats, the misuse of his power—it had all occurred in private. Verbal exchanges. Words embedded in my brain.

"By all intents and purposes, he raped you, and that's absolutely true," Sasha confirmed. "Unfortunately, it just doesn't fall under what the legal definition of rape is right now—even though he had a position of power over you."

It would come down to my word against his. Sigh.

I asked after a civil suit against Jack.

Again, Sasha suggested this wasn't a good idea. It'd be really difficult to convince a jury to sympathize with me because I'm a woman and victim-blaming is the social norm. It's worse in cases like mine, with a lack of hard evidence or documentation of explicit abuse. Nevertheless, she encouraged me to be proud of what I've accomplished: making my reports, inspiring policy changes, and being the catalyst for his resignation.

"It's been a learning experience," she said, adding, "Although, what lesson you could take from this, I don't know. Stay away from male professors? Don't trust anyone?"

We both laughed—what else could we do? She wished me well, and I thanked her. She'd been kind to me, took me seriously, and I was grateful.

With that, I told Craig I was ready to go on the record—with the condition that I'd remain anonymous.

I agreed to meet at his house on a Sunday evening. He hadn't warned me that his roommate was hosting a small party; the place was filled with people, many of whom I recognized from campus. So much for remaining anonymous.

We sat outside so I could smoke while we talked. To start, Craig had a bit of news to bounce off of me. Irene told him something she'd learned from Zach Cantor (who's taken charge of her independent study): JB had scared off a newly hired professor by quickly roping her into a sexual relationship, then dropping all contact with her. This had allegedly taken place sometime during the summer.

My face plummeted. *What. The. Fuck.*

"Oh shit," Craig realized. "You hadn't known about that?"

"No, this is the first time I've heard anything about it."

He apologized, saying he just wanted to verify the story. Then, he pulled out his recorder.

We were interrupted often by his friends, so the interview took a while, but it was fine. I appreciated the breaks. Once he'd run out of questions, we chatted casually for a bit and finally called it a night.

The story was approved for the front page. When it hit the stands across campus, I shuddered with dread, waiting for something to drop: retaliation from pro-JB students, administration, or Jack himself—anything. But, nothing happened. The few people who did approach me already knew of my involvement and just wanted to check in or praise my bravery in speaking up.

Within three or four days of the release of Craig's article, two television news outlets reached out to him for additional coverage. The first sensationalized the story as a sex scandal and falsely insinuated that Dr. Blair and I were secretly *schtupping* in his office. Gross.

A reporter from another news outlet specified they wouldn't pick up the story without a firsthand account from me. Craig asked about protecting my identity, and the reporter assured him they had methods of doing so.

I was in [the city] when Craig called. For us to make the evening news, everything had to be recorded by two PM. I only had about ten minutes to brush my teeth, throw on some clothes, and hit the road. I made good time and arrived at the station ahead of Craig. The reporter met us outside, and we got straight to it.

The interview took place in a conference room. Lights were set up to toss the shadow of my profile against the wall, and this was what they filmed. They'd talked about shooting my hands or the back of my head, but I kyboshed these ideas because I have identifying tattoos in those places. At one point, someone asked about my hat.

"Hey, I know you keep your head covered for religious reasons," Craig said, "but it might help to further disguise you if you lost the hat for the interview."

"I don't know... I think most people know I have a shaved head now."

"Oh, you do?" Craig chuckled. "I didn't know that."

I didn't budge. I was in a darkened room with three men. I wasn't going to remove my head-covering. I might as well undress in front of them.

I can't remember how long the interview lasted—maybe twenty minutes? Eventually, the reporter said the cameraman would continue to film us talking, but the mic would be turned off. Then, he turned in his chair, looked me right in the eye and said, "So, I have a question for you, off the record: why didn't you just say *no*?"

I reacted with astonishment. "How could I say *no* to him? He was my professor. I wasn't in a position to say *no*."

What a baffling question. It seems so obvious that rejecting Jack was never a real option. Surely people understand that, right? Five months before my graduation. Enrolled in four classes with him. He was my adviser. We had a good working relationship. I admired and cared for him. I'd trusted him.

When he'd hit on me, it startled and confused me because he wasn't my peer. At the same time, it was touching because he'd often said he viewed me as a peer. Plus, I always accepted everything he'd taught or told me. Confessing his feelings for me was no different. Like any other information he presented, I accepted his word and made the cognitive shifts to make space for and reflect that information in my developing worldview. In this case, instead of contributing to my education, it was a romantic connection. Basically, if he likes me, then it must be that I should like him too. And what happens after two people establish a mutual romantic interest? Well, they act on it.

Clearly, it was more complicated than addressing the matter with a simple *no*. I guess I could see how others wouldn't get it, unless they'd been similarly abused by someone who held power over them.

That night, I skipped Shabbos service to stay in and watch the live coverage. The segment was short, and the portion of the interview shown was only about thirty seconds long. I'd gotten choked up at one point, and this was the clip they chose to air. It was hard to watch.

Later on, [my friend] Stephen picked me up. We'd arranged to go by my favorite tattoo parlor so he could flip through artist portfolios and schedule a consultation. Afterward, we planned to go for a jog together.

I stepped outside of the parlor when Magda called to ask how I've been holding up as this media coverage plays out. She admitted anxiety fueled her interest, and I can totally understand this. Since everything blew up, hearing updates related to her, Jack, or general reactions to my case has helped to relieve the blustery sense of uncertainty and provided an admittedly false semblance of control.

I mentioned telling the reporter that Jack had manipulated me into submitting.

"But, Cal," she interjected, "woman-to-woman: hadn't you said that you were flattered too, that you were attracted to him?"

"Well, it's complicated, right?"

I realized it would be a struggle to make her understand, as she actually *was* Jack's peer. Though he'd abused her too, it was different because they were colleagues. She hadn't been dependent on him. He hadn't dangled the strings of her immediate future, her ability to achieve career mobility.

So, I gave up thinking of a response, and the subject was quickly dropped. It didn't need to be discussed anyway.

As we spoke, Magda began to cry. I listened stoically, though my heart painfully ballooned with empathy. What she described, I was also enduring. All of the trauma-induced symptoms: trouble sleeping, not being able to focus, the paranoia... On top of it all, the fucking disillusionment that comes with weeding out of all the lies and trying to piece reality together. You reach out to others for validation because you're uncertain about everything, yet you're also suddenly distrusting of everyone, so you struggle to accept their support. It's absolutely crazy-making, isolating, and fucking torturous. Yes, I could relate.

Magda also bristled with everyone's praise. She said it was hard to be told over and over how strong and courageous she is and how this experience would help her to help others later. That going through this would make her a better feminist and champion of women. Even if it proves true eventually, she can't fucking hear it right now.

Laughing, I confirmed I felt the same way. It seems ridiculous to be told how strong and brave you are when you're also making daily lists to remind yourself to complete simple, routine chores. We appreciated everyone's intentions, but really, there's little anyone can say that would be truly comforting. We just have to get through it.

Our conversation lasted about two hours. In the meantime, Stephen and I drove to a park and sat in the truck, smoking. While I talked to Magda, he checked his email and played a couple of games on his phone. He—the darling *mensch*—never once implied that he wanted me to wrap up the call so we could resume our evening.

I didn't feel like I could anyway. Weeks ago, I vowed to always make myself available to Magda. Firstly, we have a connection, being victims of the same man. Who else can so closely empathize with what she's going through? And secondly, I owe her. I started all of this.

Grace has called me a whistle-blower, and while this has an honorable connotation, in being the one to speak up, I've made a lot of people's lives and jobs harder. The department now has to find a new professor to replace someone with over a decade of experience. A lot of students are heartbroken and betrayed. They've lost their mentor and role model.

So, yes, it's wonderful that Jack is no longer on campus, but goddamn. Even his absence brings chaos and hardship.

As I mentioned, Irene told Craig about another professor Jack had become briefly involved with over the summer. I've since asked her to elaborate.

Irene admitted she didn't know much about it. Zach mentioned it in passing, some weeks after Jack and Magda's classroom argument. I imagine he offered this additional insight to help Irene get a sense of why the confrontation occurred.

According to Irene, Zach said JB had been sleeping with two newly hired adjuncts, but one of them took off after he stopped speaking to her (and by "took off" I mean, she refused the position, dropped the job—*took the fuck off*). I told Irene he'd been messing around with Anna recently, but she indicated the situation with the other professor took place earlier than this.

"I think it was right before classes started," Irene explained, "because she was teaching two classes, and JB had to pick up an extra class."

Wait. The Race and Ethnicity course Jack was co-teaching with Eleanor last semester? That extra class he'd freaked out about? All of the whining because they were short-staffed and needed to hire someone? All of that crap about drowning in work?

That's why?! Because he'd fucked over the unfortunate, unwitting adjunct who'd just been hired to teach these classes and scared her away from the position she'd only *just* taken?!

Holy shit. What a rapey, out-of-control scumbag.

I'd love to ask Zach about this myself, but I can't. Everyone in the department has been ordered to keep their distance from me. At least, I presume they have. Where there had been smiles, nods, and waving before, now [the professors] stare ahead as they pass me on campus, refusing eye contact and pursing their lips.

Actually, no. Zach has straight up said he can't talk to

me. He found me outside of the library smoking a few weeks ago. He nodded, put a hand over his heart, and said everyone believed me and was standing by me, but he couldn't go into further details and couldn't be seen speaking to me.

"I will tell you this," he said, selecting the words carefully. "If this semester has taught me anything, it's that your colleagues aren't necessarily your friends. It's not the same thing."

Then, he looked around, put out his cigarette, and went back inside.

3 February 2017

Current mood: tired

Current music: Edward Elgar, "Enigma Variation #9 (Adagio) 'Nimrod'"

Magda called a couple of days after my on-camera interview. I was at work and stepped outside to talk privately. A reporter from [the town's newspaper] had contacted her, but she wanted to refrain from any press involvement and told the reporter she'd ask me instead.

I mulled it over. It wouldn't kill me to do another interview, I supposed, though god knows I'm emotionally exhausted and blank, even as my nerves continue to buzz and ache. Still, after my shift ended, I called Katie, the reporter. We scheduled an interview for the following evening at the paper's headquarters downtown.

Later, I went to Amber's to babysit [my niece] so she could attend karate class. Magda rang me again, so I slipped into the kitchen to talk while [my niece] watched telly in the living room. From our conversation, I learned more outrageous, interesting shit to add to my growing collection of outrageous, interesting shit about Jack. I want to remember as much as possible, so I'll record it here:

- In early summer, Jack told me he had a growth extending from the bone in his left arm. A biopsy was done to determine whether it was cancerous. For two weeks, I was wide-eyed with trepidation, waiting to hear the results. Finally, Jack said the doctor concluded the growth was benign, and it was removed.

  I asked Magda if she knew anything about this, but she didn't. She asked if I'd seen a bandage on his arm or anything. But, Jack never took his shirt off in front of me, even during sexual encounters. I never saw his bare arms or chest. Magda confirmed he was the same way around her. In the end, he probably lied. If it were true, it makes no sense that he'd tell me, but not his long-term partner.

  Magda suspects that, in some strange way, making up this bollocks about having cancer is Jack's way of entertaining his legitimate fears about developing cancer. Who can say?

- Jack swore he didn't drink alcohol for health reasons and never drank around me. Conversely, he'd have beers with Magda when they went out. She saw him drinking a lot more since he'd started hanging out with Anna. I presume he lied to make himself seem more appealing, since I'm in recovery.

- I made a comment about Jack eating like a bird, and Magda snickered, saying he definitely had regular portions around her. Again, this was probably because he thought restricting his food intake would make him seem attractive to me. Maybe he thought it would provoke my sympathy? I have no idea, but it gives me the creeps to think he went this far to manipulate me.

- I described features of Jack's social anxiety to Magda, including how he'd reacted to the crowds in the Van Gogh exhibit at the Chicago Art Institute. I believed he avoided social situations, and this was why he and I rarely spent time together outside of his home.

  "Oh, that's crap," Magda huffed. "He doesn't have social anxiety! He and I went out all the time—met up with people, went out to eat... We never ate-in at home, unless I cooked for him." Finally, she said pointedly, "He was just telling you all of that to avoid being seen with you!" Oh, duh. How totally obvious that seems now.

- During my last visit to his house, Jack elected to show me his artwork. As I flipped through the pieces, he'd stated in this deeply vulnerable tone, "This is the first time anyone has seen this. I haven't showed this work to anyone else."

  The moment had stuck with me. So, when Magda and I began talking, I asked if she'd ever seen his artwork. It'd seemed so meaningful on his part; I was curious to know if it was authentic. But, it wasn't. He'd shared his artwork with her more than once.

- I asked if she knew much about Jack's former fiancée Teresa—how she'd died from complications relating to her eating disorder. As I described this, Magda hooted, "She didn't *die*!" He'd told Magda their relationship ended in a completely different way, adding some ridiculous story about Teresa's mother coming on to him. We determined this was, yet again, just another way to stage a bond by relating to my own struggles.

- On the night of my graduation, Jack said he couldn't spend the evening with me because he was going to have drinks with a colleague who'd been diagnosed with terminal cancer. (There's that cancer shit again). Magda said this was totally untrue. Jack had been with her and other professors that night, and no one was dying of cancer. He'd made it all up.
- Before spring break, Jack took off one weekend, saying his father was being hospitalized with intestinal issues. But as far as Magda knew, Jack hadn't been to Oklahoma for a couple of years. Neither of us could figure out where he'd been that weekend. I know he wasn't at home, because I'd stayed at the house during his absence. I was still there when he returned, bags in hand. Hmm.

We discussed Jack's aptitude for violence. He'd never physically harmed us, but was *really* intimidating when angry. Magda mentioned how Jack had punched in his rear windshield some years before. She hadn't seen him do it, but saw the aftermath. When I pointed out some bits of broken glass on the floor of his garage, he'd told me about bashing the windshield, saying he'd done so during a desperate fury over his health issues.

I told Magda about visiting Jack's house after our breakup and finding a garbage bag in the kitchen, filled with broken dishes and ripped-up books. The bottom shelf of his bookcase was cracked too. So, while the suicide attempt was a lie, he hadn't lied about smashing shit up. But, why had he done it?

Magda offered a possible reason. Jack had arrived at her house one afternoon, unhinged. She'd sat in calm disbelief as he stormed through her house, yelling about his students' laziness, their lack of gratitude. I asked when this had happened, and it turned out to be the same afternoon I'd sat in on his Sociology of Art class.

When he'd destroyed items around his house and broke his bookshelf, he'd just returned from Iceland. We were still in a relationship. Eventually, the thrill of his vacation with Magda had to dissipate and he'd have to deal with me. Perhaps he felt overwhelmed and reacted with rage. Maybe these destructive outbursts are symptomatic of Jack's frustration in being unable to impose total control over his numerous lovers. If we defy him, he just loses his shit. It's as good a guess as any.

Magda and I also concluded that Jack isn't nearly as sick as he's consistently made himself out to be, or he was downright lying. At times when he reported being sick to me, he was actually with Magda and doing just fine. She knew nothing about the emergency room visits during the spring. She knew nothing about the diagnoses he received in the summer.

However, she'd heard about the more severe, unusual stuff he'd occasionally describe, such as having what he thought were seizures. He'd talked about instances in which he'd suddenly develop confusion while driving and would hit curbs or get lost on his way home.

He'd been recounting these issues to me since spring and progressively more as the months went on; however, he'd just begun to share them with Magda, as though they were new health concerns. Presumably, as he was (probably) getting more involved with Anna (and god knows who else), he started lying more to Magda about his health to distract her from his infidelities—the same lies he'd fed me in earlier months.

And it worked—some pretty crafty shit. Magda and I never questioned him. What would we have said? "That sounds too outlandish to be true?" Called him a liar? Despite our suspicions, we never confronted him. But, have our suspicions we did.

For example, on a few occasions, Jack had said in text messages he wasn't feeling well and was throwing up, but he would try to pull it together, so I was welcomed to start heading to his house. Sometimes, I'd walk through the front door and be told he'd thrown up only minutes before. But, I *never* detected a whiff of vomit, and I know, from years of on and off purging, puke stinks. It lingers in the air like a bad dream.

Magda found herself in the exact same scenarios! Like me, she never noticed any odors or other evidence to support his stories. Yet, neither of us said anything to contradict him. What kind of people would that have made us if we were wrong? And who lies about something as serious as being *so* sick?

Nevertheless, we agreed that Jack *is* dealing with some sort of malady. I know he'd been sincere about having blood-work done in the late spring because I ran across the test results and doctor's paperwork in his kitchen. But, neither of us believe he's suffering to the severity he'd described: experiencing temporary blindness or hearing loss, seeing spots in his vision, losing control of motor function, severe memory loss, etc. It's all *drek*. His stories are just too bizarre, inconsistent, and were apparently shared at times when illness made for a convenient excuse to conceal his cheating behaviors.

He's just a fucking malingerer. And to think, all of the agonizing, the nerve-shattering anxiety I'd experienced on account of his chronic poor health, my paralyzing fears of him dying—all completely baseless.

Oh, but this shit right here? What follows is the kicker. No one saw *this* coming.

During one of our first conversations, I mentioned to Magda how Jack always visited his ex, Tracy Hines, on Sunday evenings to watch *The Walking Dead* and grade papers.

Magda interrupted, "No, no, no. That's not right. Jack has a routine on Sunday nights. He stays in and watches *60 Minutes*, followed by *The Walking Dead*, and he goes to bed early."

"What? No, I was there," I countered. "I would see him off. He left to go to Tracy's every Sunday around seven-thirty.

Most of the time, he'd even let me stay at the house until he got back, usually around ten-thirty."

Magda was blown away. "Well, that's fine. I don't care if he's going to Tracy's. Why wouldn't he tell me?"

Then, sometime last month, Magda was on campus and opted to swing by Tracy's office and ask her about it. According to Magda, this is how it went.

She told Tracy she'd heard about Jack stopping by on Sunday nights.

"Well, *yeah*," Tracy said. "That's what people do when they're in a relationship."

Reasonably, Magda was confused. "What do you mean you're *in a relationship*?"

"We're getting ready to celebrate our thirteen year anniversary," Tracy expounded. "We just got back from visiting his family in Oklahoma."

"But, how can that be?!" Magda objected. "What do you mean you've been with him for *thirteen* years? What about this complaint filed against him? What about these other students?" She provided our names.

Tracy said she knew about Zahra. Jack had talked to her about the two of them hanging out, and it was all right. She didn't say anything about me.

Magda continued. "But, he and I have been together for the last four years! Everyone knew—it was a public relationship! How could you have not known?"

At this point, Tracy shut down and grew tearful. She asked Magda to leave, and Magda complied.

I've asked [my former mentor] Charles about this while we were having coffee, because it's... WELL, COME ON. This is completely fucked!

Charles had wondered about it himself. He knew Magda and Jack were dating, but he'd suspected Jack was still involved with Tracy. Charles said he and his wife used to run into Jack and Tracy at a bookstore all of the time.

"Since when?" I asked Charles. "Over this last year?"

"Oh, yeah. We saw them there recently."

OY GEVALT! HE NEVER BROKE UP WITH TRACY. HE HAS BEEN WITH TRACY THIS WHOLE FUCKING TIME.

"I cannot believe it," Magda told me. "There's no way she didn't know Jack and I were together. Everyone knew!"

Eh, who knows? Who knows what he's been telling Tracy? I was only involved with Jack for eleven months and just in that time, my sense of reality is so warped. Mentally untangling all of the features of his deceit has been a huge undertaking.

It's just so much. Even when he didn't lie, he just didn't tell me things—all to keep me insulated from other people. Like, I found out Magda has a Jewish background, and he'd told her I was Jewish, but he hadn't shared this with me. Why? He didn't want me to have any excuse to talk to Magda, to connect with her. Of course, I'm speculating, but it makes sense, doesn't it?

Tracy may have sincerely not known about his relationship with Magda. Or if she had concerns about it, he manipulated her into believing something else. After thirteen years, Tracy probably has some whacky, codependent version of reality for which Jack is responsible. But again, who's to say? Maybe she *did* know about all of us and just didn't care, so long as Jack stayed with her. Maybe Jack convinced her to have an open relationship, and Tracy's under the impression all of his other lovers know about her. Ultimately, it doesn't matter. It's just fucked.

Magda did bring this up with Jack, though, after confronting him about me and Anna McNeil.

Firstly, he denied anything occurred between me and him. He said we'd only been emotionally intimate and shared secrets with each other, but that was as far as it had gone—which is exactly why I know what his dick looks and tastes like, obviously, because we were just "emotionally" close. Uh huh.

He fed Magda the exact same line about the extent of his involvement with Anna. He might as well have just confessed.

When she later questioned him about Tracy, Jack explained they'd broken up before he began dating Magda. But shortly after, Tracy wrote him a heartfelt letter, requesting they get back together. He submitted, but with different terms than before. He claimed they hadn't been intimate in several years, which is utterly laughable. He'd said the same thing about his relationship with Magda before we became sexually involved.

Jack basically told Magda that yes, he'd stayed with Tracy, but this should be okay since their relationship wasn't physical. And she should be understanding about that, because he felt bad for Tracy and stayed with her to avoid hurting her. Sure. Great. What a nice guy.

On a separate front, I met with Katie, the reporter for [the town's newspaper] on Tuesday. The interview went well. Before I left, Katie said she'd let me know when the story would be released—in a week or two. So, more anxious waiting.

5 February 2017

Current mood: pensive

Current music: Skinny Puppy, "Past Present"

I haven't been able to shake something Magda mentioned a couple of months ago. A friend had told her that Jack sounded like a sociopath and she should read up on it.

I considered this to be inaccurate. Too strong a word. Not quite right. A narcissist, sure. But then, Magda shared something else with me.

When she first challenged Jack about the details of my confessional message to her (in addition to her suspicions about his involvement with Anna), they'd met at his house. She'd been so distressed, she'd excused herself to vomit. Afterward, she paced around the living room, weeping as she directed questions at Jack.

All the while, he sat numbly on the couch like a *schlub*, "just taking it in." He said nothing, provided no answers.

Finally, she asked what was wrong with him—why wouldn't he react?

To this, he stated coldly, "I think I might be a sociopath." When Magda asked what he meant, he said, "I just don't feel anything."

WHOA. Goddamn.

I've only looked into this a little bit, but I think there's something to it. It would certainly explain his capacity for such widespread deceit and manipulation.

From what I've read, sociopathy is actually an informal term for what's considered antisocial personality disorder or psychopathy. People who are known to be sociopaths (psychopaths) are glib, conning and manipulative, live life on the edge (so to speak), lack remorse or guilt, are often pathological liars, have poor impulse control, lack empathy, are unreliable, blah blah blah. They tend to be criminals, con artists, or even take on "successful" positions, as they are often authoritarian or power-hungry.

Um. Holy shit.

But, I'd need to further read up on it before I make any conclusions. I'm surprised Jack would make this declaration to Magda, especially because it seems to fit. He may not have been lying!

Was he having a lucid moment of actual self-awareness—maybe similar to when he told me in September that our relationship was exploitative? Can he slip into a fleeting state of empathy and, even if just for a moment, understand how his behavior might actually fucking *devastate* another person? Or, was this just another form of deflection, a way to avoid responsibility for his behaviors?

Why else would he say it? It's possible he was making an

informed judgement. Jack does have some background in psychology; it was his second undergraduate major.

We'll never know for sure, but it's interesting (and blood-chilling).

I think his paintings actually support the notion. When Magda revealed she too had seen his artwork, she added how she didn't quite get it—not that she didn't grasp his intent, but didn't know why the subject matter was so compelling to him.

He says his work is interpretative of power and masculinity. Almost all of the pieces depict distorted male profiles with accessories generally associated with masculine power and authority, such as suit ties with bulky knots, oversized cowboy hats, or crowns. I can't recall a single painting or drawing in those stacks that wasn't an abstract portrait of a domineering man's face.

Then, it clicked. "Magda, holy shit! Doesn't that make so much more sense now?"

After a pause, she gasped, "Oh my god, I hadn't thought of that—but you're right!"

He was painting his *reflection*. All of those darkly obscure, intimidating male portraits... He probably had over a hundred of them buried in all of those portfolio cases.

My skin crawls just thinking about it.

7 February 2017

Current mood: tired
Current music: Jacob Hoffman with Kandel's Orchestra,
"Doina and Hora"

I called [my ex and best friend] Bevel earlier, just to *kvetch*. I'm experiencing a lot of anger and self-pity. Tomorrow, Alex and I are flying to Washington, DC. While I attend the AWP

Conference, he plans to go museum-hopping. Kamyar is joining us on Saturday, which is exciting, as we haven't seen each other in a couple of years. I've been looking forward to the trip for months, but now that we're hours away from taking off, I'm apprehensive. I worry I won't be able to enjoy myself or absorb much because I'm still struggling with these new trauma-induced symptoms. The jumpiness, the cognitive fog, the difficulty reading others or reacting appropriately in social situations—it's not very conducive to meeting new people, networking, or (hopefully) seeing friends.

It pisses me off. I just want to detach, have fun, and reclaim a part of myself. The most important part, the thing that most makes me *me*, the artist—the *writer*. Yet, here I am, and I'm afraid I won't be able to embrace the experience because of what that monster has done.

Talking to Bevel was grounding. "Hey, it's okay," he soothed. "You can't beat yourself up for feeling sorry for yourself. It's natural."

Reactions like this are expected, he went on. I'm not wrong; it *is* unfair, and I *didn't* deserve this. I'm a good person, and it's not my fault someone took advantage of my love, loyalty, and trust. It shouldn't stop me from continuing to be that person, and it won't, but fuck. It still hurts so deeply, so badly.

"You have to keep in mind that it's only been three months," Bevel added.

This really helped, actually. Three months is not enough time to be okay, but I've made progress. My counselors have said so, but they've also had to remind me to be patient and not to rush my recovery. Like, why am I beating myself up for having a difficult evening? Instead of allowing myself to be upset, I'm upset with myself for being upset. I just want it to be fucking over and done with, and I'm pushing it, and I shouldn't. I have to let myself heal—gradually.

For instance, Alex and I haven't made love for weeks. I felt empowered for a spell, but I can't bring myself to do it now. I know this is normal; just another example of how the healing process isn't linear.

There was one day—maybe nine or ten months since I'd last drank—when something unforeseen and terribly stressful occurred. Instead of reacting with an intrusive urge to drink, I simply took the steps to calm myself and tackled the issue. It wasn't until later—when I realized I hadn't even thought about drinking—that I understood: I'd finally reached the other side, and now my recovery was based on maintenance.

These circumstances are very different, but reflecting on my recovery has helped me cope with these symptoms—many of which I experienced in early sobriety, such as mild cognitive impairment, disturbed sleep, etc. I guess... Well, I look forward to the realization that weeks or months have gone by and I haven't thought of Jack at all—that I don't wake up in cold sweats or cringe at the thought of being touched. That Alex is able to kiss me without inspiring panic. That I can go places without constantly checking my surroundings for Jack or his car.

God, I hope this trip goes well. Maybe once we get there and the conference kicks off, I'll melt into the experience, and everything will be temporarily forgotten, or at the very least, be unthreateningly far away.

16 February 2017

Current mood: inspired

Current music: Ours, "Live Again"

Katie's article was released yesterday. She apologized for the delay; she'd been waiting on comments from expert sources. I read the article this afternoon, and I'm really pleased with it. It's the most critically written, yet thoughtful coverage of my experience to date.

I've been writing! I started a historical fiction piece about a Jewish farming family, with the older sister as the first-person narrator. I'm already so pleased with it.

Our trip was amazing. Throughout the entire weekend, I was bursting with excitement and gratitude. I saw several friends from prior conferences and have made new ones. And I had a wonderful time with Kamyar when he came up on Saturday, staying late enough to have dinner with me and Alex—my darling, beautiful partners. I'm so lucky to have such incredible people in my life. Them and the rush of inspiration I have now—these are some of the aspects of my life that fuel me to persevere.

The conference was *exactly* what I needed. Honestly, I feel more myself than I have since I can remember—certainly since before December 2015, when that *ganif* first hit on me.

I just wanted to make a quick note about Katie's article, how rejuvenated I feel after the conference, and how pleased I am to be writing again.

I feel so relieved and hopeful. Even if this joyful motivation doesn't last—and it won't, because nothing does—I'm thankful. I plan to milk these feelings for as long as I can, even if it only lasts a few more days.

WELL, IT'S COMPLICATED, RIGHT?

"As social beings, we live with our eyes upon our reflection, but have no assurance of the tranquility of the waters in which we see it."

-Charles Horton Cooley

"I'm not interested in myself per se. I'm interested in myself as a theme carrier."

-David Shields, *Reality Hunger*

"I don't want to reread this letter —I am sending it as I have written it— Nevertheless I am as it were dimly aware that there are some cold and rational people who would say on reading it —'she is raving'— My sole revenge is to wish these people —a single day of the torments that I have suffered…then we should see whether they wouldn't be raving too."

-Charlotte Brontë, to her professor

■

In recent years, Chris has done most of my tattoos. Although he has a formidable appearance as a stocky, middle-aged metalhead, he conducts himself with self-conscious sensitivity. He calls me "buddy" and never touches me without warning.

On the day of this appointment, the city was heat-swept, streets and occupants scorched. I wore a pair of cutoff shorts and a flimsy tank top and carried a tote with a change of clothes to wear to Shabbos service afterward. My sleeve was tucked into my armpit so Chris could press the stencil of a barred owl across my right breast, opposite of the pigeon he'd tattooed the year before. Once the tracing was applied, I approved its location in the mirror, laid down on the table, and reminded myself to breathe from the belly.

Chris led his needle over the outline. "So, what's been going on, Cal? It's been a while."

I groaned. "This last year has been completely fucked. I wouldn't even know where to start."

He hummed in agreement. "Well, we're going to be here for a least a couple of hours."

I gave an abridged version: my professor had seduced me; he'd been abusive; I reported him; it was in the local news; a bunch of other professors and students were swept up in the scandal—some have lost their jobs, including him—and now, in light of it all, the university was amending their policies.

"Goddamn, dude," Chris marveled. "But, you know what? I've heard this shit so many times from my female friends who've been to college."

I gaped at him. "For real? You mean, about their professors taking advantage of them?"

"Yeah," he said gravely, pausing to mop ink from my breast

with a paper towel. "Just for example, a good friend of mine got into the Art Institute. It was a big deal, and she's a fucking great artist. But, one of her professors got to her, and it fucked her up. She had to drop out."

"Holy shit." I exhaled and squeezed my hands to keep from shaking.

"Like I said, that's just *one* example." Chris sat up and caught my eye. "Seriously, I hear this shit *all of the time*."

I clammed up then, and Chris drove the conversation elsewhere so I might laugh at his soft-hearted shenanigans over a recent weirdo girlfriend and the chaos of moving into a new house with his ridiculously huge record collection. I commented here and there, but as the tattoo progressed, I eventually buried a grimace in my forearm and tried to meditate beyond the pain.

*

In truth, I'd begun to notice the same. As I confided in a trickle of friends or kindly acquaintances, many of them gasped with recognition. They knew a family member or friend who'd been through something similar in college, or it had happened to them. One woman told me she was the product of such a relationship. "My mother was my father's student—it's how they'd met. He was abusive; really, he was a bastard, and I can say that now that he's dead."

During a coffee date with a former classmate who'd started teaching herself, she described how she, as an undergraduate, was also ensnared by a professor. "He said he would leave his wife for me," she lamented. "I was so young, you know? I believed him. But of course, he only strung me along."

As these admissions were spoken, the tone became a quiet pleading. It's something secretive that still buzzes with tragic embarrassment—like an instance of naïve, childhood cruelty, such as discovering baby frogs near a pond and pulling off their legs. Except, we speak from the frog's perspective, and *would you believe me if I said that while I wanted to be a frog, I didn't ask to have my legs ripped off?*

Trauma and chronic strain usually leave people feeling alone, set apart, exceptional in their suffering. I was no different. I felt alien and misunderstood. Still, to have been victimized by my professor—is that not rare?

Apparently, no. Nothing about my experience is unique. Everything about it follows a web of intersecting parallels that account for every aspect of my experience and provide answers to the stock questions most—if not all—abuse survivors ask themselves.

How did this happen? Why? How could someone do this? What kind of person would do this to someone else? Why me? What did I do wrong? What were the red flags, and how did I miss them? And now that it's over, why am I so fucked up? How long will this last?

Once the worst of the acute shock wore off, I started exploring these questions by resuming the tools of my disciplines: critical thought, scholarly research, as well as curiosity and imaginative musing. I knew my foundations—what I'd been taught or taught myself. I knew how to reinvent questions so they could be studied from a scientific perspective. I knew to look for patterns and consider variables.

I began haunting the halls of local libraries. I probed indexes and skimmed abstracts. I printed off mountainous stacks of peer-reviewed articles, photocopied entire book chapters. I scrawled notes, underlined text, and chased citations. I watched countless hours of documentaries and filmed lectures, and sheepishly engaged expert professionals for clarification.

What follows is the product of those research efforts, wherein I regard my involvement with Jack as a kind of case study—a lens through which psychological and sociological realities are defined and unraveled. I've isolated these into seven primary points of discussion, beginning with unseen, cognitive processes and expanding until aspects of higher education are considered.

Every human being is subject to the same bewildering, appealing, and harrowing forces. Each one of us is on display to the other, and sometimes, analysis of the stranger best communicates truths about our individual and collective selves. Although the specifics will vary, here are my truths, reconciled alongside some theoretical assertions so that they might be analogously felt and, hopefully, understood.

1. Errors of Cognition

The human brain is an extraordinary product of mammalian evolution. Unlike other primates, we have the capacity for critical and symbolic abstract thought, as well as self-reflective consciousness (or, the ability to ponder features of our very existence). In spite of this exceptional ingenuity, our brains seem determined to sabotage us. Humans are incredibly susceptible to warped perceptions, mistaken judgments, and errors of cognition. We are, for all intents and purposes, hardwired for irrationality.

Even our tendency toward illogical thought is an adaptive feature. In order for us to swiftly and routinely process vast amounts of information, humans have developed a system of unconscious, automatic mental short-cuts, known as cognitive biases. Without these short-cuts, it would be damn near impossible for us to make timely decisions or make sense of our social environments. So, while cognitive biases allow us to disseminate information quickly, they also predispose us to faulty conclusions about ourselves and the world around us.

Dr. Jonathan Howard (2018), a neurologist and psychiatrist, writes that although being referred to as biased feels like an insult, "having biases does not make us immoral or flawed." Instead, he likens biases to blind spots in our vision, impossible to notice unless they're pointed out. "To say we are biased simply means we all see the world from a specific vantage point, based on our beliefs, desires, personality, past experiences, and culture" (Howard, 2018).

To combat bias, we should explore the thinking mistakes they can lead to; the information they prevent us from gathering, or the perspectives they obscure; and attempt to mitigate these effects (Howard, 2018). "This is easier to do with some biases than others, but preventing bias all together is not an option" (Howard, 2018). Acknowledging our cognitive blind spots can help us to subvert the impulse to adopt them. This practice, Howard (2018) says, "should contribute to your humility, not your confidence." In other words, learning about biases shouldn't be used to assert how correct our beliefs are, but to realize the ways in which we might be wrong.

This is immensely difficult, for instance, since we are predisposed to evaluate our beliefs by consciously looking for, or unconsciously gravitating toward, evidence that supports them. This is known as confirmation bias: "once we have formed a view, we embrace information that supports that view while ignoring, rejecting, or harshly scrutinizing information that casts doubt on it" (Gardner, 2008). The relevance of the thought—whether it is about something trivial or important—makes no difference; "once a belief is established, our brains will seek to confirm it" (Gardner, 2008).

I perpetuated this bias when I became aware that Kayla's boyfriend "Bob" was actually Jack. When I'd discussed the matter with Mikki, she pointed out that, though I had every right to be upset with Kayla for lying, I should also be concerned with the inappropriateness of Jack's actions. Yet, I'd disregarded Mikki's remarks, as they didn't align with my preexisting conclusions about Jack's character.

It certainly didn't end there. Throughout the course of my involvement with Jack, I succumbed to a number of psychological tricks aimed at rationalizing his behavior and its impact on me, as well as justifying my decision to participate in the relationship. Unfortunately, this cognitive trickery only served to fuel an irrational set of perceptions in which Jack's abuses escaped me, unrealized fully, until I spoke to Zahra.

*

Confirmation bias is sometimes the byproduct of cognitive dissonance. According to Festinger's theory, cognitive dissonance is an unpleasant state of mental tension caused by people's awareness of inconsistency among beliefs, attitudes, or actions (Smith, Mackie & Claypool, 2014). For instance, "if we believe X, but have done something that is incompatible with X," we experience a kind of uncomfortable mental clash known as dissonance (Mook, 2004). To avoid this tension, people will respond by reducing the dissonance, either by adjusting their belief or attitude, or altering their behavior. But, because behavior requires more effort to change than shifting one's attitudes, "the tension caused by the differences between important actions and attitudes is often reduced by adjustments we make to our thinking; not to our behavior" (Smith et al., 2014).

People will and do experience cognitive dissonance frequently. At any given moment, we might find ourselves stumbling into new information or situations that challenge our self-schema (i.e. the core beliefs we hold about ourselves). So naturally, I experienced cognitive dissonance about Jack. In the beginning, this state of tension arose from my beliefs about professor-student relationships versus my decision to be in a relationship with my own professor. To preserve my sense of integrity, I told myself while yes, it's unethical for faculty to date students, Jack and I were an exception. As the relationship progressed, the tension centered between what I thought about Jack as a person versus how his behaviors actually made me feel.

As described in my diary, Jack habitually latched onto me in his office during our Monday afternoon appointments. In truth, these exchanges had not been entirely enjoyable. Within such a tight space that signified his authority over me, his embraces and deep kisses felt all too forceful, making me feel small and trapped.

Worse were the couple of occasions in which he masturbated in front of me. My immediate reactions were shock, fear, and then confusion. The flagrant disregard for the setting and the task at hand—discussion of my coursework—came off as disrespectful to me and to the terms of his position.

In these moments, I churned with internal conflict, and the way I chose to elude this feeling was to convince myself that I *liked* it. I kissed him back. I didn't push his hands away. And when he touched himself, I tried to watch. Afterward, I blushed, telling my friends what had happened, and giggled devilishly at their disapproving groans. But, I knew it was wrong, and if I'd accepted how these in-office acts genuinely made me feel, I too would have shuddered and groaned with disapproval.

Festinger (1957) suggests that "motivation and desired consequences may also be factors in determining whether or not two elements are dissonant." This claim presumably led to the understanding of a psychological phenomenon known as effort justification. According to Nicholson and Lutz (2017), "Individuals experience dissonance arousal when they consider abandoning a project, task, or even a relationship into which they have put extensive time, effort, and resources. As a result, they begin to more strongly prefer the object or scenario into which they expended their resources or efforts in order to justify their behaviors and reduce dissonance." Put more succinctly, if someone goes through a difficult or painful experience in order to attain something, it becomes more attractive (Tavris & Aronson, 2007).

Dating Jack was incredibly arduous. It grew increasingly more stressful as the months passed, and yet, I never considered leaving him. Even after he'd broken up with me, I was determined to be a close friend. I simply held out, believing life would eventually settle down and we'd have sufficient time and emotional reserves to dedicate to each other. I loved Jack harder, in a sense, because doing so reduced my dissonance and justified the substantial amount of time, focus, commitment, and self-esteem I was investing in him. The option to give up never crossed my mind.

*

Dissonance reduction may also help to shelter oneself from threats to their self-esteem. The inconsistency, then, arises from our beliefs about our own character in comparison to our actions: as Mook (2004) illustrates, "I am an honest, sensible, kind person," versus "I have done this dishonest, foolish, cruel thing." To preserve self-esteem and reduce dissonance, individuals generally respond by perceiving their actions in a positive light. The idea is that dissonance reduction operates "like the burner on a stove, keeping our self-esteem bubbling away" (Tavris & Aronson, 2007). On the other hand, if someone suffers low self-esteem, dissonance reduction may result in thoughts that validate their negative self-image, called cognitive distortions.

As a term, cognitive distortions has come to describe a variety of systematic thinking errors. Typically, these "appear when information is biased or inaccurate," and are "often directly associated with negative mood states" (Lewis, 2014). The concept was originated by psychiatrist Aaron Beck through his work with depressed patients. While Beck identified six cognitive distortions to start, more have been classified using his methodology. Common examples include overgeneralization (drawing a general conclusion based on an isolated event), personalization (assigning responsibility to events outside of one's own control), and emotional reasoning, magnification, and minimization.

Consider how I reacted when Jack revealed his proposal of marriage hadn't been literal. Though I was angry with him, I was also despondent, blaming myself. "Oh, but can I *really* be so shocked?" I wrote in my diary, "No one has ever *seriously* wanted to marry me." This is an example of emotional reasoning: when one assumes their emotional reactions reflect the true situation (Beck & Pretzer, 2005). Not only had Jack made me feel unworthy of marriage, his statements also fueled my impressions of total worthlessness. And I accepted these because they validated intrusive, negative beliefs I already struggled with about myself.

My anxiety also led to magnification and minimization. In the weeks immediately following graduation, I noticed Jack had grown distant. He stopped inviting me to sleep over and made fewer plans to hang out. I asked if he felt ill and if this was causing him to favor isolation, and he agreed. So during this time, whenever we experienced exceptionally fun or romantic interactions, I viewed these as proof that our relationship was good, then diminished the significance of anything that contradicted this belief. Thus, I treated some aspects of our situation—independent of their *actual* significance—as very important (maximization) and others as trivial (minimization) (Beck & Pretzer, 2005). Doing so allowed me to avoid the more hurtful implications of Jack's changing behavior.

I point this out in order to emphasize how someone who is already depressed, anxious, or suffering low self-esteem is particularly vulnerable to abuse (though, it goes without saying that these antecedent issues should never be used to reason why someone is abused). Individuals who already don't think highly of themselves will likely tolerate messages of the same sentiment from someone else, especially persons they love and trust. Indeed, plenty of research has found correlations between low self-esteem, trauma, and abuse. One study of abuse survivors conducted by Dutton and Painter (1993) found that women with the lowest self-esteem tended to experience the most trauma and were more attached to their abusers than women with higher self-esteem.

This isn't to suggest the presence of low self-esteem can predict someone's responses to an abusive partner or their reluctance to separate from them. On the contrary, having high self-esteem might contribute to a victim's denial of their abuse by engaging a bias: they believe they're not the type of person who would allow themselves to be abused; therefore, their partner isn't really being abusive (Nicholson & Lutz, 2017). Of course, this is illogical. Anyone, under the proper conditions, can fall victim to intimate partner abuse.

It's worth mentioning that while cognitive distortions are typically associated with negative moods and thoughts, this isn't always the case. They can also be representative of efforts to preserve a positive spin on someone's idea of self and their circumstances. This, too, can prolong someone's relationship to an abuser—by misconstruing events and interactions optimistically, despite contradictory evidence.

*

Of all the cognitive tricks I used to manage my anxiety and confusion, rationalization was activated the most. From when Jack first flirted with me and as the relationship unfolded toward its eventual end, I clambered to make excuses for him.

I know him. I've known him for years. He's a good person. He's not hurting me on purpose. He wouldn't use me.

He's afraid of disappointing me, and his fear is holding him back.

He meant it when he said it, and now he's changed his mind—but he's scared to admit it because he's embarrassed and doesn't want to hurt me.

Rationalization occurs when "apparently logical reasons" are given to justify problematic behavior and to defend ourselves "against feelings of guilt, maintain self-respect, and protect oneself from criticism" (Rationalization, APA, 2018). I also experienced denial, which involves ignoring or refusing to acknowledge unpleasant thoughts, feelings, or events via excluding these perceptions from my immediate consciousness. So, even though I was aware Jack's actions were hurtful, I denied malicious intent on his part because I didn't want to believe it.

Rationalization and denial are common examples of ego defense mechanisms: psychological strategies meant to shield against anxiety, unacceptable impulses, and to preserve one's self-schema. In addition to being provoked by internal conflict, "they may be aroused by whatever is perceived as dangerous to the person's survival, acceptance, and security in the social world" (Hentschel et al., 2004). Defense mechanisms are somewhat similar to cognitive bias in that they support our ability to navigate reality; however, they manifest out of the inherent need to counteract uncomfortable stimuli, rather than the necessity to speedily process information. Though defense mechanisms have been found to activate cognitive distortions (Batmaz et al., 2016), defenses usually occur on an unconscious level, while distortions are conscious—albeit automatic—thoughts.

The conceptualization of ego defenses originated around the turn of the 20th century with Sigmund Freud and the newly founded field of psychoanalysis. His daughter, Anna Freud, later expanded on his research, writing the first definitive book on the subject: *The Ego and the Mechanisms of Defence.* Her contributions are exceptional because she shifted the view from psychopathology to adaptation. She recognized that defenses allow all individuals to cope with the burdens of external reality and are not strictly a feature of the psychologically ill, impaired, or distressed.

The theory of ego defenses has expanded throughout the century. Beginning with the ten prominent defenses A. Freud describes in her book, others have been identified, such as intellectualization (addressing the emotionality of a subject through a purely intellectual lens) and altruism (meeting one's own needs by fulfilling the needs of others). In the 1970s, psychiatrist George Eman Vaillant proposed a classification scheme, grouping defenses within a four-level hierarchy: psychotic, immature, neurotic, and mature. "At the lowest level, the mechanisms distort reality, at the highest, they bring about its integration with interpersonal relationships and feelings," and at intermediate points, "defenses alter distress and modify the experience of feelings, and may appear odd, inappropriate, or socially undesirable from an outside point of view" (Hentschel et al., 2004). For instance, use of humor as a defense is considered a mature mechanism, while passive aggression is immature. Denial is categorized as psychotic, given how this defense disrupts one's understanding of reality. Neurotic defenses are also fairly common—such as displacement (avoiding problematic impulses or emotions through redirection)—and offer temporary relief from external strain, but can lead to dysfunctional thinking patterns if engaged long-term.

Ego defenses are yet another cognitive tool humans instinctually rely on to ease anxiety and resist difficult feelings. Like other errors of cognition, they can disrupt one's ability to make sound judgments. As Hentschel et al. (2004) emphasize, "To be sure, there is a price to pay for reliance upon defense mechanisms. It is exacted in the form of reduced awareness of both self and environment."

Like cognitive biases and distortions, defense mechanisms are another means by which people in abusive relationships psychologically protect themselves. Defenses can offset negative emotions, and allow individuals to cope with their circumstances and maintain a positive impression of their partner. This is possible because defense mechanisms are activated unconsciously, and over time, the thoughts associated with them become normalized, making it harder for the victim to perceive the abuse or acknowledge it when its remarked upon by others. According to Hentschel et al. (2004), "Defense mechanisms involve manipulation of threatening representations, even to the point of making them disappear," while the coping component provides individuals with a false sense of control.

Habitual use of defense mechanisms may be one reason many people remain committed to abusive partners. "If they feel 'trapped' in the relationship, they may be inclined to change their negative attitude pertaining to the relationship or abuse, whether they know it or not" (Dare et al., 2013). Once someone adopts measures that prioritize a positive outlook, they will continue to have these positive feelings toward the relationship, "due to the human nature of wanting to remain consistent with our thoughts and actions, therefore reducing dissonance" (Dare et al., 2013). This doesn't mean individuals come to regard the abuse as acceptable or become complacent; rather, they've unconsciously found comfort by reducing the dissonance associated with the abuse—a shift in attitude when enacting a change in behavior is more difficult or even dangerous.

Evolutionary biologist Robert Trivers (2011) writes, "So powerful is our tendency to rationalize that negative evidence is often immediately greeted with criticism, distortion, and dismissal so that not much dissonance need be suffered." This is true even when the consequences of dodging our mental tension result in prolonging our exposure to harm. I suspect one reason for this is that our survival drive is mostly tied to our need to cope with immediate stressors or threats.

Logical assessment of long-term outcomes takes a backseat to enduring a moment of crisis. In instances of sudden pain and fear, we respond with defenses meant to shield us from thoughts that would further overwhelm us, fueling a state of powerlessness and panic. When looked at from this perspective, it makes more sense how people remain in abusive relationships. Intimate partner abuse tends to be episodic rather than constant. Psychological abuse, specifically, is often subtle and entails manipulation, making it more challenging to detect outright. Therefore, instances of abuse—blatant or otherwise—can come to be perceived as something one simply tolerates, excuses, or refuses to see in order to resume the usual, more pleasurable hallmarks of an intimate relationship.

At first, this may sound puzzling or contradictory. How can someone recognize that abuse is occurring, while also convincing themselves that it isn't? Trivers (2011) explains this, stating that "true and false information may be simultaneously stored, only with the truth stored in the unconscious mind and falsehoods in the conscious." In effect, defense mechanisms provide a means to deal with uncomfortable mental tension by keeping one's own mind in the dark. The thoughts that surface seem accurate and sound, while the hard truths of one's reality go unrealized, buried deep in the psyche.

*

In his book, Festinger (1957) makes several references to cigarette smoking to illustrate the process of cognitive dissonance. A smoker who knows the health risks posed by their habit may reduce dissonance by quitting. Or, since it requires less effort than behavioral changes, they might rationalize their smoking instead: "you only live once," or "you're going to die someday anyway." While this is an effective way to describe cognitive dissonance, Festinger failed to take into account nicotine addiction. Most people understand smoking is bad for them, but halting this behavior is infamously difficult because nicotine is a powerful drug.

The same can be said of someone stuck in an abusive relationship. Even if an individual is physically able to escape with relative safety, they may fail to do so because they are, in effect, hooked. Research demonstrates that we become addicted to our romantic partners, and this can occur regardless of the presence of abuse.

The area of the brain that encourages a human to complete a survival-based action—such as eating, drinking, or having sex—is called the survival-reinforcement circuit (Inaba & Cohen, 2014). When a potent psychoactive substance activates this neuro-pathway, the result is a feeling of satisfaction, a "high," or physical and emotional pain relief, which prompts a "go" switch in the brain, urging the user to consume more (Inaba & Cohen, 2014). Normally, the accompanying "stop" switch tells the person a need is satisfied and they can cease to perform the action. But, with increasing drug consumption, this "stop" switch gets disabled. The survival-reinforcement and control circuits of the brain become hijacked and subverted, eventually causing the user to feel as though their survival depends on more and more of the drug. At the subconscious level, the overriding message is "If you don't do it again, you will die" (Inaba & Cohen, 2014).

Try to reimagine this last paragraph with some modifications in word choice: *love* and *partner* in place of *psychoactive substance*, *drug*, and *user*. The internal processes are, more or less, the same.

According to Burkett and Young (2012), "When we fall in love, we experience an exquisite euphoria, loss of control, loss of time, and a powerful motivation to seek out the partner...The psychology of human love and drug addiction share powerful overlaps at virtually every level of the addictive process, from initial encounters to withdrawal. A preponderance of evidence from human studies and animal models now demonstrates that these overlaps extend to the level of neurobiology as well, where virtually every neurochemical system implicated in addiction also participates in social attachment processes." Of the neurochemicals included in their review, Burkett and Young (2012) note the release of dopamine and oxytocin in social bonding—the same neurotransmitters stimulated by drugs like alcohol, cocaine, and ecstasy. Burkett and Young (2012) even suggest that prescription drugs used to help individuals through drug withdrawal might also be effective treatment for persons grieving the loss of a loved one.

Emerging research has also linked social stress and increased levels of oxytocin. One such study of mice revealed the release of this neurochemical a few hours after a stress-induced event (Guzmán et al., 2013). Parallels were drawn between their findings and previous links to oxytocin and its "fear-enhancing effects in humans" (Guzmán et al., 2013). The implications of this are fascinating, since oxytocin is a hormone primarily associated with social bonding—sometimes colloquially referred to as the "cuddle" or "love hormone." Scientists now recognize that "during times of low stress, oxytocin physiologically rewards those who maintain good social bonds with feelings of well-being," but during periods of "high social stress or pain," it may stimulate someone's need for social contact (DeAngelis, 2008).

These conclusions can also help explain why victims become attached to their abusers. For one, individuals can get addicted to their romantic partners. Then, because abuse often involves both coerced isolation and feelings of isolation, this often causes the victim to feel, during periods of exceptional stress, that the only person who can comfort them is the person who hurt them in the first place. Presumably, this encourages the practice of conflict-resolution and self-regulation through maladaptive coping defenses—denial, rationalization, and the like—as the victim struggles to regain feelings of love and security.

Taken all together, these neuropsychological processes are indicative of what is known as trauma bonding. Psychologists Donald Dutton and Sally Painter introduced this theory to account for prevailing attachment in abusive relationships. A prerequisite for traumatic bonding is the presence of a power imbalance, wherein the abuser dominates and controls their partner. There also has to be a pattern of first pleasant, then upsetting interactions, followed by a period of relief or "cooling down." By Dutton and Painter's (1993) assessment, this cycling between negative, hurtful and positive, pleasurable experiences with a romantic partner mimics that of a psychoactive drug stimulating the reward-survival pathway. This is further amplified by the release of feel-good bonding hormones. "This cycle of dependency," Dutton and Painter (1981) state, eventually creates a "strong affective bond," as the victim develops a deeper need for the high-power partner.

In reflecting on these concepts, I can see how my responses to Jack parallel addiction. I think most people who've been in love can relate to feeling obsessive about or intoxicated by their romantic partners. This is followed by a kind of helpless void (withdrawal) when they can't see their partner for a prolonged period of time, or at a time when they need to be comforted. Adding abusive elements to the mix complicates this reliance, causing desperation, a sense of being out of control. In this state, it's no wonder individuals will respond through negative thought distortions and defense mechanisms, even if doing so is irrational and, ultimately, self-destructive.

*

Sociologist Erving Goffman (1961) notably stated, "There seems to be no agent more effective than another person in bringing a world for oneself alive, or, by a glance, a gesture, or a remark, shriveling up the reality in which one is lodged." In my case, Zahra was the agent who transformed the meaning of my experiences, effectively shriveling up my reality in the process. Hearing Zahra's story permitted me to evaluate Jack's actions as they might affect another person and how such actions were unethical and misleading.

Suddenly, I knew he'd lied and led me on. He *was* in the habit of sexually pursuing his students, and there *was* concern about his fidelity. Because Zahra's account was impartial to mine, yet confirmed my fears, I was shoved outside of the irrational set of perceptions both imposed on and nurtured by me. As Trivers (2011) might say, the truthful information finally began to migrate into my conscious mind. Only then, after eleven months of combatting cognitive dissonance, I gained a sense of objectivity over my impressions of Jack, and what I saw was deplorable.

I would spend the next several months apologizing to others who'd been swept up by the drama. "You have nothing to be sorry about," was a common, gentle reply.

"I'm just so embarrassed," I repeated, agonized. I was, in essence, apologizing for my human brain and all of its frustrating, innate vulnerabilities. I felt so, so stupid. What I failed to understand was just how complex my cognitive realities are and made even more so through the trauma bond I'd developed to Jack.

We process information and emotions so rapidly that it's possible to experience different forms of cognitive errors simultaneously. For example, we might respond to a cognitive distortion through bias. Or, we might express a number of defensive mechanisms after a single event. To maintain a sense of security in ourselves and our relationships, we succumb to inherent mental short-cuts, leading to conclusions that seem rational on the surface, though the opposite is true. It's unsurprising, then, that so many of us become victims of deceitful trickery; we're already designed to trick ourselves.

2. Manipulation and Psychological Abuse

My counselor Heather expressed disgust over victim-blaming during one of our early sessions. People often pronounce victims "should have known" the abuser was capable of such behavior, or they "should have seen it coming." She said these responses are terribly flawed, negating the fact that the majority of sexual abuse or assault victims are targeted by persons close to them, such as neighbors, friends, and relatives. Nor does abuse generally occur at random or with easily perceived warning. Most predators groom their victims or focus their exploits on individuals who are already dependent on them in some way.

We discussed how Jack's behavior over the years could reflect potential grooming efforts. This was really upsetting; to think his kindness and praise were part of a greater agenda to eventually seduce me. He'd made me feel superior to my classmates when he complimented my intellectual abilities, and confided in me about his health and his frustrations with other students. When doing so, he'd displayed a unique trust in me by using phrases like "just between us" or "because I view you more like a peer than a student..." Likewise, the slack he'd given me on my late homework, the books he'd gifted me, and even my good grades—all of it might represent his attempts to mold me for abuse.

Yet, none of these statements or actions raised alarm or seemed unusual. I had no idea that I was his prey.

*

Manipulation is a basic survival tactic, arising from humans' relationship to their environment and the objects therein.

Many times, these objects are alive, such as plants, animals, and other people. As summarized by Buss et al. (1987), "manipulation of living objects may be defined as the various means by which organisms influence and exploit the sense organs and behavioral machinery of other organisms." Throughout our lives, we're often subject to interactions wherein we're compelled—either consciously or otherwise—to manipulate another person to preserve our best interests.

Though manipulation has a negative connotation, the phenomenon itself isn't innately malicious. Many forms of manipulation are harmless, such as when a child pleads for a new toy until a parent agrees to buy it for them. Such instances of manipulation differ from that of exploitation. Discerning between the two depends on 1) whether an asymmetry of power exists between parties, and 2) the consequences, and how these cause intended, unintended, or latent harm toward the manipulated parties. When individuals or groups of people have suffered violations to their ability to subsist or practice autonomy in order to benefit persons with designated power over them, then exploitation has occurred.

The parent can be annoyed by their child who is utilizing manipulation in hopes of getting a toy, but the action is innocent because it fails to undermine the parent's autonomy. Too, the parent has power over the child, which can rebuff the child's efforts. And finally, despite being the manipulator, the child is the most vulnerable party in this scenario, as their well-being is dependent on their parent's discretion. So, if the parent felt the toy was inappropriate for the child, it's their responsibility to off set potential harm by refusing to purchase the toy. Such factors are important to note when distinguishing between innocuous versus harmful forms of manipulation.

Take lying, for instance. Lying is a common manipulative technique, considered to be "a deeply ingrained human trait" (Bhattacharjee, 2017), and isn't always intended to be hurtful.

In fact, some lies serve a positive social function, ensuring comfortable interactions between people. We lie to each other to express politeness, to avoid petty conflict or hurting someone's feelings, or to make each other laugh. For reasons of self-preservation, we lie to deflect embarrassment or judgment, escape awkward situations, and hide our flaws or inadequacies.

The designs of most lies are innocent, which is good news since the average person lies about once or twice per day (Bhattacharjee, 2017). Separating minor falsehoods from serious transgressions can be determined in the same way that manipulation is distinguished from exploitation: by judging the stakes and the potential for injury. To illustrate the difference, imagine finding out a friend had lied about what they ate for lunch, and compare this to being told your doctor was practicing medicine under a forged license. The first lie is frivolous, annoying; the second is an example of fraud, and its implications are far more disturbing.

What if you discovered that someone you loved had fabricated much of their life story, passing it off as their reality? What if their lies were elaborate and suppressed your ability to make independent, informed decisions about yourself, your lifestyle, and your involvement with them? To this, journalist and abuse survivor Abby Ellin (2019) says, "That's exploitation, and it causes real damage."

*

Within the context of interpersonal relationships, psychological manipulation is characterized as applying undue influence through mental distortion and emotional exploitation with the intent to seize power, control, and other rewards at the expense of another person. Most commonly, abusive manipulation "involves ethically suspect behavior such as deceiving...undermining autonomy, or bypassing or subverting the [victim's] rational capacities" (Gorin, 2014). Clinical neuropsychologist Grant Sinnamon (2017) says this is done in such a way that the victim's own moral, ethical, and social compass is undermined or redeveloped "in favor of accepting the predator's objectives as appropriate, legitimate, and even desirable aims." In this way, the manipulation is exploitative because it suppresses the manipulee's ability to express autonomy and execute reason in their decision-making.

Although manipulation is typically viewed as covert (in that the target doesn't realize they're being manipulated), some forms of manipulation are more obvious, like "guilt-tripping." In this case, someone is aware they're being made to feel guilty; however, this understanding doesn't always interrupt the intended outcome, as the manipulee feels guilt and acts on it (Barhill, 2014). Blatant manipulation may also reflect basic social or cultural dispositions, such as a man buying flowers for a woman who has rejected him in an attempt to sway her decision. On the other hand, an individual may employ more intricate methods, such as faking interest in a hobby enjoyed by the manipulee as a way to obtain their trust. Covert manipulation is considered the favored approach by abusers, as they are more likely to successfully influence someone who doesn't realize they're being manipulated.

Psychological manipulation is steadily gaining more recognition as a form of intimate partner abuse. Many types of manipulative trickery have been labeled by psychologists, social workers, and domestic violence advocates so that they are becoming more widely known by the general public. For instance, I wrote in my diary about me and Phoebe being gaslighted by Jack, which is characterized by statements and behaviors aimed at disorientating the other person by causing them to question their own memory or overall sense of reality.

In addition to this, I've come to realize how Jack employed a range of other manipulative tactics to exert control over me, first as his student and then as his intimate partner. My research on this has been immensely relieving in that it has validated my suspicions about particular aspects of Jack's behavior. Then again, it's also troubling to be confronted with evidence that speaks to just how profoundly manipulative he was toward me and others.

*

I've mentioned Jack's use of grooming; this occurs when an individual purposefully gains the trust and dependence of another, causing them to become acquiescent to abuse. Grooming is a slow, methodical process that often involves staging emotional bonds with a victim or making claims to relate to them, prompting a sense of connection and subsequent loyalty. Excessive declarations or displays of affection and flattery (i.e. "love-bombing"), gift-giving, professing secrets, granting favors, and special treatment are common indications of grooming, and are a means to foster commitment and obedience from a victim.

Sinnamon (2017) explains how "grooming may involve weeks, months, or even years of preabuse preparation," and "generally progresses through a series of stages during which the sexual predator uses a number of specific techniques to mask their intentions and prime their target for abuse." As relayed by Salamon (2011), these stages have been categorized as: identifying a target victim; "collecting information about the intended victim so that the abuser can utilize that information to manipulate the target; filling a need by acting in a supportive, nurturing manner"; lowering the victim's inhibitions; and finally, introducing the abuse.

Grooming is an insidious form of abusive manipulation, colloquially likened to "brain-washing" or psychological "programming." It's the same type of systematic abuse that disingenuous self-help and wellness gurus, cult leaders, pedophiles, human traffickers, pimps, and recruiters of child soldiers implement to gain the complacency of their victims, influence their beliefs and actions, and desensitize them to mistreatment. While much of the literature on sexual grooming is focused on the exploitation of children, adults can be and are frequently victimized in this way. Compared to that of children (which is unlawful and inarguably abusive), adult sexual grooming is harder to recognize, since it involves individuals of legal consenting age and appears to begin like any normal relationship. Regardless, as Sinnamon (2017) points out, "the grooming process used by sexual predators on children and adults is essentially the same, focusing on emotional and psychological manipulation tactics."

People who are selected for grooming by sexual predators tend to have physical, social, or interpersonal vulnerabilities. They may be socially isolated, culturally disadvantaged, physically disabled, have psychological or learning exceptions, or suffer mental illness, addiction, low self-esteem, and financial troubles. (However, confident, socially advantaged individuals can and do fall victim to abusive grooming as well.) Most predators are also inclined to imbed themselves in environments where inherent disparities of power between themselves and their targets can be exploited based on age, performance of gender roles, level of expertise, and access to information and resources. Inserting themselves within these so-called "hunting grounds" can allow offenders to legitimize their proximity to susceptible persons through socially applauded occupations, such as those of coaches, clergymen, counselors, teachers, health care personnel, or social workers. Given the helping roles associated with these positions, grooming behaviors can be easily masked, granting predators the availability to instigate abusive manipulation under the guise of concern or assistance.

"The challenge with 'grooming' behaviors," Sinnamon (2017) continues, "is that, at least in the early stages of the process, the actions undertaken in an honorable versus nefarious interaction may be indistinguishable. This is because exploitative grooming often takes the shape of a deliberate process of creating a strong, positively reinforced relationship, in which trust is garnered and intimate interactions are normalized." Since the positive attentions are not offensive or seem inappropriate to start, a victim rarely understands they're being taken advantage of until much later, as the abuse becomes more overt, increasing in frequency and severity. But, because they have invested trust in or grown reliant on their abuser, they're likely to cope with the abuse through cognitive distortions and defense mechanisms. After all, the victim has no way of knowing the relationship was staged from the beginning.

*

Jack had incorporated grooming techniques into our interactions for several years. By the time he made sexual advances, I was putty—softened, shaped, and bound to him. His friendly, empathetic persona permitted me to let my guard down around him. While I'm a candid person anyway, I felt comfortable being more forthcoming with Jack about the specifics of my life in comparison to other professors with whom I felt close. In doing so, I unintentionally armed Jack with details about my preferences and insecurities, which he used to manipulate me.

Our elopement plans may be one example of this. Jack knew I'd been devastated when my engagement to Cody fell through and that I planned to wear my wedding dress to the graduation ceremony. By proposing, Jack ensured some complacency by exploiting this tender subject and baiting me with the promise of fulfilling a previous desire of mine. Of course, he never meant to follow through with our plans, and it was only a couple of months before I understood we weren't going to get married. Still, for that short time, I was exceptionally obliged to him. If his intentions were to keep me dreamily distracted and—more importantly—silent until after I graduated, he was successful in this.

Most of Jack's compliments were designed to soothe my areas of self-doubt and boost my self-esteem. Well aware of my history of disordered eating and body dysmorphia, he never ended a meeting without telling me how "healthy" I looked or how "well" I seemed. Once the private visits at his home began, he expanded on this flattery, noting his admiration for my appearance with statements like, "You always look so put-together," and "I've always liked your fashion sense and how you dress yourself." On a few occasions, he said, "You have the body of a dancer"—and how my heart had fluttered!

Likewise, he'd targeted my intellect and creative writings. I was constantly told how brilliant I was, how interesting and clever. Repeatedly, Jack said I was one of the smartest people he knew—smarter than his colleagues—and one of the most intelligent pupils he'd ever encountered. My ideas were rarely challenged and my writing was never criticized. When I read my prose or poetry to him, he hummed and gasped with approval. Really, I've never known a better cheerleader of my academic and creative pursuits. Because I have always struggled to believe in my abilities and fear failure over most things, this enthusiastic battering of support was intoxicating—yes, addictive.

Once I was hooked, and Jack and I had entered our secret relationship, the seductive grooming continued. He also began to feed me more details about his life. These stories were mostly heartbreaking, and yet, despite the painful circumstances he'd suffered, he assured me that sadness had not left him jaded. Instead, he saw himself remaining sensitive, loving, and receptive to the emotions of those around him.

Being the big softy that I am, I ate it up. I ached on his behalf, believing in his anguish, his loss. How could I have known he was lying? Who would lie about being chronically ill, losing so many loved ones to sudden death or cancer, or struggling to remain lucid through fierce bouts of suicidality?

Not Jack—not this warm, kindly man I'd grown to love and trust so deeply.

To get concessions from their partners, abusive manipulators will commonly elicit their sympathies and stroke their protective, nurturing sensibilities. By portraying themselves as victims or malingering (i.e., feigning illness or exaggerating symptoms of illness for personal gain), abusers can encourage codependency in that their partners are more likely to sacrifice their wants and needs to appeal to those of the abuser. When met with accounts of suffering, the manipulees are likely to respond charitably, sensing a duty to perform favors and see to the biddings of their poor darlings. To fail to do so could impart feelings of guilt, as if they were contributing to their partner's hardships. By depicting themselves as weak, the manipulators can further disguise features of their exploitation. Their partners are less likely to recognize their abusers are exercising power over them because they perceive them as physically or emotionally fragile.

"Playing the victim" and portraying himself as an invalid were additional forms of strategic dishonesty Jack practiced. His propensity for deception was breathtaking—pathological. Ranging from withholding pertinent information, to exaggeration of facts, to elaborate story-telling and play-acting, Jack deliberately prevented me from having an accurate understanding of him or our arrangement as a whole. In retrospect, Jack's deceit was the framework from which he enacted the majority of his manipulation, including the establishment of his victim persona, gaslighting, and many features of his grooming efforts. In the end, if it had not been for the mastery of his lying, I doubt he would have successfully achieved his goal of sexually exploiting me.

Because it undermines the manipulee's ability to execute autonomy or make informed choices, deception is considered a form of psychological manipulation. To this point, philosopher Trudy Govier (1998) states, "Lying indicates a willingness to mislead and manipulate the other person, and the one who is lied to has [their] autonomy diminished insofar as [they have] acquired inaccurate information about the world." In essence, abusers create a one-sided version of reality, designed to exert control over their partner and to take advantage of them. If knowledge is power, so then will a disparity of power inevitably manifest in relationships wherein someone consistently lies to their partner.

*

The emotional impact of discovering deception within intimate partnerships was investigated in a study by McCornack and Levine (1990). Their results suggest that it tends to result in "an intense and predominately negative emotional experience...The degree of relational involvement, importance attributed to the act of lying, importance of the information that was lied about, and suspicion all played significant roles in influencing the emotional intensity of responses" (McCornack & Levine, 1990). A couple of these negative emotions were reported as shock and uncertainty, and occurred even when someone was already suspicious of being lied to by their partner.

Additional research shows that individuals can manifest symptoms of post-traumatic stress disorder (PTSD) when a partner's deception is finally uncovered or disclosed. One study with the wives of deceptive, sex-addicted husbands equates the confession to a crisis; the authors conclude "the event of initial disclosure is indeed a traumatic event, resulting in significant trauma-related symptoms and functional impairment" (Steffens & Rennie, 2006). After learning of her husband's infidelities, one woman from their sample is quoted as saying, "I was shocked. I threw up, couldn't sleep, couldn't eat, cried constantly, couldn't work" (Steffens & Rennie, 2006).

Having a traumatic response to deception is possible because our reality is, in large part interpersonal, shaped by the narratives of those around us and by the messages we absorb from our social worlds. As clinical sociologist and psychotherapist Amber Ault explains, "Human reality is mostly built on agreements that we have with other people about what's happening and what's real and what's true...So, when we have conceived an interpersonal reality and taken it to be true, it's very traumatizing to discover we've been operating out of a false set of assumptions, that without our consent, we've been living a lie through someone else's manipulation" (Ellin, 2019).

In the mid-1990s, psychologist Jennifer Freyd introduced the concept of betrayal trauma, arguing "how certain categories of adult experience entailing interpersonal betrayal can be understood as types of trauma exposures" (Brown & Freyd, 2008). Betrayal trauma (BT) occurs when individuals or institutions on which a person is dependent break an explicit or implied social agreement, resulting in a traumatizing violation of trust (Freyd, Klest, & Allard, 2005). This includes exploitation and abuse at the hands of persons in positions of power, care, or responsibility over the victim, such as clergymen, health care providers, parents, etc. The specifics of the trauma may not "threaten death or physical injury, but can be damaging to well-being, relationships, self-concept, and beliefs about others and the world" (Freyd et al., 2005). Research has also shown correlations between BT and physical illness, psychological distress, and mental health issues (Freyd et al., 2005; Brown & Freyd, 2008), including symptoms of PTSD.

Nevertheless, survivors of BT don't always qualify for a diagnosis of PTSD as outlined by the fifth edition of the American Psychiatric Association's *Diagnostic and Statistical Manual of Mental Disorders* (*DSM-5*): the standard, authoritative text used by clinicians to identify psychiatric disorders. As determined by the *DSM-5*, for an individual to be given a PTSD diagnosis, they must meet Criteria A, which reads, "[exposure to] death, threatened death, actual or threatened serious injury, or actual or threatened sexual violence" (APA, 2013). This prerequisite has stirred controversy and creates ethical conundrums for mental health practitioners. Certainly, individuals will suffer violations that don't involve an overtly violent threat to their physical safety, and still respond with the same "intrusive symptoms, emotional numbing, and automatic hyperarousal" as those who've had their lives or bodily safety threatened (Brown & Freyd, 2008). Presumably, most clinicians sense a principled need to overlook Criteria A to validate the traumatization of their patients and facilitate their treatment.

While I agree that Criteria A deserves criticism, I think it's worth noting the history behind its inclusion as a diagnostic feature. PTSD is a relatively new diagnosis; it was established in the 1980s, due to the lobbying efforts of combat veterans who sought to legitimize the psychological effects of their wartime experiences. For their purposes, Criteria A is a reasonable precedent. In recent decades, however, trauma research has exploded. There's now an overwhelming amount of empirical evidence to demonstrate how human tribulation besides that of warfare or exposure to overt physical or sexual violence can manifest the same pattern of symptoms. Thus, recommendations to further revise the *DSM*'s guidelines are warranted.

Based on Freyd's theory, one could reason that PTSD accounts for my reactions to Jack's abuses, which originate from the betrayal of his status as a helping professional. My counselors have reached the same conclusion, given what I've gone through and the symptoms I've displayed. Besides this, I will later discuss rape trauma syndrome, outlining how this explains more specific impacts on my physical and mental health.

*

Grooming, manipulation, and deception fall under the canopy of psychological abuse. Also called emotional or mental abuse, psychological abuse involves subjecting an individual to actions and messages that result in psychological harm, distress, or trauma. Bifulco and Moran (1998) write that "while most people have a reasonable understanding of what constitutes physical or sexual abuse, the identification of psychological abuse remains more elusive." This may be due to the fact that psychological abuse is most often subtle in nature, varied and multifaceted, and can exist independently of violence (Bifulco & Moran, 1998; Marshall, 1996). Because there are innumerous tactics a person could conceivably use to psychologically mistreat their partner, researchers identify abuse based on how specific behaviors cause harm. As psychologist Linda Marshall (1999, 1996) says, "The abuse is in the effect of the act."

From her research into the subject, Marshall (1999, 1996) confirms that psychological abuse against women can be overt or subtle, and that differences between types are marked by an observed potential for harm, as well as the victim's ability to describe the act and their feelings attached to it with relative ease. Subtle abuse is defined by its difficulty in being discerned and described by the victim. This is, in part, because subtle abuse can be performed in ways that can be inferred as caring or romantic. Marshall (1999) points out that "even the most violent men do not always inflict psychological abuse with an aggressive or dominating style," and goes on to add how men are often very gentle or loving when they enact various forms of psychological abuse. Importantly, Marshall (1999) also says that "because subtle acts of psychological abuse are more intangible, they are more likely to harm a woman's sense of self and her mental health and well-being more than her perceptions of the relationship and her partner."

Marshall's definition of subtle isolation is noteworthy. Most abuse research designates isolation as a person's obvious attempts at suppressing their partner's access to others, such as restricting their car or phone use. However, Marshall (1999) introduces subtle isolation as the alienation or psychological distance from others and even from oneself, and emphasizes how this has remarkable effects on a victim. Marshall (1999) states that "sustaining this type of subtle psychological abuse could result in a woman feeling as if she were alone or different from others even if she has a wide circle of friends. It could also keep her from enjoying the small, private pleasures most women enjoy (e.g., taking a long, hot bath)."

To encourage further research on psychological abuse, Marshall developed the Subtle and Overt Psychological Abuse of Women Scale (SOPAS)—a tool explicitly designed to assess previously under-documented forms of psychological abuse of women by their male partners. Broken down into subscales, SOPAS is used to measure the following abuse items: dominate, indifference, monitor, and discredit (overt); and undermine, discount, and isolate (subtle). From her own applications, Marshall's (1999) results "clearly show that an expanded view of psychological abuse is warranted," and that "subtle forms of psychological abuse had an effect more frequently than overt psychological abuse, violence, or sexual aggression."

For the sake of these pages, I've reimagined an abbreviated list of SOPAS items (Marshall, 2000) in relation to what I experienced with Jack:

Overt

Dominate

- used an offensive or hurtful tone when I expressed myself or my concerns
- got angry or hurt when I talked about our relationship
- made me feel like nothing I said would have an effect on him

Indifference

- acted like I didn't matter (unless it suited him to do so)
- ignored and avoided me

Discredit

- told others things that made me look bad—lied to others about my actions
- told me what he liked about me, only to get upset at me for the same things
- overemphasized my emotionality

Subtle

Undermine

- made me worry about my health and well-being
- made me worry about whether I could care for myself
- made me feel guilty about things I had or hadn't done
- made me question myself, making me feel insecure and less confident
- made me feel ashamed of myself

Discount

- acted secretive and kept things from me
- did things that made me feel small

- acted like I could do what I wanted, but then would get upset when I did
- made me feel like there was something wrong with me emotionally
- did or said things that hurt my self-respect

Isolate

- discouraged me from talking to people he knew
- made it difficult to talk to others
- pointed out how he was the only one who truly understood me
- tried to keep me from showing certain feelings

I didn't include Marshall's overt subscale *monitor* above, since Jack rarely bothered to track my movements, activities, or relationships with others. But, he didn't have to. As long as I believed the threats to my academic success, he could trust me to keep our intimacy a secret. As long as I accepted the awful, unflattering portraits he'd painted of other professors and administrators, he knew I would keep my distance from them. And as long as I believed he alone held the key to my future happiness, he could rely on my devotion.

There are several other items in SOPAS that matched Jack's behavior (though, I was unable to classify within the subscales). These would include instances in which Jack played games with my head; encouraged me to do something, only to make it difficult for me to do; changed his mind about something, only to tell me when it was "too late"; became more upset than me when I talked about my feelings; made me choose between things he wanted and things I wanted or needed; interrupted or sidetracked me when I was doing something important; and tried to convince me something had occurred the way he described it, when I knew that it wasn't true (Marshall, 2000).

Because abuse is thorny and often elusive, even if we make it a point to look for "red flags" in our partner's behavior, many of these can be tough to spot or easily excused. I think it's best to focus instead on how someone's conduct makes you *feel*—that immediate gut response—instead of trying to examine the behavior itself. This may be easier said than done; love is one hell of a drug, and like any other drug, it can numb us of difficult feelings and impair our thinking. But, it's possible, as long as we're willing to prioritize ourselves in the face of someone else's demands, and respond with self-preserving actions instead of problematic shifts in our thinking.

To finish, I'd like to share a quote that reads as both a cautionary piece of advice as well as a means by which healthy and collaborative relationships can be measured. David Royse (1994), a professor of social work, says that "abuse is present in any relationship where your loved one does not show concern for your problems, allow you to express your feelings, or treat you as an equal. Healthy relationships should not be characterized by feelings of competition, anger, manipulation, disappointment, or distrust. Instead, they should bring happiness, affection, harmony and tranquility into our lives—frustration and hurt ought not be the constant products of a loving relationship."

3. Rape

I was at Alice's house when I first breached the topic. Some weeks had passed since I'd made my reports to Eleanor Parsons and Linda Barrow, and first spoke to Magda. I remember taking off my hat and rubbing the stubble of my shaved head.

Alice sat across from me on an overstuffed, red leather couch. We each huddled beneath blankets to fight off the chill in the house, the chilling subject matter.

My mouth was a spout of nervous rambling. "Besides the power imbalance, consent requires both parties to be *informed*, right? Like, knowing if your partner has an STI or is married or something, and making a decision to have sex or not based on that information."

"It wasn't like he just didn't tell you," Alice said. "He actively lied when you asked."

"Right! Because if I'd known he'd done this with other students, or if I'd known he was still dating Magda, I would've *never* consented to *anything*." I paused to pick at the frayed ends of my blanket. "So, does that explain why I'm reacting this way, or why I've been such a fucking disaster for the last few weeks—or really, this whole time? Like, my body and my subconscious are reacting to the reality of the situation before I've consciously understood what was going on? Isn't that something they say—the body knows?"

"Yeah, there's some truth to that."

I threw the hem of the blanket off my lap. "So, is *that* what's happening? Am I reacting like a rape victim? *Am* I a rape victim?"

"It's just like you said: you weren't able to give informed consent," Alice affirmed. "He *raped* you. You've been raped many, many times."

*

Rape trauma syndrome (RTS) refers to the reoccurring pattern of immediate and long-term physical, behavioral, and psychological consequences of surviving rape. The symptoms of RTS overlap with PTSD, so it is not viewed as a separate disorder; rather, the condition was proposed to address the specific ways that survivors of rape manifest symptoms of PTSD.

Research indicates that 94 percent of rape survivors will experience RTS in the weeks immediately following an assault, with 35 percent suffering prolonged rape-induced PTSD (Resick & Schnicke, 1996; Foa & Rothbaum, 1998), although some studies have concluded that this number is as high as 50 percent or more (Bisson, 2007).

After my conversation with Alice, I did an internet search of "rape symptoms." I compared my symptoms to the information guides that popped up, and later confirmed these through clinical sources. While I wasn't exhibiting many of the physical signs (as these included bodily harm sustained during a violent assault), I was expressing most of the behavioral and psychological indicators of RTS:

Physical Symptoms

- nausea
- tension headaches
- sleep disturbances, such as difficulty falling or staying asleep, being
- awoken by nightmares, or feeling exhausted and sleeping more than usual
- eating disturbances, such as loss of appetite

Behavioral Symptoms

- crying more than usual
- difficulty concentrating
- stuttering or stammering more than usual
- being restless, agitated, and unable to relax; or just sitting around and moving very little
- exaggerated startle response

- isolating from others; or, socializing more than usual (often due to fear of being alone)
- becoming more watchful and alert
- increased irritability or anger
- sexual dysfunction, including fear of sex and loss of interest in sex
- loss of interest in hobbies or other pleasurable activities
- blunted affect (i.e., a reduction in the display of emotions)
- self-harming behaviors

Psychological Symptoms

- disorientation and bewilderment
- intrusive thoughts (i.e., sudden, distressing involuntary thoughts, images, ideas, or feelings related to the rape)
- flashbacks
- nightmares
- dissociation (i.e., mild to severe detachment from immediate surroundings, physical and emotional state, or sense of identity)
- unable to feel certain feelings, like happiness, or feeling "flat" or "numb"
- mood swings
- anxiety (or increased anxiety)
- developing fears of things related to the rape or rapist
- fear of future prospects, or feeling uncertain about the future
- distorted perceptions (i.e., changes to previously held beliefs)

- paranoia
- feeling depressed, sad, or having thoughts of suicide
- feelings of humiliation and shame
- feeling "different," or distant from others
- feelings of helplessness and powerlessness
- loss of self-respect or self-confidence (Terry & Cling, 2004; Allison & Wrightsman, 1993; Hansson, 1992; Peterson, Prout, & Schwarz, 1991)

The onset and progression of RTS may be divided into two stages: the acute crisis stage and the reorganization stage. The first refers to the immediate and short-term effects of the rape, including those that echo the victim's state of shock. According to Allison and Wrightsman (1993), at this stage, the most commonly reported symptoms are anxiety and fear, which suffers a victim's cognition (e.g. racing thoughts and flashbacks) and their ability to have restful sleep, and produce physiological reactions like trembling, a racing heart, body pains, and muscle stiffness and numbness. Other initial effects fall into five categories, as defined by Allison and Wrightsman (1993): shock, denial, and disbelief; emotional and personality disruptions (such as presenting with confusion or disorientation, or loss of affect); self-blame or guilt; regressing into a state of helplessness and dependency; and distortion of prior beliefs.

Also called "the recoil stage," the reorganization stage describes the period whereby a survivor begins to rebuild their sense of security and control, and restore order to their life. Within this period, "the essential adaptive task for the rape victim is to attribute meaning to the experience in such a manner that their lives are reorganized in a positive direction" (Peterson et al., 1991). "This task," Allison and Wrightsman (1993) state, "can take anywhere from a few months to years for completion, if, indeed, completion and closure ever do occur." The reorganization stage is additionally concerned with prolonged symptoms or permanent personality and lifestyle changes. Common reactions include persisting emotional and behavioral disruptions, development of phobias, and drastic lifestyle decisions like relocating, switching jobs or schools, or altering one's appearance.

Although most survivors report relief from the more debilitating, shock-associated symptoms after three months (Kilpatrick, Veronen, & Best, 1985), the severity and longevity of each stage differ from person to person. It's not unusual for survivors to exhibit symptoms from both stages simultaneously. The onset of responses can also be delayed or emerge gradually. For example, while survivors might experience little sexual dysfunction at first, this symptom may present months or even years later. Many survivors develop social anxiety and begin to isolate. If left untreated, these symptoms may, over time, result in agoraphobia or other similar conditions.

Recovery can be slow, unpredictable, and depend on a multitude of variables, such as the age of the victim, the nature of the assault, the victim's relationship to the offender, the presence of community supports, the cultural background of the victim, and so on. All told, the degree to which a person suffers RTS is subjective. Some survivors are deeply impacted and their struggles last for years. Others exhibit few symptoms and retain functionality or recover with notable ease. However, studies reveal that nearly all rape survivors will exhibit RTS symptoms during the acute crisis stage, with the vast majority going on to experience rape-related intrusive thoughts, feelings, and nightmares, as well as avoidant behaviors after three years (Kilpatrick et al., 1985). Some researchers surmise that rape survivors may form the largest group of persons suffering with PTSD (Basile, 2005), and according to Terry and Cling (2004), "rape victims suffering from PTSD tend to have more severe symptoms than individuals whose

PTSD is due to other stressors."

The latter assertion is a sensible one. Rape is unlike most forms of traumatization because "no other crime offers a similarly personal and intimate violation to the self" (Allison & Wrightsman, 1993). Furthermore, rape victims tend to be regarded with less sympathy than victims of other crimes or trauma types. Harmful social perceptions fuel the stigmatization of rape survivors, despite persistent efforts of advocates, clinicians, and social scientists. These include damaging and biased assumptions—that victims play a role in their rape, or lead offenders on and are therefore either responsible for their rape or deserve it; victims always retain the power to stop offenders; the assault cannot be considered rape if the offender was known to the victim or previously intimate with them; and that most accusations of rape are false (Basile, 2005).

Because society is quick to assume rape is the victim's fault, "feelings of self-blame are often induced or amplified," as well as feelings of "humiliation, embarrassment, anger, guilt, [and] shame" (Peterson et al., 1991). Accessing resources and legal aid poses additional hurdles, if sought out at all. In order to seek support, treatment, and legal representation, the survivor risks exposing themselves to painful scrutiny. Between the devastating consequences of being raped and societal views on rape and rape victims, it's understandable why survivors would suffer higher rates of PTSD than those whose trauma types aren't as heavily stigmatized. Not only do survivors suffer the effects of being raped, they're also forced to navigate re-traumatizing ignorance and stereotyping in their communities and the greater public.

*

After some online study of RTS, I brought it up with my counselor Heather. She concluded the nature of my symptoms—

their severity, abnormality, as well as the correlation of their onset with Jack's behavior toward me—were consistent with the diagnosis. This opinion was shared by Sonya, the counselor I saw at the women's center, and another clinician I worked with the following year.

Only after hearing Heather's input did I feel confident enough to include this information in the victim impact statement I shared with Linda, Eleanor, and Dean Witterman. Nonetheless, a review of this document reveals some hesitancy. Instead of saying, "I believe Dr. Blair raped me," I wrote, "I feel raped." Both statements are true, but my diction shows an attempt to distance myself from totally accepting my trauma as rape or accusing Jack of being a rapist.

Why would I do this? In retrospect, I believe I'd succumbed to cognitive dissonance. I was well aware of what I was going through. I had a diagnosis. Yet, I grappled with my preexisting notions of what constitutes rape—therein lying the catalyst for my mental tension. I considered myself a victim of *something*, but was it accurate to call it *rape*? On the other hand, how could I be manifesting symptoms of a syndrome related to rape trauma if what occurred to me couldn't be described as *rape*? What the hell *is* rape anyway?

From what I've since gathered, the interpretation of meaning normally attached to this word is continuously debated, leaving its definition vague or simplistic. Many point out that if we rely on legal classifications of rape, we'd embrace malleable, socially constructed ideas about an act that are historically oppressive. As Estelle B. Freedman (2013) says, "the history of rape consists in large part in tracking the changing narratives that define which women may charge which men with the crime." What we now accept as instances of rape are quite new understandings. Until the recent past, for example, it was legally permissible for a man to rape his wives, domestic servants, slaves, and even his children, as these persons were considered his property.

Marital rape specifically wasn't recognized as a crime until laws began to shift in the late 1970s, with the last American state outlawing marital rape in 1993. A number of states still make exemptions, such as if a wife is drugged and raped by her husband, it is not considered rape. Several states require rape between spouses to have been physically violent, and don't take into account other forms of coercive control. Even with the passage of acquaintance rape laws, research shows that jurors are less likely to be convinced that a rape occurred if the perpetrator was known to the victim (Fields & Kirchoff, 2011). This is an incredibly problematic statistic, since the vast majority of victims are acquainted with their assailants prior to the assault. Too, despite rape shield statutes, a victim's sexual history or opinions regarding their sexual character continue to be allowed as admissible evidence in rape trials. So, while efforts at reform have been made, our legal culture continues to reflect conflicting, harmful conclusions on what constitutes rape, who can be raped and by what means, and is still influenced by medieval codes of law.

It's no wonder rape continues to be an elusive concept with a variety of differing, sometimes contradictory or exclusionary meanings. For instance, some activists disapprove of the American federal government's definition of rape. Before 2012, rape was previously restricted to an event in which a male forcibly penetrates a woman's vaginal canal with his penis. The definition has been revised and expanded, so it now reads, "the penetration, no matter how slight, of the vagina or anus with any body part or object, or oral penetration by a sex organ of another person, without the consent of the victim" (United States Department of Justice, 2012). This is a considerably more appropriate characterization, as it now recognizes such cases of male-on-male rape, rape by foreign object, etc. However, many feel this delegitimizes assertions of rape made by individuals who were coerced into penetrating another person or into providing or receiving oral sex.

To obscure the matter further, rape statutes differ from state to state, so what may constitute as rape in one state may not in another. The terms *sexual assault*, *sexual battery*, *sexual imposition*, and *criminal sexual conduct* are applied rather than *rape*, while many argue that these qualifiers are not interchangeable and carry separate, though related definitions. States like California, Indiana, and Tennessee have separate criminal statutes for both rape and sexual battery. Other states apply degrees of severity to rape, such as New York and South Dakota, which account for the nonconsensual nature of the act for reasons such as the victim's age, the perpetrator's use of force, and so on.

In my home state of Kansas, criminal rape statutes are as follows:

> (a) Rape is:
>
> (1) Knowingly engaging in sexual intercourse with a victim who does not consent to the sexual intercourse under any of the following circumstances:
>
> (A) When the victim is overcome by force or fear; or
>
> (B) when the victim is unconscious or physically powerless;
>
> (2) Knowingly engaging in sexual intercourse with a victim when the victim is incapable of giving consent because of mental deficiency or disease, or when the victim is incapable of giving consent because of the effect of any alcoholic liquor, narcotic, drug or other substance, which condition was known by the offender or was reasonably apparent to the offender;
>
> (3) sexual intercourse with a child who is under 14 years of age;

(4) sexual intercourse with a victim when the victim's consent was obtained through a knowing misrepresentation made by the offender that the sexual intercourse was a medically or therapeutically necessary procedure; or

(5) sexual intercourse with a victim when the victim's consent was obtained through a knowing misrepresentation made by the offender that the sexual intercourse was a legally required procedure within the scope of the offender's authority (Kan. Stat. Ann. § 21-5503 (West {2012}).

While the statute seems fairly cohesive, it was largely because of these descriptions that I was unable to pursue legal action against Jack.

"He raped you," Sasha, the legal assistant, had said. "Unfortunately, it just doesn't fall under what the legal definition of rape is right now."

So, if I were to (gladly) scrap legal classifications, where would that leave me in terms of establishing an inclusive but more precise definition?

*

Popular discussions of what rape means often contain terminology that causes further deliberation. This includes language like *capacity*, *active agreement*, *consent*, and *coercion*. To reach a well-rounded understanding of rape requires explanation of these constructs and how these contribute to its definition.

To start, *capacity* refers to an individual's ability to comprehend both the manner and repercussions of their decisions. Examples of persons who lawfully cannot consent to sexual acts are children, the developmentally disabled, and those under the influence of mind- and mood-altering substances.

It's usually considered rape when such persons of limited or reduced capacity are subject to sexual acts (though, as noted above, this is unfortunately not always the case). When all parties have enthusiastically and freely agreed to engage in a sexual interaction, they are exercising *active agreement.* Likewise, *consent* is understood as an individual's approval to willingly participate in a sex act.

Consent can be communicated through nonverbal cues and actions, though frequently emphasis is placed on consent as a verbal contract. One reason for this is that sexual preferences vary, so what one partner may enjoy, another may dislike. While there are universal physiological signs of sexual arousal, acute stress response—also called "fight or flight"—manifests in many of the same ways: increased heart rate, flushed skin, trembling, shallow breathing, etc. Therefore, an individual who wants to halt a sex act and withdraw their consent can actually come off as aroused when they are, in fact, stressed. As a result, it's suggested that if someone isn't clearly expressing eager involvement, the sexual interaction should be interrupted until their consent is verbally reaffirmed. The exchange could otherwise slip into a grey area where the hesitant party can emerge feeling coerced. To reduce the risk of harm, pro-consent activists encourage parties to reach a dependable level of mutual trust and use open communication prior to sex, in addition to practicing empathy and common sense during sex acts.

With this being said, verbal or behaviorally implied consent isn't enough to qualify a sex act as genuinely consensual or void of coercive measures. Stating "yes" or actively partaking in sex can and does occur under duress. Individuals will often "freely and enthusiastically" concede when they feel that to do otherwise may result in violence or other hardships. I've heard many people describe feeling too scared to ask their partner to stop, or say they "just laid there and took it" because they didn't want to risk upsetting their partner.

Such instances cannot be ruled consensual, as these persons felt pressured or submitted out of fear. So, while attaining a person's verbal consent is a helpful rule, it's a superficial way to determine what sexual interactions are or are not consensual.

In my opinion, although a lack of consent can establish rape in many instances, more significance should be placed on coercion as a means to determine what sex acts are rape. Simply put, to *coerce* is to compel by threat (Burgess-Jackson, 1999), and extends to use of overt and subtle threats toward a victim's physical, psychological, emotional, and financial well-being. For our purposes, *coercion* also refers to a set of interpersonal tactics by which an individual employs aversive behavior to access sex. Such threats and coercive tactics are meant to impose a sexual exchange and obtain a victim's compliance via undermining, reducing, or eliminating their autonomy.

According to Snyder and Dishion (2016), coercive behaviors "may be direct and include physical threats and aggression, verbal threats and disparagement, opposition and noncompliance, and emotional manipulation and control." Most of these examples are overtly harmful; however, many manifestations of coercion are not blatantly obvious to the victim or close observers. For example, the use of physical aggression is always coercive, but not all forms of coercion are violent or hostile. Such distinctions need to be made in order to understand the extent to which someone can be raped.

In her book *Rape: Sex, Violence, History*, scholar Joanna Bourke (2007) writes how "the harm of rape can be triggered without the employment of brute force. Violence is often the *means* of violation, but the harm of rape may exist independently of violent means." Moreover, it's in the best interest of the rapist to use nonviolent forms of coercion to gain a victim's submission. As Burgess-Jackson (1999) points out, they "[have] reason to prefer coercion to force; it produces the same benefits with fewer cost." Too, as Bourke (2007) says, "Subtle intimidation...is often more effective in producing the docile body of the victim," adding that coercion may include generating a sexual encounter through the use of manipulation, emotional blackmail, and deceit.

Snyder and Dishion (2016) expand on this, stating, "Coercion can also take more indirect and subtle forms such as love withdrawal, lying and deception, third-party character denigration, and rejection or exclusion in social groups in which relationships are key to adaptive functioning. In some cases...individuals may even 'coerce' their romantic partner into acquiescence through manipulative affection." To the latter point, Snyder and Dishion (2016) note how "coercive behaviors may be shaped and maintained by positive reinforcement," as it can lead to "increased cooperation and compliance" on the part of the victim. Flattery, excessive compliments, and other means of seductive trickery can be categorized as coercive behaviors when they're performed with the intent to persuade an otherwise unwilling partner into agreeing to sex acts.

Because subtle coercion can appear benign, the perpetrator's goal of hijacking their victim's autonomy is incredibly difficult to infer. Thus, the coercive nature of the sexual interaction is usually only recognized in its aftermath, as the victim comes to realize their violation in relation to subsequent actions displayed by the rapist. These may include continued deceit, psychological abuse (such as gaslighting and intimidation), stonewalling communication, and abandonment (e.g., "ghosting").

*

This topic is as complicated as its countless, possible manifestations. Like most social realities, the concept of rape is a construct and subject to interpretation. To summarize it wholly and effectively would be a terrific challenge. As Freedman

(2013) puts forward, "*Rape* remains a word in flux," and "contestations over the meaning of sexual violence will continue as long as social inequalities...characterize American life."

I previously quoted how abuse is determined based on its effects on the abused, and I believe this rule absolutely applies here. An individual who identifies with a traumatic sense of violation after a sex act, and thinks of themselves as a rape victim is, in my opinion, just that. In other words, if someone *feels* raped, they probably *were* raped—regardless of legalized technicalities or societal criteria. Instances of rape are often too diverse to be standardized, and attempts to do so have only continued to fuel scholarly quarreling about what it means and who can claim it as an experience.

All considered, I support Bourke's (2007) definition, which "merely states that a person can claim that a particular 'sexual' act is rape if it is non-consensual, unwanted or coerced, *however they defined those terms.*" Characterizing rape in this way places the burden of meaning on the individual survivor and their interpretation of events. I think this is the most appropriate way to understand rape because, frankly, no one has the right to define another person's experiences or their aftermath.

I recognize my assertions are unconventional. In telling my story, others have questioned me: "But, can you *really* call it rape? Weren't you in a relationship? Didn't you consent?"

I understand their confusion, their reluctance. I have felt and lived it too. After all, I'd loved Jack entirely. I saw him as a partner, a soulmate. Though he'd wooed me through fanciful lies and smothered me with sweet nothings and esteem-boosting compliments, he'd never gripped my shoulders and held me down.

But, I also know this to be true: I never consented to a sexual relationship with a stranger, a possible psychopath. I never consented to psychological abuse—to the exploitation of my body and soul. Yet, this was my reality. Quite simply, if

I hadn't been groomed, deceived, and coerced, I would have never acquiesced to his sexual advances, nor would I now have a diagnosis of PTSD.

4. Psychopathy

After making my reports, I'd wondered if a mental health disorder could explain Jack's actions and some of the unsettling oddities in his personality. These suspicions solidified when Magda said Jack had admitted as much to her, stating, "I think I might be a sociopath." I later asked my counselors what they thought, and they agreed this could be true.

Before this section unfolds, I need to give disclaimers. Even after months of research, my conclusions about Jack's mental health are hypothetical. Most of the data available to me is limited to my own selective observations, combined with the details I've been afforded by Magda, Phoebe, and others. I've come to believe Jack is a successful psychopath, but I can't know for sure if this is accurate. While I *am* a licensed substance use disorder counselor and author with a background in sociology, I'm *not* a clinical psychologist.

Also note that I take the subject of mental illness very seriously. The stigmatization of the mentally ill is a persistent societal problem; its harms disproportionately affect women, people of color, immigrants, homosexuals, gender non-conforming persons, and the poor. Psychopathy is especially misunderstood and widely misused. Like other psychiatric conditions, it's often applied as a means to dehumanize an individual—to cast them as "evil," and set them apart from the rest of "good" society. I'm uninterested in perpetuating these narrow-minded and dangerous attitudes. What's good is subjective, and anyone is capable of evil under the right conditions. Some people simply perform what's viewed to be evil more than others, but this doesn't make them any less human.

I included this section because I would be remiss if this book didn't include some psychological examination of Jack. It speaks to one of the many paths I've trekked during my post-abuse, truth-interpreting journey. But unlike the other sections, what's proposed here regarding Jack is rather speculative.

*

The fifth edition of the *Diagnostic and Statistical Manual of Mental Disorders* (*DSM-5*) begins its definition of antisocial personality disorder as "a pervasive pattern of disregard for, and the violation of, the rights of others that begins in childhood or early adolescence and continues into adulthood" (APA, 2013). Diagnostic criteria are indicated by criminality, deceitfulness, impulsivity, irritability and aggressiveness, reckless disregard for the safety of self or others, consistent irresponsibility, and lack of remorse (APA, 2013). For someone to be considered for this diagnosis, they must be at least eighteen years old and have a history of conduct disorder in adolescence—which involves "a repetitive and persistent pattern of behavior in which the basic rights of others or major age-appropriate societal norms or rules are violated" (APA, 2013).

Although these features seem pretty straight forward, they've been subject to criticism. Practitioners and other specialists in the field of abnormal psychology often dispute the standard qualifiers of antisocial personality disorder (APD), such as criminality, the perceived absence of a conscience, and the prerequisite of antisocial symptoms before the onset of adulthood. Most experts seem to agree this disorder falls on a kind of web-like spectrum. This would account for overlapping symptoms, as well as variations in attitudes and behavioral patterns, and the degree to which these are displayed.

While the *DSM-5* refers to APD as synonymous with psychopathy (and sociopathy, for that matter), there is enough divergence in underlying mechanisms—and facets within those—to justify differentiation between what's understood to be APD and what's understood to be psychopathy. Generally, making a diagnosis of APD is relatively simple because it's mostly based on an individual's behavior. Psychopathy is more elusive, as it is defined by interpersonal and emotional conduct, as well as behavior (Kosson, 2013).

Determination of APD emphasizes features like criminality and irresponsibility. But, this neglects interpersonal and affective facets most usually exhibited by those understood to be psychopathic, who also may have symptoms like criminality and irresponsibility, though not always. Along these lines, Blair, Mitchell and Blair (2005) propose a separation of "reactive aggression" (emotional or impulsive) and "instrumental aggression" (purposeful and goal-orientated). Persons with APD frequently express reactive aggressive behaviors, while psychopaths are more instrumentally aggressive. Still, as Schouten and Silver (2012) point out, the two aren't mutually exclusive; it's the psychopath's heavier reliance on instrumental aggression that sets them apart.

Hervé (2007) best summarizes the differences, stating that "although most individuals with psychopathy qualify for a diagnosis of APD (i.e., both display antisocial conduct), most individuals with APD are not diagnosed as psychopathic (i.e., they do not display the interpersonal and affective features of psychopathy)." Hence, many have argued in favor of establishing psychopathy as its own disorder—separate from, though related to, APD.

This is important to note since Jack may not—at first glance—seem to demonstrate enough of the stereotypical signs of APD to justify a diagnosis. However, he would only need to fulfill three of the seven diagnostic criteria, which the *DSM-5* expands on through a discussion of associated features. Here are those descriptions I witnessed in Jack:

> *"Persons with this disorder disregard the wishes, rights, or feelings of others. They are frequently deceitful and manipulative in order to gain personal profit or pleasure (e.g., to obtain money, sex, or power). They may repeatedly lie, use an alias, con others, or malinger. They may engage in sexual behavior...that has a high risk for harmful consequences.*
>
> *"Individuals with antisocial personality disorder show little remorse for the consequences of their acts. They may be indifferent to, or provide a superficial rationalization for, having hurt, mistreated, or stolen from someone (e.g., 'life's unfair'...). These individuals blame victims for being foolish, helpless, or deserving their fate...; they may minimize the harmful consequences of their actions; or they may simply indicate complete indifference. They generally fail to compensate or make amends for their behavior. They may believe that everyone is [out to get them].*
>
> *"[They] frequently lack empathy and tend to be callous, cynical, and contemptuous of the feelings, rights, and sufferings of others. They may display a glib, superficial charm, and can be quite voluble and verbally facile...These individuals may also be irresponsible and exploitative in their sexual relationships. They may have a history of many sexual partners and may never have sustained a monogamous relationship...[They] may also experience dysphoria, including complaints of tension, inability to tolerate boredom, and depressed mood" (APA, 2013).*

One major factor for a diagnosis of APD is the preexistence of conduct disorder in childhood or adolescence. To this, Jack disclosed tales both privately and during in-class lectures where he self-identified as a troublemaker in his youth. Examples of this involved rowdiness in school, disdain for authority, and some unlawful behavior, like stealing and selling drugs. Ironically, I cannot be sure these stories were authentic, given Jack's rampant dishonesty. It's wholly possible that Jack, as an adult, engaged in unlawfulness I'm unaware of, as revealing this to me could have compromised his charming performance of a good yet tortured soul. Then again, as other researchers have argued, individuals don't necessarily have to exhibit criminality in order to be diagnosed with psychopathy.

So, which is it? Is Jack antisocial or psychopathic?

I believe he potentially meets the criteria for APD because he embodies enough of the diagnostic features to warrant a diagnosis. The descriptions I've pulled from the *DSM-5* mostly reflect Jack's interpersonal and emotional expressions, in addition to some behavioral symptoms. This could classify Jack as a psychopath, given how experts pose categorical determinations between APD and psychopathy.

It's not a simple matter of choosing which symptoms Jack displayed and building a case from there. After all, everyone is known to lie from time to time, or to exaggerate their sickness pains for sympathy. At some point, most people find themselves feeling entitled and will make declarations about how unjust life seems. Anyone can succumb to stress or forgetfulness and withdraw from responsibilities or seem unreliable. When faced with consequences or conflict in our relationships, all of us have become defensive and made attempts to avoid blame.

But, the average person doesn't display these attitudes or traits to the degree that it appears symptomatic of a pathological condition. For example, I was first diagnosed with major depression around the age of eleven. Having depression doesn't mean I sometimes feel sad or hopeless. To receive this diagnosis, I had to have expressed a prolonged, unyielding sense of sadness or hopelessness that defied rationale—along with a slew of other indicators. It's with the same consideration that I've reviewed Jack's profile. His extensive perpetuation of the features associated with psychopathy is why I believe he may qualify for the diagnosis.

*

In his book *The Psychopath of Everyday Life*, psychiatrist Martin Kantor (2006) reasons for the existence of a mild form of psychopathy, which "closely resembles a personality disorder," while severe psychopathy involves psychosis and the propensity for violence. Others have come to the same conclusion, such as Robert D. Hare, foremost researcher of contemporary psychopathy studies, who refers to mild psychopaths as "subcriminal," "successful," or "white-collar psychopaths." "These individuals are every bit as egocentric, callous, and manipulative as the average criminal psychopath," Hare (1999) writes, "however, their intelligence, family background, social skills, and circumstances permit them to construct a façade of normalcy and to get what they want with relative impunity."

Kantor (2006) suggests that though mild psychopathy has a relationship to APD, there are notable differences. For one, he points out how individuals with APD are usually very impulsive. On the contrary, mild psychopaths are "often quietly and resolutely calculating, and desire and retain the ability to think about the future and plan ahead" (Kantor, 2006). Similarly, while the behavior of those with APD can cause them to become socially ostracized, mild psychopaths can maintain close relationships, albeit as a means to fulfill their own needs. Kantor argues that mild psychopaths have the ability to love or feel guilt, but these feelings are generally applied as defense strategies. If confronted, "they might apologize to those they have wronged, even though their apologies have no practical effect on their subsequent behavior" (Kantor, 2006). In other words, they can sympathize enough to offer apology, but not to the extent that they will modify their behaviors.

As clinical psychologist Scott Lilienfeld (2016) puts it, psychopaths tend to be reliably unreliable, meaning they are sometimes trustworthy (or loving, comforting, etc.) and sometimes not. Because they may be remorseful and make promises to change, this allows them to avoid culpability and prolong their relationships through what psychologists call the variable-ratio reinforcement schedule, or unpredictably reinforcing positive (or negative) responses in others. "[Psychopaths] tend to keep people hooked—in their friendships, in their romantic relationships, in the workplace—on the variable reinforcement schedule," Lilienfeld (2016) states, adding how "those are the very schedules that are the most difficult to extinguish; they are the ones that keep people busy in casinos. And psychopathic people tend to do that, because they get our hopes up, crush our hopes, and get our hopes up again, and so on."

Jack's malingering and insincere claims of suicidality have also historically been documented as manipulative tactics frequently used by psychopaths. In his famous work *The Mask of Sanity*, psychiatrist Hervey M. Cleckley (1988) outlines the clinical profile of a psychopath, including "false threats of suicide rarely carried out" as a common behavioral characteristic. Unlike malingering, faking suicidality hasn't continued to be associated with APD in the *DSM-5*, but despite this, researchers continue to include this manipulative ploy, in addition to malingering, as a behavioral feature of psychopaths (Schouten & Silver, 2012).

Overall, the mild psychopath is host to maladaptive traits—expressions of which are subdued in comparison to their typical antisocial counterparts or extreme psychopaths (such as serial killers, who are deemed "unsuccessful" or "true" psychopaths). The mild psychopath can and will draw attention to themselves, but tend to be less outwardly offensive or dangerous. Schouten and Silver (2012) refer to this group as "almost" psychopaths and explain how they, "like true psychopaths, may engage in socially unacceptable and sometimes illegal conduct, and...may be self-centered, egotistical, and indifferent to the needs and emotions of others." The only real difference lies in the degree of intensity or frequency of their inappropriate behavior and emotional dysfunction (Schouten & Silver, 2012). While parasitic and exploitative in their relationships with others, they are less likely to commit major crimes, like murder.

Kantor (2006) and Schouten and Silver (2012) also propose that the antisocial conduct of the mild or almost psychopath may be selectively expressed based on their social environment. This can account for how they're able to positively uphold the behavioral expectations of some social statuses, but deviate radically in others (i.e., a corrupted, violent law enforcement officer who behaves as a genuinely loving husband and father at home). Because they can function normally in most instances or mimic normality when necessary, these psychopaths can avoid detection.

Expanding on this, Lilienfeld (2016) presents the concept of persona—a mask behind which people hide their true selves—and how the elusiveness of the successful psychopath has inspired many folk prototypes: the two-faced person, a wolf in sheep's clothing, and the social chameleon. The message of these folk characters is that there are people out there who're not as they seem, and as a result, we can be fooled or tricked (Lilienfeld, 2016). Such individuals conceal their true selves, making their intentions exceptionally difficult to discern. Even as they cause harm to the people around them, the psychopath's ability to deceive and manipulate others allows their deeper selves to go unrecognized.

*

About a year after reporting Jack, I had a brief conversation with Zach Cantor. We'd run into each other on a stretch of sidewalk outside of the campus library, cigarettes dangling from our fingers. I can't recall how the subject came up, except that Zach had expressed some frustrations with the job.

"I wonder if it wasn't working here that made him act the way he did," he proposed. "This place is just...oppressive."

"What, like strain theory?" I asked.

Zach nodded. "I've taught in several universities, but I've

never been somewhere like this. And Jack worked here for, what? Fifteen fucking years? That changes a person."

Brow wrinkled, I shook my head. "I don't know. I mean, that might explain some of it, but from the research I've done, I think he was probably a psychopath. He seems to fit the criteria."

"Well, you would know better than me, unfortunately." He flashed me a look of sympathy before dropping his cigarette and stomping out the cherry. "I will say this, though: I can't wait to be out of here. I've been looking for other positions ever since all of that went down."

I can appreciate where Zach was coming from. No one wants to accept that they were duped. Once we've gotten close to someone, even after coming to view them as a villain and severing ties, it's hard not to believe there might be a kernel of goodness somewhere inside of them, and that external forces were responsible for inspiring their nefarious behaviors.

The general premise of strain theory addresses how individuals within certain social structures may be pressured into deviant behavior. (Someone who lives in poverty and takes up drug-dealing as a way to combat their socioeconomic circumstances is a commonly cited example.) In Jack's case, the stress of teaching and achieving tenure (and all this requires), combined with a repressive work environment might account for how he developed a taste for sexual exploitation. Perhaps his abuses were a way to garnish positive stimulation, blow off steam, and maybe reap some personal benefits in a high-pressure, sometimes unpleasant institutional career.

After some thought, I disagree. I don't believe Jack started out as a pro-social do-good professor who was gradually shaped into a scumbag by academia. For one, he'd been sexually preying on students and colleagues for several years. And what about all of the other genuinely good people employed at that university who had been there longer, taught the same number of classes, and had just as many—if not more—responsibilities as Jack did? Someone like my mentor Charles, who lectured full-time, served as a sponsor for student projects and organizations, showed up for recreational events, and outside of campus, was the primary financial provider for his wife and children, and still had to schedule time to work on his own creative writing.

What the hell was Jack's excuse? Just imagine: Jack's locked the office door. On the other side of his desk, he's squished himself against the wall. His clothing loosens and parts to expose his erection. He starts jacking off, only to begin sobbing, "I'm sorry! I'm under so much stress—academia's making me do this!"

Never happened. No, he had total control over his actions. He wasn't a desperate man.

It could also be said that power corrupts. An immense body of literature clearly demonstrates how some individuals in positions of power will use their influence and authority in self-serving ways to the detriment of others. Professors aren't politicians, celebrities, or *mafiosi*, but they will have charge over dozens of students at any given moment. Maybe over time, Jack grew relaxed in his roles and took advantage of his status to manipulate others for sex, whereas at the beginning of his career, he wouldn't have done so. Yet again, I don't believe this is the case.

The Stanford Prison Experiment is arguably most responsible for projecting the "power corrupts" message into modern popular consciousness. Since its execution in 1971, the experiment has been subject to mass criticism and accusations of fraud, given psychologist Philip Zimbardo's deeply flawed methodology, which included his reliance on anecdotal evidence and the lack of a control group, among numerous other issues. In recent years, Zimbardo himself has since backtracked, claiming the experiment was meant to be viewed as a "demonstration," rather than a scientifically valid study (Resnick, 2018).

Twenty-four male volunteer applicants were accepted into the experiment. Half were randomly assigned to be "prisoners," and the rest were assigned to be "guards," with six participants held as substitutes to step in as needed (Haslam & Reicher, 2017). A mock prison, including an observation block and a few small cells, was constructed in the basement of Stanford University's Jordan Hall. Zimbardo remained on site during the study to act as "superintendent."

Into the second day, the mock prison became a hellish place, as guards were later said to have internalized their authoritative roles and began to subject the prisoners to abuses. Prisoners were taunted, verbally accosted, and humiliated. They were made to do repetitive, alienating tasks; ordered to do push-ups with a guard's boot pressed into their backs; or commanded to clean their toilets with bare hands. After a few days, five participants had suffered enough distress, they requested to be released early. Another went on a hunger strike. Although the study was meant to last two weeks, it was abandoned after only six days.

Zimbardo believed "the extreme behavior witnessed in the study could not be explained simply as manifestations of participants' deviant personalities" (Haslam & Reicher, 2017). Instead, he testified to "situational hypothesis," suggesting the behavior of the guards was a result of the implied pathology of their social context. "The mere act of assigning labels to people, such as 'prisoners' and 'guards' and putting them in situations where these labels acquire validity and meaning, is sufficient to elicit pathological behavior," Zimbardo (1971) concluded.

Eh, or maybe not. While there's a lot of solid scholarship on role theory, drawing this conclusion from the outcomes of the Stanford Prison Experiment is ill-formed at best. For instance, Zimbardo was found to have interfered with the volunteer guards, influencing their behavior through directives and revealing his research intentions. By acting as superintendent, it's very likely his presence affected the actions of the participants. (This is known as Hawthorne's effect: the understanding that people will modify their behavior when they know they're being observed.) And finally, subsequent, variant research models have failed to replicate Zimbardo's original findings (Haslam & Reicher, 2017). Of all criticisms of the "demonstration," I feel this the most telling.

So, what does this have to do with psychopathy?

Before the student volunteers were recruited for the study, they underwent a screening process. One aspect of this was a psychological assessment, which determined the 25 participants had normal levels of authoritarianism (Haslam & Reicher, 2017). Thus, Zimbardo insisted the personality dispositions of his volunteers didn't factor into their actions during the simulation.

Following this, Carnahan and McFarland (2007) designed an experiment to investigate if students who independently volunteer for a study of prison life possess characteristics associated with abusive behavior. They solicited participants by placing adverts in newspapers that were "virtually identical to the ad used in the Stanford Prison Experiment" (Carnahan & McFarland, 2007). The primary advert read: "Male college students needed for a psychological study of prison life," while the second advert, used to assemble a control group, omitted the phrase "of prison life" (Carnahan & McFarland, 2007). Respondents accepted into the study then underwent a battery of psychological assessments. In their summary, Carnahan and McFarland (2007) report that volunteers who responded for the prison study "scored significantly higher on measures of the abuse-related dispositions of aggressiveness, Machiavellianism, narcissism, and social dominance and lower on empathy and altruism, two qualities inversely related to aggressive abuse." The overall presumption is that because prison settings are associated with aggression and authoritarianism, individuals who personally value such traits were attracted to the study.

Another report aimed at investigating the potential for power to corrupt had similar conclusions. By analyzing the results of both a field survey and lab experiment, DeCelles et al. (2012) demonstrate how "the psychological experience of power enhances moral awareness among those with a strong moral identity, yet decreases the moral awareness among those with a weak moral identity." When assigned scenarios meant to promote a sense of power, DeCelles et al. (2012) found the individual's preexisting morals could predict their self-interested behavior, with the latter being defined as "actions that benefit the self and come at the cost to the common good." The authors conclude that "power both corrupts people and enables people to benefit the common good by corrupting those with a low moral identity and enabling those with a high moral identity" (DeCelles et al., 2012). So, yes, power corrupts. But, it tends to corrupt those who are already prone to corruption.

Being a professor, working in an institutional setting, and having power over his students didn't mold Jack into a psychopath. It's more likely he already was one. Academia simply provided him with a cover and an easily accessible pool of victims—a "hunting ground," as previously mentioned.

Competitive business positions, community leadership roles, and helping professions are common fields of employment for successful or mild psychopaths. Ultimately, I think their chosen profession depends on what type of exploitation the psychopath is most interested in, as well as their personality and the resources available to them. An affluent "corporate" psychopath who lusts for upward mobility and accruing wealth may commit white-collar crimes, such as embezzlement or insider trading—crimes that can affect the livelihoods of thousands of people. Conversely, a psychopathic sexual offender may work as a civil servant, teach Sunday school at their local church, and commit sexualized violence against individuals under their care. As psychologist Kevin Dutton said in an interview, "Any situation where you've a got a power structure, a hierarchy, the ability to manipulate or wield control over people, you get psychopaths doing very well" (Crawford, 2012).

Much of this is possible because our society values traits associated with psychopathy: charisma, confidence, assertiveness, industrious thinking, egotism, and the ability to remain calm under pressure. For everyday life, these characteristics are helpful; in positions of leadership and authority, they are often necessary and certainly rewarded—which makes sense. We're more likely to back a manager or political candidate who is charming and unfazed by stress. We're more easily swayed by someone who seems to know what they're talking about and believes in what they say. And we're expected to revere those who have accessed positions that demand trust from the people they serve.

It's unfortunate because in the right hands and applied for the right reasons, leadership status can support our collective common good. In the wrong hands, the consequences are vast and detrimental.

*

Sometime in January of 2017, I met with Grace Driscoll to discuss the goals of an independent study. During our conversation, I mentioned how Jack had told Magda he thought he was a sociopath.

Nodding, Grace said firmly, "*Believe him*. People will tell you who they really are, if you listen to them. If Jack said he's a sociopath, it's probably true."

Later, as I waded through the literature, Grace's advice

was a continuous echo. Nonetheless, I was hesitant to think of Jack as a psychopath. Perhaps I was entertaining popular myths associated with this term, such as psychoanalyst David Kosson (2013) humorously attempts to dispel when he says, "Psychopathy is widely misused, right? So, if you're not careful, you might get the impression that psychopathy is mainly a disorder of serial killers who like to play with dolls."

On the contrary, as Hare (1999) warns, "Psychopaths are often witty and articulate. They can be amusing and entertaining conversationalists, ready with a quick and clever comeback, and can tell unlikely but convincing stories that cast themselves in a good light. They can be very effective in presenting themselves well and are often very likeable and charming."

The unfortunate truth is that psychopaths are not strictly nocturnal phantoms whose obvious crimes are uncovered only in their aftermath at daybreak. In reality, they can be elusive, complicated individuals. They can be charismatic, but restrained, coming off as kind, gentle, or sensitive. They can have families, form loyalties, engage in community service, and be prized employees. They can inspire others to be socially conscious or motivate them to commit acts of beauty. They laugh; they cry—they are human.

So it was with Jack. He was well-liked and respected. He attracted the admiration of his students, colleagues, and, really, the majority of people who came into contact with him. He was soft-spoken, disarming. He was handsome and quietly eccentric. He made people feel valued and safe. He seemed an empath.

Beneath it all, he proved a liar. A con artist. A malingerer. An abusive intimate partner. A rapist. In total, a successful psychopath. A viper in a sweater vest.

I've decided to follow Grace's advice and to believe Jack, just this once. He said he thought he was a sociopath, and from what I've gathered, the research supports this.

5. Obedience to Authority

What if Jack had *not* been an abuser, rapist, or potential psychopath, and we'd found ourselves sharing romantic interest—what then? Would our relationship have been well-adjusted and mutually beneficial? Might we have fostered equality despite our designated statuses of student and professor?

In hindsight, no. I believe this to be overwhelmingly improbable.

Jack had maintained that he viewed me as a peer, yet I didn't always feel comfortable treating him as such. I was exceptionally hesitant to raise objection when he acted in ways that were hurtful or seemed unreasonable. On the occasions I managed to do so, I planned these difficult conversations carefully, first processing my frustrations with friends, and later, rehearsing questions and explanations of my feelings to ensure I sounded mature, sensible, and clear. I had to practice courage to follow through because, ultimately, I was afraid of how he'd react. Even as my intimate partner, he still intimidated me.

I think this would have been the case even if Jack had been a good man and truly thought of me as his peer. Normal romantic give-and-take is based on mutual consent by people of equal status, wherein the boundaries are fully understood and accepted by both partners. But, this give-and-take is not possible in student-faculty relationships because the power disparity is too great. If someone has designated power over their partner, inconsistencies in equal treatment are inevitable. The imbalance can cause the low-power partner to unintentionally assume a subsidiary role.

This can occur even after the discrepancy is leveled, as partners can—unconsciously or otherwise—assume attitudes and behaviors previously associated with their high- and low-power positions. As Irons and Schneider (1999) put it, "Even in the best-case scenario, when both parties believe that they are making a free choice to get sexually involved, unconscious forces are influencing that choice and making it likely that sooner or later one or both will be adversely affected. Long after the professional relationship has terminated, these same forces may still be in place."

*

Sociologists and social psychologists recognize a "role" as the expected pattern of behavior expressed by an individual based on their status. "Status," on the other hand, refers to "any of the full range of socially defined positions within a large group or society" (Schaefer, 2009). A role is not merely a label, but a comprehensive set of actions socially recognized as befitting a particular status. Individuals fulfill a number of statuses at any given moment. Many are fluid or overlapping, conflict with each other, or can be viewed as contradictory (such as a car mechanic who works part-time as a fashion model). Statuses can be temporary or fixed as well. For example, the statuses I personally embody are that of a daughter, sister, auntie, friend, intimate partner, substance use disorder counselor, writer, worship attendee, etc. If I left my job and allowed my license to expire, I would no longer be a counselor, but for having (and having had) siblings, I will always be a sister.

Vandenburgh (2004) says that roles exert considerable force over our beliefs and actions. "They are instructions we absorb about the ways to fit into a given group or setting," he explains, adding how "the group's expectations of the ways the individuals are to act, feel, or think places considerable limits on behavior" (Vandenburgh, 2004). Acknowledgment of roles as both a social reality and theoretical concept has led to the development of role theory. According to Biddle (1986), "Role theory concerns one of the most important characteristics of social behavior—the fact that human beings behave in ways that are different and predictable depending on their respective social identities and the situation...Role theory may be said to concern itself with a triad of concepts: patterned and characteristic social behaviors, parts or identities that are assumed by social participants, and scripts or expectations for behavior that are understood by all and adhered to by performers."

Consider my list of statuses and try to imagine the social environments wherein I may or may not perform the roles associated with these. If I am at work, I wouldn't assume the same set of behavioral scripts I would be expected to take on during a Shabbos service. At my workplace, it would be inappropriate for me to welcome clients with a Hebrew or Yiddish greeting, followed by a hug or a kiss, whereas this is customary at my synagogue. Likewise, I wouldn't approach a fellow congregant in the same manner as my coworkers or our patrons. To respond to someone's "Shabbat shalom" with a simple "Hey there," and then resist an affectionate touch would certainly inspire judgment or concern.

My conduct also will shift to reflect the particular type of relationship to the individuals in my presence. When I'm hanging out with my brother Sam, I definitely wouldn't treat him the same way I treat my partners Alex and Kamyar. Although Sam and I have an intimate relationship, it's rooted in a familial bond, rather than a romantic one. The way I speak to Alex or Kamyar is specific to our relational context. If I'm trying to get Sam's attention, I wouldn't squeak or meow at him, though I routinely do this around my lovers. Instead, I'd call, "Eh, bro!" I could make these frivolous sounds at Sam, but he'd probably just laugh with confusion and make fun of me.

These are just two examples of countless scenarios in which my conduct is both dictated and restricted by my social roles. The same prescriptive rules of behavior apply to all individuals in society, with our everyday activities falling into patterns of socially categorized expectations. These behavior patterns—performance of roles—help preserve social interactions and social structures; in sum, they function to keep our social lives and society at large organized and predictable (Schaefer, 2009).

With this in mind, consider how someone is likely to act in the presence of an authority figure. Few people would feel comfortable treating their parents the same way they treat their friends, classmates, or coworkers. Similarly, the ways in which the average person is expected to behave around their employers, religious leaders, or in the company of law enforcement differs greatly from the ways they will act around anyone who has no prescribed power over them. This occurs because human behavior is also shaped by the hierarchical statuses of individuals within the groups we inhabit. As Schaefer (2009) says, "People we think of as peers or equals influence us to act in particular ways; the same is true of people who hold authority over us or occupy awe-inspiring positions."

The latter is a necessary factor in examining how my status as a student influenced the ways in which I participated in the relationship with Jack. Because his status ascribed him power over me, it impeded my ability to behave around him in the same ways I would around a romantic partner like Alex, who has no assigned power over me.

I took my status as a student seriously, meaning I placed priority on the behaviors socially expected of students. I saw my self-worth reflected in my academic performance. I fretted over my coursework, was active in classroom discussions, voluntarily met with professors for extra help, and took their suggestions to heart. Moreover, I concerned myself with their opinions of me, not only as their student, but as a person in general, since academics were an important part of my identity.

Regardless of my personal investment in the roles of a student, I—like all people in our society—was socialized from an early age to respect authority figures. Our social life is structured by power relations (Plummer, 2010), in which power and submission act as a form of social cohesion. These power relations exist at every level of social interaction, from the two-person dyad to our involvement in broader societal institutions.

In effect, our social interactions often appear as an interconnected series between order-givers and order-followers (Tolbert & Hall, 2009). The basic function of organizational hierarchy is to maintain social order. And despite how one feels about our current systems of power, individuals thrive on positive assurance and the predictability of patterns. We tend to avoid conflict, as it would disrupt the status quo and invite uncertainty into our interactions with others. Such is the basis for the majority of our social norms and mores. As a consequence, to revere power through displays of compliance is a vital, highly-emphasized norm, and resisting the guidance of authority figures is seen as an act of deviance—and in our society, deviance is rarely rewarded or seen as virtuous. It can often result in difficult corrective or interpersonal consequences.

*

Stanley Milgram's collective work on obedience to authority is arguably among the most influential psychological research in recent history. Born to Holocaust survivors, Milgram's experiment began as an attempt to understand how average citizens came to participate in genocide and other atrocities in Germany and their allied countries. Although Milgram himself drew parallels between his findings and the actions of regular people during World War Two, Burger (2009) advises, "one must be cautious when making the leap from laboratory studies to complex social behaviors such as genocide."

For Milgram's initial experiment, a man in a grey technician's coat played the part of the "experimenter." Research subjects ("teachers") were asked to read a series of word exercises to another participant (a "learner") and to administer electric shocks when he failed to answer a question correctly. Unbeknownst to the teachers, the learner was an actor and wasn't actually connected to any source of electricity. The puppet shock generator had labeled switches ranging from 15 to 450 volts. When switches were flipped, a buzzing sound was produced and pilot lights corresponding to each switch were illuminated for the benefit of the actor (Milgram, 1963).

The actor gave convincing cries of pain from the next room when "shocked." As the intensity of the electricity was increased, the actor pleaded for the experiment to stop and even pretended to become unconscious. Although the unwitting teachers expressed great reluctance to continue directing shocks, most did so under the experimenter's authoritative command, which comprised of concise directives, such as "please go on" and "the experiment must continue." In the end, 65 percent of the teachers proceeded, directing what they earnestly believed was a life-threatening 450-volt electric shock to the learner (Milgram, 1963; Martin & Hewstone, 2003).

The results of Milgram's original and follow-up experiments continue to disturb social scientists and stir debate. Many of these criticisms are certainly warranted. Retrospective scrutiny show flaws in Milgram's methodology, the most obvious being his use of deception and his failure to ensure the emotional welfare of subjects, many of whom were distressed by the experiment. In addition, "there was not one experiment, but over twenty of them," involving different variations, altered scripts, and even different actors" (Perry, 2012). At first glance, this seems counterintuitive to performing a sound, scientifically valid study. However, Alan Elms (2009), an assistant of Milgram, has defended these variants, explaining how they used "several clusters of experimental conditions" and that "data from different conditions were compared with a baselines control condition."

Historical sociologist Walter Garrison Runciman (2000) asserts that "in follow-ups to the Milgram experiment, it has been shown that people are consistently disposed to discount or misinterpret it. We don't, it would seem, want to face up to just how conformist we are: we systemically underestimate the strength of the external pressures to which we yield in our apparently spontaneous decisions about how to behave in company. The choice may be in the individual mind, but the power is in the social group." Perhaps the criticism is less about Milgram's research process, and more to do with how his conclusions cause people to question themselves—their limitations and capabilities—and makes them deeply uncomfortable.

Despite the controversy, Milgram's work has been canonized and is frequently cited to illustrate the influential force of an authoritative presence on the average person. Most crucially, researchers have used variant paradigms in subsequent experiments to test and ultimately confirm Milgram's original findings (Blass, 2000), giving credence to obedience to authority as a psychological mechanism. The overall results are the same: most individuals tend to comply with authority, even if doing so will have harmful results.

From what I've read, the most distressing of these replicate experiments involved asking participants to deliver real shocks to a puppy dog (Sheridan & King, 1972). The labels on the shock generator were exaggerated so in actuality, the puppy received relatively minor shocks, enough to cause it to yelp in pain, bark, and begin to run around. Still, 77 percent of participants completed the experiment, though many of them exhibited obvious signs of tension and some complained of stomach pains or began to weep (Sheridan & King, 1972).

More recently, social psychologist Jerry Burger designed a partial replicate of Milgram's experiment. To meet current ethical standards, Burger employed several strategies to safeguard participants from psychological distress, such as screening out volunteers who indicated a history of mental health issues. Burger's experimenter also relayed the same authoritative script used by Milgram. But unlike Milgram, Burger's experiment was ended at the 150-volt level, when the actor-learner began complaining of heart issues and making demands to be relieved. This was so whether the teacher refused to continue by this point or after having already pressed the 150-volt switch. Ultimately, 70 percent of participants continued beyond the 150-volt level and had to be stopped by the experimenter (Burger, 2009). "Although changes in societal attitudes can affect behavior," Burger (2009) concludes, "my findings indicate that the same situational factors that affected obedience in Milgram's participants still operate today."

As unsettling as this seems, deeper investigation of Milgram's notes and further research provides some hopeful silver linings. Using Milgram's work to fuel the assumption that people might helplessly slip into some robotic state wherein they can do nothing else but submit to authority is false and misleading. Rarely is anything about human psychology or behavior that simple. As Slater et al. (2006) propose, "It could be argued that rather than obedience, this was a matter of participants being willing to put up with their own discomfort for the sake of honoring their agreement to be a participant in the experiment. Similar arguments have been made in relation to the original experiments by Milgram—for example, that his subjects were not necessarily being obedient, but were deferring to the expert scientific authority; in other words, since the behavior of the experimenter indicated that nothing out of the ordinary was happening, this signaled to the subjects that everything must be going according to plan."

Through his variant studies, Milgram did record certain

conditions that predicted reversal findings: if the teacher and actor were in the same room; if the experimenter was absent from the room, or if they were replaced by a plainclothes teacher-actor; if an additional, defiant teacher-actor was present—in these scenarios, participants tended to *disobey* orders. This indicates the physical environment and the configuration of social relationships play an important part in determining "which voice the participant will heed and which they will ignore" (Reicher & Haslam, 2017). I feel the most telling variable directly relates to whether the experimenter fronted as a legitimate or expert authority. When this was the case, the rates of obedience tended to be high. Regardless of whether this reflects true obedience or deferring to authoritative expertise, the result is the same.

The sway of expert-based power was revealed through another experiment designed to explore the relationship between nurses and doctors. This field study was arranged at three psychiatric hospitals, one of which was set as the control. An actor posing as a doctor telephoned an on-duty nurse and requested her to give an excessive dose of medicine to a resident patient. During the call, he explained how he was running late for his shift, but would sign the medication order once he arrived. However, this arrangement was problematic as it violated hospital policy, the doctor was unknown to the nurse, and the medication was not approved for use at the hospital. For reasons of safety, researchers decided to use a harmless placebo drug (Hofling et al., 1966). An observer also stood by, prepared to intervene before a nurse could administer the placebo to the patient.

At the two hospitals where 22 nurses received orders from anonymous actor-doctors, only one of them refused to follow through with the order (Hofling et al., 1966). Interestingly, at the control hospital, nurses were given a questionnaire describing the same scenario and were asked to speculate how they thought they would react. Ten out of these twelve nurses reported that they wouldn't follow through with the doctor's telephone orders (Hofling et al., 1966).

These results clearly show a remarkable difference between self-reported attitudes and actual behaviors when it comes to defying authority. To this point, social psychologist and Holocaust survivor Thomas Blass (2000) writes, "Being enlightened about the unexpected power of authority may help a person to stay away from an authority-dominated situation, but once he or she is already in such a situation, knowledge of the drastic degree of obedience that authorities are capable of eliciting does not necessarily help to free the individual from the grip of the forces operating in that concrete situation; that is, to defy the authority in charge."

Some sociologists have developed a concept similarly concerned with how obedience is expressed during interactions with representatives of legitimized power structures (e.g., military personnel with respect to their commanding officers). Authorization as a social process refers to how individuals and groups from a subordinate status comply with superiors, under threat of sanction or judgment, and even when directives are obviously corrupt or morally questionable. Kelman and Hamilton (1989) expound on this, stating that "individuals characteristically feel obligated to obey the orders of the authorities, whether or not these correspond with their personal preferences. They see themselves as having no choice as long as they accept the legitimacy of the orders and of the authorities who gave them...Often people obey without question even though the behavior they engage in may entail great personal sacrifice or great harm to others."

*

In comparing these concepts to my experience, I believe they can explain my submissiveness with Jack. The obedience to authority mechanism might account for why I was compelled to accept him as a potential romantic partner after he expressed a sexual interest in me. I was under no obligation to do this, but at the time, I felt obligated nonetheless. Resisting him would have equated to resisting my education. I also presumed he wouldn't have provided the option of intimacy between us if it weren't meant to benefit me in some way—and what is more beneficial to a person than love?

When he detailed the risks that would befall me if anyone learned of our relationship, I never doubted him. As a student, I was ignorant of the grey areas in faculty policy and enforcement, whereas he was a professor and had more access to this specialized knowledge. In addition, I'd always felt discouraged from asking for extra details about him and simply accepted what he told me as the truth. Questioning him was a nerve-wracking prospect. It was much easier to soothe my internal tension through authority bias and to simply have faith in Jack's narrative, even as I rumbled with suspicion and hurt.

To further complicate matters, by the time Jack began inviting me to his home, I was well into a routine of doing what he asked of me, having been his student and advisee for several years. This is important, since social psychologists have speculated how this may be a contributing factor to Milgram's rates of obedience. Burger (2009) discusses how the high rates of obedience could be contributed to the incremental nature of the shocks, and states "we know from a great deal of subsequent research that this type of gradual increase in the size of demands is an effective tactic for changing attitudes and behaviors." He also identifies how humans have a need for consistency and a self-perception process, and it could be that the subjects came to view themselves as "the kind of persons who follow the experimenter's instructions" (Burger 2009). I, too, regarded myself as a good student who followed her professor's instructions, which eventually progressed from enrolling in the classes he suggested, to complying with whatever sexual position he wanted at the time.

Consistency, for me, meant acquiescence.

Interestingly, Milgram (1974) has also pointed out that "although a person under authority performs actions that seem to violate standards of conscience, it would not be true to say that he loses his moral sense. Instead, it requires a radically different focus. He does not respond with a moral sentiment to the action he performs. Rather, his moral concern now shifts to a consideration of how well he is living up to the expectations that the authority has of him."

I recognize this shift in priorities all too well. Once resolved to the seeming inevitability of the relationship, I began to constantly worry about what Jack might think of me. Preserving his high opinion became the central focus for my ensuing actions. I started wearing makeup to campus. I groomed more frequently and found myself eating less—due in part to my anxiety, but also because I wanted to remain slim and desirable. I worked harder that semester than ever before. I took on more extracurricular projects, spent hours crafting my weekly article and chapter reviews, and dedicated weeks to research papers and final reports in the hopes of tailoring them to perfection.

On the surface, these adjustments may seem positive; however, this preoccupation had negative effects. I neglected personal aspects of self-care to make time for tasks directly relating to Jack. I also became impatient with Alex, Alice, and others when I felt they were imposing on my ability to prioritize Jack. In all, I was incredibly distracted because I didn't want to fail Jack or give him cause to reject me.

*

Shortly after the release of Craig's article in the student newspaper, I saw my friend Taylor in the library. She told me she'd overheard a couple of professors talking in the cafeteria. "They were saying that you should have known what was going on. Like, students are all adults, and if you're old enough to be in college, you should have known what you were getting into."

"Um, no," I said. "How could I have known?"

"Right!" Taylor huffed, throwing up her hands. "I just wanted to yell at them. It just pissed me off so much. He totally *lied* to you. That's what they don't understand. There's so much more to it than what people think."

The opinion of these unknown professors is demoralizing and ignorant—a rejection of the powers of human psychology and socialization. Too, the professors fail to note another remarkable point about my case: as a student, it's not my responsibility to be conscious of the problems that manifest from having sex with my professor; rather, it's a professor's obligation to be aware of them and to prevent a sexual relationship from taking place.

I'd always assumed that when Jack spoke to me, he told the truth. And I had to believe the things he said were factual to facilitate my education and academic feats. After all, this had evolved from within higher education, where obedience to authority is both expected and encouraged.

As students, we clearly understand that faculty and administrative staff dominate the campus and that their leadership is due to their advanced knowledge and expertise. The asymmetry between statuses is legitimized 1) because authorities are accepted as honorable, expert agents of the institution, and 2) because students face real penalties for disruption from their roles, such as poor grades, financial waste, and the loss of access to various systems of support. Furthermore, genuine learning cannot occur if students feel, at any point, they might be misled by their professors. A principal aspect of the college experience is that students must safely rely on their professors to be academically successful, and that their professors refrain from abusing this inherent trust.

6. Helping Professionals and the Ethics of Sexual Boundaries

The term *helping professions* broadly refers to occupations that provide specialized, expert support for the physical, psychological, intellectual, and spiritual welfare of individuals, families, or communities. These positions are generally centered on addressing difficulties in the lives of the help-seekers, giving information and guidance, and encouraging healthy changes and personal growth. Typical examples are social workers, therapists and counselors, clergy and other religious leaders, healthcare professionals, and schoolteachers. However, other jobs involve the consistent use of helping skills like active listening, empathizing, conflict resolution, etc. Such trades, due to the nature of their responsibilities, are also considered helping professions, such as lawyers, athletic coaches, human resources personnel, law enforcement officers, and college professors.

Most helping professionals are cautioned to avoid multiple relationships with their clients, patients, patrons, dependents, or consumers. Also called "dual relationships," Corey et al. (2015) specify that multiple relationships "occur when professionals assume two or more roles at the same time or sequentially with a client." This entails taking on more than one professional role or combining the professional role with a nonprofessional relationship, such as imparting services to a friend or relative, borrowing from or loaning money to a dependent, and becoming emotionally or sexually involved with them (Corey et al., 2015). More colloquially, "conflict of interest" might be used to describe some types of multiple relationships, though not all, as conflicts of interest don't always involve individuals from contrasting modes of power.

Karen S. Kitchener has spent much of her career exploring ethics within the field of psychology and has discussed the risks posed by dual relationships. In a highly influential article, Kitchener (1988) makes references to role theory, arguing that in dual role relationships, role expectations "conflict or compete with each other...Conflict occurs when expectations associated with one role require behavior of a person that is to some extent incompatible with the behavior associated with another role. Competition occurs when the individual does not have the time or energy to adequately honor the expectations associated with both roles." With this overlapping of roles comes the predilection for frustration, anger, and resentment, as well as confusion about what is appropriate behavior (Kitchener, 1988).

"Based on role theory," Kitchener (1988) continues, "three guidelines can be used to differentiate between dual role relationships that have a high probability of leading to difficulty and those that are less likely to be problematic. First, as the incompatibility of expectations increases between roles, so will the potential for misunderstanding and harm...Second, as the obligations of different roles diverge, the potential for divided loyalties and loss of objectivity increases...Last, as power and prestige between the professional's and the consumer's role increase, so does the potential for exploitation and an inability on the part of consumers to remain objective about their own best interests." Kitchener (1988) concludes that given the potential for harm, all multiple relationships can have problematic consequences; thus, being proactive about avoiding these issues is crucial for ethical professional conduct.

The rationale to be committed to professional boundaries and abstain from multiple relationships is founded in the possibility of misusing power to influence or exploit dependents (Corey et al., 2015). On the surface, it may be easy to recognize the inherent power status of some helping professionals over others. Police officers obviously have more authority than the average citizen, as do doctors over their patients. A pastor may be seen to have less influence over congregational members in comparison. Yet, regardless of how thickly or faintly some hierarchal lines are drawn, the power helping professionals hold over patrons cannot be erased.

To illustrate the point, when Linda Barrow recommended I visit the women's center for counseling, I discovered that a long-time friend of my mother's worked there. Before Sonya was assigned as my counselor, I'd asked Mom's friend if she could see me. I thought I'd feel more comfortable describing my pains to her than to a stranger. But, she apologetically turned me down. She couldn't take me on as a client, as it would have been impossible for her to treat me with impartiality. Because she was Mom's close friend, this may have also influenced my willingness to disclose certain things to her.

Similarly, after my little brother was arrested several years ago, my father reached out to a friend, who also happened to be an outstanding local attorney. He replied sympathetically and offered to make a referral, but he couldn't take on the case himself. One of the reasons he cited was how being well-acquainted with our family would make it difficult for him to work objectively on my brother's behalf.

In these instances, the focus on maintaining professional boundaries with me and my family was necessary to ensure we received the best possible services. Thus, we were sheltered from the implications of multiple relationships by being encouraged to seek other professionals who could guarantee neutrality while addressing our needs.

*

College and university professors are, first and foremost, educators, yet they frequently take on additional roles for the betterment of their students. They act as counselors, life coaches, mentors, and case managers, and may provide legal advice or connect students with local social welfare agencies. The performance of these extra roles is rarely viewed with suspicion; indeed, many assume these actions are within the range of their duties. And perhaps this is true, and such roles are appropriate as long as they're carried out with ethical care.

Still, it begs questioning: given their authoritative power and the architecture of their work, why aren't professors consistently held to the same ethical standards as other helping professionals—as other educators? Specifically, why is it that helping professionals are, in general, instructed to avoid sexual intimacy with help-seekers, but practitioners of higher education are an exception?

Across the helping professions, representative organizations and associations promote codes of ethics or ethical principles that their members and the professional community at large are obliged to follow. Most explicitly prohibit sexual relations between providers and their patrons, as with the following examples.

- The American Medical Association requires physicians to abstain from sexual interactions with concurrent patients, relaying how such interactions may exploit patient vulnerabilities and prove detrimental to the patient's health care and general well-being (AMA, 2016).
- The Rabbinical Council of America's Codes of Conduct states that romantic relationships with persons with whom a rabbi serves "are subject to power imbalance and should be avoided" (RCA, 2018).
- The American Psychology Association prohibits psychologists from becoming sexually involved with clients, students, supervisees, or anyone else over whom they hold evaluative authority (APA, 2017).

- The National Association of Social Workers bans sexual activities and communication with concurrent and former clients or client's relatives, and are warned against providing services to individuals with whom they've had previous sexual involvement. Social workers who act as educators or supervisors are also forbidden from sexual relations with "supervisees, students, trainees, or other colleagues over whom they exercise professional authority" (NASW, 2017).
- The National Association of State Directors of Teacher Education and Certification acknowledges "there are no circumstances that allow for educators to engage in romantic or sexual relationships with students," and stresses the potential ramifications of entering into such relationships with former students (NASDTEC, 2015).

The average person would agree it's inappropriate for a high school teacher to engage in sexual interactions with a student, even if the age disparity is slight and the student is of lawful consenting age. When the public has been made aware of such cases, the intimacy is scandalized and met with outrage. Several states have passed laws criminalizing sex acts between high school teachers and students, such as Georgia, Kansas, and Michigan. These and many other states have also passed laws restricting or prohibiting sexual relationships between other types of helping professionals and those they are meant to serve: police officers and those within their custody, corrections officers and inmates, and psychotherapists and their clients.

Society as a whole appears to acknowledge the elevated risk for sexual exploitation of help-seekers by helping professionals. Unfortunately, this consensus isn't as widely reflected in higher education regarding sexuality between professors and their students. And why not, if the power differential and potential for abuse is the same?

For comparison's sake, the statement of professional ethics held by the American Association of University Professors (2009) says that professors should "demonstrate respect for students as individuals and adhere to their proper roles as intellectual guides and counselors. Professors make every reasonable effort to foster honest academic conduct and to ensure that their evaluations of students reflect each student's true merit...They avoid any exploitation, harassment, or discriminatory treatment of students."

While AAUP notes the need for professors to be considerate of their status, they don't recognize a professor's authoritative power, nor the potential risks of developing multiple relationships or engaging in sexual activities with students. Maybe this is implied, as the AAUP warns professors not to exploit students. But, when sexual relationships aren't explicitly prohibited, what's to deter professors from seducing students—from using their power and influence to harass, intimidate, groom, or otherwise coerce students into sex acts?

To their credit, the AAUP has released statements urging universities to formulate policies on consensual faculty-student sexual relationships. But, why stop there? Instead of leaving it up to individual colleges and universities to devise policies, why not promote the wide spread adoption of this position by including it in their statement of professional ethics? From what I can tell, unlike other helping fields, academia seems resolved to bicker rather than take a collective stance on the issue. In the meantime, the students suffer the consequences—the realities of which are often neglected or outright denied.

It's not as if no parallels have been made regarding professors as helping professionals or the exploitative risks posed by sexualizing their students. To the contrary, numerous academics and researchers would attest to this potential for harm. After dedicating years to the assessment of helping professionals accused of being sexually inappropriate, Irons and Schneider (1999) agree that relationships of unequal power include professors and students. "These are all relationships that are fiduciary, bounded, and involve sacred trust, relationships in which the person in greater power has an implied duty to act in the best interest of the other person...and these best interests do not include a sexual relationship" (Irons & Schneider, 1999).

This view is also relayed by the Rape, Abuse & Incest National Network (RAINN)—the most prominent anti-sexual violence organization in the United States. On their website, RAINN (2018) confirms that "sexual exploitation by a helping professional includes sexual conduct of any kind between a professional and the person seeking or receiving a service. Helping professionals include doctors, therapists, professors... and any other professional who offers a helping service."

*

Introducing sexuality into any relationship will create irreversible changes. Perspectives are altered by the influx of new feelings, addictive hormones, and the deeper understanding created when two people explore each other's bodies and physiological responses—those of which are most intimate and vulnerable. The budding romance takes precedence, and the couple's personal priorities shift at the expense of their other relationships and responsibilities. In effect, sexual relationships are often messy. As the couple tries to determine a new rhythm to their interactions, they will suffer from miscommunication, infringe upon each other's personal boundaries, and the like. It takes time and invested effort to nurture healthy, balanced romantic relationships.

Still, most relationships fail. One survey of heterosexual couples determined about half of them had broken up before a year had passed, while a third terminated the relationship within the first six months (Sassler et al., 2016). When a relationship is ended, people often find it difficult to maintain a rapport with their former partner. Most require a cooling period before exploring the possibility of a platonic relationship, if they're able to reconnect at all. People hold grudges. Sometimes, it's hard to move on. As they say, love hurts. They also say, don't shit where you eat. Hence, in many professional settings, romantic relationships between peers or colleagues are frowned upon or prohibited given how disruptive they can be, and how they can interfere with job performance and overall morale.

I can speak to these troublesome realities. Several years ago, I worked at a brand-name fashion outlet. There, I learned how to expertly fold clothes; I also met Huascar, who joined our staff for the holiday season. He and I began dating after discovering we had mutual interests—most notably creative writing and being drunk.

After six weeks, Huascar abruptly dumped me and began dating another one of our coworkers. As one can imagine, the store was a delightful working environment. On the sales floor, I was distracted, quietly boiling with disgust and often coped by guzzling vodka in my car during breaks. Huascar eventually quit, and we met up a time or two afterward, but these exchanges ended in drunken arguments, followed by nasty, character-defaming text messages that read like short, poetic essays.

It took a couple of years before we reconnected as friends, having shaken off our more unhealthy dispositions by then. Every once in a while, we still apologize to each other for having been so toxic when we dated, if we're not laughing over the stupidity of it all.

Now, imagine if there had been a disparity of power, and Huascar had been a manager. He would have controlled my schedule, pay grade, and overseen performance reviews. I would have been subject to his discretion, which could never again be impartial after having pressed his nakedness into mine and drank up my sad, alcoholic brays. I would have had to escape the threats to my financial and emotional welfare by finding another job. But, what if I couldn't?

Moreover, what if there was more at stake than my financial security, but my physical, psychological, and spiritual health too? What if my right to immediate resources was on the line? What if my overall life goals and access to upward mobility were at risk of being interrupted, damaged, or lost? Unfortunately, I can now speak to these realities as well.

Given how routinely sex complicates matters between ordinary couples, it should be obvious why sexualizing the helping relationship is viewed as the most problematic boundary violation (Corey et al., 2015). There are several reasons to warrant this conclusion. According to Irons and Schneider (1999), the authority of the professional and their intellectual and educational advantage are critical features of their power over the help-seeker. Many professionals also have the upper hand in age and level of life experience, which can increase the imbalance of power. In addition, Irons and Schneider (1999) note how "the person with greater power is generally in possession of more personal information about the other person than vice versa." This means they can make more educated decisions about the trajectory of the relationship than the patron.

Conversely, the help-seeker has a reliance on the professional to treat needs they're unable to address on their own. This causes them to be inherently vulnerable, as they are dependent on the professional's knowledge, leadership, and guidance. Because of the professional's status, the help-seeker is also psychologically subject to the obedience to authority mechanism. Having been socialized to revere authority, they're susceptible to following through with commands, even in the face of damaging personal consequences. As Irons and

Schneider (1999) put it, they have a naturalized tendency to defer to the professional's judgment, to please and trust them.

Since the professional's status impresses upon the help-seeker's reasoning and ability to exercise absolute autonomy, this arguably acts as a form of coercion. Under these conditions, they can't express genuine consent. The power disparity matched with the help-seeker's vulnerabilities undermines their ability to make fully informed and empowered choices, which includes consenting to sex acts with the helper.

This is still the case even if the dependent themselves breach the topic of sex or make attempts to initiate erotic contact. As Corey et al. (2015) write, "Professionals cannot argue that their clients seduced them. Even if clients behave in seductive ways, it is clearly the professional's responsibility to establish and maintain appropriate boundaries." They're in charge, after all.

Helpers exploit their dependents for a variety of reasons. Their abusive behaviors may be indicative of mental illness and addiction, problems with impulse control, or naivety to the importance of appropriate boundaries. They may crave nurturing due to personal loss or crisis, or are self-serving and feel entitled to having their desires met. Many helpers violate sexual boundaries because they crave power and control, and aspire to further realize this by sexually dominating their dependents. In the course of their work, Irons and Schneider (1999) determined that about a quarter of professionals met these criteria. This population of helpers were documented to have sexually exploited patrons through physical force, blackmail, intimidation, and other types of coercion (Irons & Schneider, 1999). This falls in line with something previously stated: helping occupations are attractive to sexual predators, since these jobs guarantee contact with a pool of trusting, reliant individuals ideal for grooming and abuse.

To reiterate, helpers must be conscientious of possible

conflicts of interest or multiple relationships, and uphold professional boundaries and express care without becoming emotionally attached. Doing so ensures they can provide services effectively, and prioritize the health and safety of the help-seeker. Therefore, sex is especially destructive to the helping relationship, completely inhibiting the professional's objectivity with respect to the patron and the fulfillment of their needs. Once a helper and help-seeker establish a sexual connection, the original goals of the relationship take a back seat or dissolve completely, as their new roles as sexual partners assume priority. More often than not, this has extensive, devastating effects on the dependent's well-being.

*

Much of the literature that investigates the effects of sexualizing the helping relationship is specific to psychotherapy and counseling. Studies have demonstrated that clients who experience sexual misconduct by their therapists "suffer dire consequences" (Corey et al., 2015). Pope and Vasquez (2011) outlined how these psychological injuries tend to fall within ten general categories: ambivalence, guilt, emptiness and isolation, sexual confusion, impaired ability to trust, confused roles and boundaries, emotional lability, suppressed rage, increased suicide risk, and cognitive dysfunction "frequently in the areas of concentration and memory and often involving flashbacks, intrusive thoughts, unbidden images, and nightmares."

In a landmark study, Bouhoutsos et al. (1983) surveyed 559 clients who'd had some form of sexual contact with their therapist, ranging from "merely proposing sexual relations," to fondling and kissing, to intercourse," with rape reported in two percent of cases. Bouhoutsos et al. (1983) determined 90 percent of respondents were adversely impacted, with ill effects including increased depression, significant emotional disturbances, increased drug and alcohol consumption, and abandonment of treatment. Eleven of the clients were hospitalized and one percent committed suicide (Bouhoutsos et al., 1983). Given these responses, Bouhoutsos et al. (1983) plainly state that "sexual intimacy is extremely disruptive to therapy," and affirm "the harmfulness of sexual contact in therapy validates ethics codes of the mental health professions prohibiting such conduct."

More recently, Eichenberg, Becker-Fischer, and Fischer (2010) reviewed responses from 77 victims of therapeutic sexual abuse and found that 93 percent reported experiencing feelings of guilt and shame, increased depression, isolation, suicidal tendencies, and PTSD. "Overall, 86.5 [percent] of the people who participated in the survey stated that the sexual contact with the therapist had negative consequences for them, of these 93.3 [percent] state problematic consequences" (Eichenberg et al., 2010). Participants were asked if they had thought about taking legal action against their therapists, and 68.8 percent said they'd never considered it (Eichenberg et al., 2010). This was mostly explained by the participants' fear of the steps required to file reports and self-described lack of courage or sense of complicacy. Three respondents specified that "they saw no point in taking legal action, partially due to either weak evidence or lack of it" (Eichenberg et al., 2010).

These studies are based solely on the effects of sexual misconduct in a therapeutic context, while the abuse I sustained was perpetuated by a college professor. Therapist-client and professor-student dynamics differ in many respects; nevertheless, as Kolbert, Morgan, and Brendel (2002) propose, "there are major similarities between the client-counselor and the faculty-student relationship. Both types of relationships involve an inherent inequality in that one individual is seeking a service (counseling or education, respectively) from another individual. The consent of the person with decreased power (client or student) to enter nonprofessional relationships is not valid if he or she is motivated by fear of the negative consequences of noncompliance (termination of counseling for the client or adverse repercussions for the student)."

This perspective is shared by Biaggio, Paget, and Chenoweth (1997), who also remark on the inherent inequality between therapist-client and faculty-student relationships. "There are several bases of power," Biaggio et al. (1997) write, "and therapists and faculty alike may exercise these various types of power over their subordinates: reward power (by dispending approval and grades), coercive power (by disapproving or devaluing actions), referent power (by serving as a role model), information and expert power (by possessing knowledge and the authority to dispense it), and legitimate power (by having an implicit contract to provide a service)."

Due to these parallels, I believe the data on therapist-client sexual abuse is useful in that it indicates how students may respond to professorial sexual abuse—an opinion commonly mentioned in related studies. Empirical research on the consequences of faculty-student sexual contact is quite limited. On the other hand, abundant research has demonstrated the harm other helping professionals cause when they sexualize relationships with their dependents, and how this harm warrants a violation of professional ethics and even criminalization.

*

Over the course of my studies, I became friends with a few professors. Between classes, we fell into impromptu kvetching sessions, or met off campus for coffee and hung out at conferences. We disclosed our fears and insecurities, fragments of our domestic lives, financial concerns, and personal goals. We gave and received advice, gossip, sympathy, and encouragement.

Some might point to this and note a blatant contradiction, bearing in mind the ethics of multiple relationships. But to their credit, I feel my interactions with these professor-friends were acceptable, even personally beneficial, because certain safeguards were in place.

Primarily, the prospect of sexual intimacy was completely absent from our exchanges. I was never invited into their homes or other private spaces. If I happened into a class with one of my professor-friends, I did not expect, request, or receive special treatment. We didn't interact outside of the classroom or off campus as long as I was enrolled in their courses, regardless of whether we had done so before. The fluctuation in boundaries went unspoken; it was just common sense.

As described earlier, the work of professors encompasses an inherent multiplicity of combined, overlapping roles and responsibilities, referred to as role blending (Corey et al., 2015). This leaves professors subject to forming multiple relationships with students. However, role blending is not necessarily problematic, nor are all multiple relationships fundamentally destructive. On the contrary, some secondary relationships can complement or enhance the aims of the primary relationship.

Professors are encouraged to take students under their wing, serve as role models and mentors, and provide emotional support and advice on personal matters. Most former students can reflect on their academic careers and recall professors who positively influenced them. I know several people who would have left their major or dropped out of school if a professor hadn't stepped in, nudged them in the right direction, empathized with their struggles, and expressed faith in their abilities. Faculty, too, can be motivated by students. Forming bonds with them can be a rewarding hallmark of the job, and can deflect aspects of burnout or career fatigue.

Taken all together, professor-student multiple relationships are often unavoidable, regarded as a normal and healthy feature of higher education, and can be fulfilling for both parties—as long as the professor is careful and proactive in their approach. As Corey et al. (2015) write, "Functioning in more than one role involves thinking through potential problems before they occur...Whenever a potential for negative outcomes exists, professionals have a responsibility to design safeguards to reduce the potential for harm."

Role blending becomes destructive when the professor's involvement with students impairs their judgment or ability to effectively impart knowledge or evaluate student progress, or results in harm or exploitation. This can be avoided if faculty recognize the vulnerability of their students and remain cognizant of their power over them. While they may be tempted to deny the impact of their authority, doing so creates a psychological gateway through which boundary violations are inevitable (Garrett, 2002), the worst of these being the sexualization of the helping relationship.

*

Higher education is an unusual institution. Others typically have a distinctive hierarchical structure wherein individuals' roles are pronounced and employees are subject to oversight by superiors. College professors, however, have a tradition of autonomy and self-regulation in their classrooms, which is commendable and essential to the academic endeavor, as long as faculty use their professional autonomy legitimately (Dziech & Weiner, 1990). Self-determination allows professors to experiment with pedagogy and engage the teaching philosophies they deem best. It can also promote values of creativity, innovation, and eccentricity amongst faculty.

Because the college or university environment lacks clearly defined professorial roles, this leads to confusion over what behaviors may or may not be appropriate. Most interactions in an institutional setting or with the agent of an institution follow a predictable script. If someone enters a doctor's clinic, they can expect to provide an ID and proof of insurance or medical coverage—if they have it—fill out necessary paperwork, and be prodded with questions relative to their physical health. Along the same lines, when someone's car is pulled over by a law enforcement officer, they presume the officer will ask to see their license, registration, and proof of insurance, followed by the officer's explanations as to why they were stopped. A college campus, in comparison, has very few reliable, predictive scripts outside of the classroom.

Moreover, when a dependent feels they've been wronged by other institutional authorities, the steps by which they report grievances are generally better understood, if not outlined within an informed consent process. For instance, if a doctor or nurse fucks up, someone might place a call to a patient advocate or visit their hospital's administrative offices. If a law enforcement officer breaks from protocol, a complaint can be filed with the department chief or Internal Affairs. When a lawyer or therapist harms someone, the state regulatory agencies can be contacted outright; sometimes, the complaints become a matter of public record. Though it's not guaranteed anything will come of it (since disciplinary actions usually favor the higher-power professionals), at the very least, the grievance procedures are more straightforward as these follow a more apparent chain of command.

This isn't readily reflected on college campuses where professors act with more impunity and department heads have leadership roles that rarely involve implementing disciplinary measures. The layout of the campus itself can further disrupt the communication of grievances, as deans and other administrators may be relegated to offices separate from those occupied by the faculty persons they're meant to supervise. Since students aren't always sure who oversees who, they may share concerns with faculty or staff members who have no authority to act on their behalf. Faculty are often just as confused about how to make referrals when students confide in them—even those subject to mandatory reporting.

In reporting Jack, I spoke to five individuals in five differing faculty or administrative positions before ending up in a meeting with Dean Witterman, the person who directly managed Jack. Think about that. Imagine, too, if I'd become disillusioned by the process earlier on and given up. Nothing would have been done—no resolution.

Unlike other types of helpers whose duties are dictated through their expertise, the work of professors is more nebulous. "The original purpose of academia was to educate and pursue knowledge," Dziech and Weiner (1990) remark, "but in the last half of the twentieth century the mission has become much less clear...Not only are many faculty members ambiguous about what they are supposed to be doing, they are equally uncertain about how to do it." To become a college professor, one must exhibit proficiency in a specific discipline or field of study. This may or may not involve graduate or doctoral courses in pedagogy and teaching theories, let alone instruction in basic counseling models. As Dziech and Weiner (1990) point out, "The advising of students requires skills in counseling and psychology which faculty never study, so many of them improvise as they go along. Often the results are disastrous." Surely, if professors aren't familiar with even the most basic of counseling practices, they're likely to struggle with appropriate boundaries. Many lacked training in teaching principles before becoming professors and, more or less, figured it out as they stumbled through their first few semesters.

Many professors begin their careers as graduate teaching assistants (GTAs), which involves performing many of the same duties as faculty instructors: teaching introductory or laboratory courses, leading workshops, writing and grading exams, holding office hours, and issuing final grades. However, a study involving 261 GTA respondents—about 84 percent of whom were doctoral students—found that only a third were required to take a teaching readiness course, less than six percent had taken a course in ethics, and almost half reported having never received supervision (Branstetter & Handelsman, 2000). Almost 83 percent stated they planned to teach at the college level in the future, though only about twenty percent felt they had received adequate training (Branstetter & Handelsman, 2000).

To complicate matters further, Dziech and Weiner (1990) explain that "the complexity of the faculty role is compounded by the notion that faculty must nurture as well as educate students...When a professor assumes or is told that he should foster the moral, social, and spiritual as well as intellectual development of students, he can lose sight of the proper limits of his interest and authority. The distinctions between his professional jurisdiction and the student's private life become blurred, and a faculty member can readily convince himself that he is acting appropriately when he may be in fact violating the parameters of proper relations with students." Although role blending in higher education presumes a personal connection between a professor and student, when there's no established process for how to navigate this secondary relationship safely, even the most compassionate and well-intentioned educators can inadvertently confuse, harm, or burden their students. Worst of all, "the professor whose intentions are less honorable can take advantage of the situation" (Dziech & Weiner, 1990).

Between the peculiarities of higher education, the uniqueness of professorial self-determination and diffused oversight, and the paradoxical roles matched with an astonishing lack of training, it's unsurprising this group of helpers isn't subject to the same scrutiny and standards of ethical conduct as other helping professionals. But, this isn't to say that they shouldn't be—far from it.

*

Human beings are fallible creatures. Dodging the emotional storm of interpersonal connection is something few of us are always equipped to do and do successfully. It's impossible to evade our inherent propensity for social bonding, and developing feelings for individuals we consistently interact with is bound to happen at any job. To preserve the helping relationship and prevent boundary violations, there are steps that helpers can take.

First and foremost, helpers should take adequate care of themselves and engage in stress-reduction techniques and self-care. Failing to do so can impair their job performance and ability to uphold ethical behaviors. Practicing self-compassion, mindfulness, and emotional regulation allows helpers to acknowledge and address difficult feelings as they arise. Helpers are generally encouraged to seek therapy to off set the psychologically taxing aspects of their work, especially during periods of personal crisis, loss, or exceptional stress.

If a helper finds themselves developing sexual feelings for a dependent, these require examination. The helper should meditate on their attraction to see if these feelings are a result of their own needs going unfulfilled or are exemplary of deeper personal issues they haven't fully resolved. Next, they should speak openly about their sexual interest with a superior or under the care of a therapist or counselor. When these feelings are explored in a safe setting, professionals are more likely to manage them constructively (Corey et al., 2015). Ignoring, denying, and regarding their attraction as taboo only allows these feelings to go untreated, which can strain interactions with the dependent. Finally, it's important the helper tackle their feelings without sharing them with the help-seeker, if at all possible. Doing so can unnecessarily confuse or burden the help-seeker, or unduly influence their own feelings toward the helper. Shifting blame or fault onto the help-seeker is never ethically sound; it's the helper's responsibility to handle their own emotions.

Surely, if these proactive measures are expected of other helping professionals, it's not asking too much of college professors to adhere to them as well. Ultimately, professionals of any field would benefit from self-care, keeping healthy boundaries, and therapeutic support. I refuse to believe these practices are unfair to expect of professors, who would benefit from them, along with the students they assist, mentor, and teach.

7. Professor-Student Sexual Intimacy: Attitudes,Outcomes, and Policy

In the summer of 2018, I volunteered to help a couple of friends move. Once the contents of their house had been relocated into a truck, I led a broom through the barren rooms and ended up in the kitchen. Sarah, an acquaintance of mine, had just arrived, holding sponges and bottles of cleaner. We hadn't seen each other in a while and began to catch up as we scrubbed cabinets and counters.

I briefly described what I'd gone through with Jack. Sarah gasped and divulged her own account of being sexually harassed by a psychology professor. Even though he'd retired and she'd graduated years ago, he still found ways to show up in places where she worked and persist in his mistreatment.

As we traded horror stories, another acquaintance, Ollie—who happened to teach at the university—hung in the doorway, listening. When I commented that I felt these abuses were vile and unacceptable, Ollie interjected, "Well, I know *you* had a bad time, Cal, but I don't think those kinds of relationships are *always* inappropriate."

Stunned, my throat gummed up. Sarah and I exchanged a solemn glance, and the conversation ended.

Oy vey. If only my involvement with Jack could be neatly

summarized as "a bad time." I haven't spoken to Ollie since. I wish their students the best.

To be fair, Ollie isn't the only person who's said this to me (nor the only professor, for that matter). I suspect one reason for this belief is due to how historically commonplace these relationships appear, immortalized by the arts and entertainment industry. Student-educator intimacy has become a tiresome cliché—another form of forbidden romance to be sensationalized, glamorized, and gradually normalized. The imbalance of power is often portrayed as something to overcome, rather than respect. Love and sex win in the end. The best resolutions are pleasant and optimistic.

I fully understand that my "bad time" with Jack isn't synonymous with all professor-student relationships. As Barbella (2010) says, "Although popular culture generally dramatizes the sexiness, romance, and humor of student-professor liaisons that is not to say that situations worthy of a romantic comedy are not occasionally found in real life too. Some professors and students can and do conduct enjoyable and fulfilling relationships with each other and are able to part ways amicably when the relationship runs its course. Some students look back on their amorous relationships with professors as a cherished and valuable part of their college experience." However, my concerns aren't motivated by the "some students" who benefited from dating their professors, but by those who've had the opposite experience and why.

Ollie's opinion is shared by many academic scholars and other professionals in higher education. They point out how sexual connection is unavoidable in spaces where groups of people convene. They argue that sexuality plays an important role in university life and that romance between instructors and students may enhance the learning experience. They also believe that banning or restricting such relationships infringes on personal liberties: their right to privacy and freedom of speech.

In her book *Teaching Community*, renowned scholar bell hooks (2003) says, "The erotic is always present—always with us...The implications of entering intimate relations where there is an imbalance of power cannot be understood." Hooks (2003) also writes that "passionate pedagogy in any setting is likely to spark erotic energy. It cannot be policed or outlawed...Just as it is important that we be vigilant in challenging abuses of power where the erotic becomes a terrain of exploitation, it is equally important to recognize that space where erotic interaction is enabling and positively transforming...Desire can be the democratic equalizing force—the fierce reminder of the limitations of hierarchy and status as much as it can be a context for abuse and exploitation."

I respectfully disagree with hooks on a couple of points. I believe there *is* enough scholarship that attests to the repercussions of differing power statuses in intimate relationships, as I've touched on in this text. And while I agree it's impossible to police or outlaw feelings, regulating behavior is an entirely separate matter.

With regards to desire, philosopher Amia Srinivasan (2020) offers a different view: "Teachers and students are divided by a profound *epistemic* asymmetry. Teachers know and understand certain things; students want to know and understand those same things. Implicit in the student-teacher relationship is the promise of at least a partial equalization of that asymmetry; that the teacher will confer on the student some of his power and help her become, along a certain dimension, more like him. In the best cases, students find this asymmetry intoxicating, frustrating, and an occasion for desire—that is, a spur to learning. When the teacher takes the student's longing for epistemic power and transposes it into a sexual key, allowing himself to be—or worse, making himself—the object of desire, he has failed her as a teacher. And this is so even if the student has fully and enthusiastically consented."

Moreover, bell hooks approaches her perspective as a professor, and one who has dated a student herself. "From the start we had conflicts about power," she says, adding that "the relationship did not work, yet we became friends" (hooks, 2003). She also qualifies her actions, explaining how she and the student didn't enter into their relationship while he was actively studying under her because she didn't want to "bring that dynamic either into the classroom or into my evaluation of his work" (hooks, 2003). All the same, I find it telling that she quotes her student-lover as saying, "I was young and inexperienced and even though it was exciting that you desired me, it was also frightening" (hooks, 2003). Maybe it's just me, but I don't think fear should be present at the onset of a romantic relationship.

Lastly, hooks touches on a popular argument that forbidding these relationships infantilizes students and prevents them from expressing sexual agency. "Extreme supporters of such bans represent students as children and professors as parents. They see any erotic bonding between the two as symbolic incest" (hooks, 2003). I appreciate why this comparison would cause some to balk with disgust, yet what hooks refers to as symbolic can translate into social situations where one person has expert power over another. Of all of the roles assumed by professors, many mimic typical behaviors of parents toward their children, such as expressing care and providing guidance and advice. This increases a student's risk of transference, or unconsciously identifying faculty as parental-like figures and acting accordingly, which can deepen their dependence on a professor.

A university employee (who asked to remain anonymous) told me how "a lot of students leave home to go to college. They move away from their families. It makes sense that professors would become placeholders for their parents. They fill that parental void." Of the mentor-protégé dimension, Bellas and Gossett (2001) express a similar sentiment, speculating that "professor-student relationships are more akin to parent-child relationships than are most other types of romantic relationships." Perhaps it's exactly because these parallels inspire an icky feeling that they deserve closer attention, rather than assuming this dynamic is abstract and may have no bearing on faculty-student interactions.

The age disparity between students and faculty can further the likelihood of transference. The average age range for undergraduate students enrolled in public universities lands between 18 to 24 years. In most states, at the age of 18, an individual is assumed to have a functional understanding of themselves and their actions and consequences. This age standard serves a practical legal purpose; it doesn't necessarily speak to an individual's grasp of adulthood.

Psychologist Jeffrey Arnett has coined the term "emerging adulthood" to describe the transitional period between adolescence and early adulthood. He proposes that, unlike previous generations, individuals now aged 18 to 25 or even older, assume hallmarks of adulthood erratically or at a slower pace. These include major life events like independent living, marriage, parenthood, and career achievement. Arnett (2015) offers five main features of emerging adulthood: identity exploration; instability (in love, work, and place of residence); growing self-focus; feeling in-between (neither adolescent nor adult); and optimism about possibilities. Individuals within this exploratory, fluid period of life view themselves as being "on the way to adulthood—but not there yet" (Arnett, 2015).

While not entirely adult, college students are not children and shouldn't be infantilized unfairly. Still, as Margaret H. Mack (1999) remarks, they don't enter college or graduate school as fully developed individuals. "The institutional hierarchy that distinguishes faculty from students may reinforce other imbalances due to gender, age, and experiential differences...Because the faculty member and his or her colleagues are responsible for grading the student, for writing recommendations, and for providing references that will impact the student's life and career, the faculty's institutional role enacts a power imbalance even when faculty and students are close in age or of the same sex" (Mack, 1999).

I also struggle with the notion of student agency. Because of the psychological mechanism of obedience to authority, I don't believe it's possible for students to effectively express self-determination with faculty, even if the student feels they're making autonomous decisions. Giving consent doesn't dispel the potential harms a sexual relationship can bring to the student or into the academic setting. The student is unlikely to be able to predict the consequences of their diminished power in the relationship, rendering their consent superficial. Furthermore, as Bellas and Gossett (2001) put forth, "Agency on the part of the student does not eliminate the possibility that a professor might have exerted subtle pressure on the student to become involved or to stay involved longer than the student desired. Neither does it eliminate other power issues from the relationship."

Among their duties, professors are expected to support students as they develop decision-making skills and explore their autonomy. So then, making the claim that students are fully autonomous, while learning how to be autonomous, is pretty absurd.

Academics who've had—or wish to preserve the ability to have—sexual relationships with students are motivated to believe these relationships are acceptable. This is understandable, as all of us are psychologically driven to defend our actions and beliefs. But, when individuals in positions of authority promote their interests over those of the people they serve, the results are destructive. By holding a magnifying glass to this population of potential young lovers and illuminating their personal and social vulnerabilities, the academics' arguments are revealed as superficial and idealistic at best, and at worst, rooted in selfish lust.

*

According to Kitchener (1988), "Role theory tells us that expectations are not consistently perceived; thus, even though professionals may believe their actions are consistent, students, clients, and other consumers of their services may not perceive them in the same way." So, even if faculty and administrators have tolerant or supportive attitudes toward student-professor relationships, the students themselves may view them as problematic. Several studies have determined this to be the case.

Ei and Bowen (2002) surveyed the opinions of 480 undergraduates regarding five types of student-instructor relationships. Responses revealed that students held no strong opinion about student-instructor business involvement (such as a student babysitting for their professor), and felt off-campus group activities between students and professors were completely appropriate. The three other types viewed as generally inappropriate included doing favors for faculty and activities where the faculty person and student were alone together. "Sexual relationships were rated the least appropriate," with no significant difference of opinion detected based on class standing, which Ei and Bowen (2002) believe supports "the argument that students develop appropriate attitudes about these potentially difficult relationships early in, or prior to, their academic career."

Another study involving 158 undergraduates examined a wider range of potential student-faculty relations: business, counseling, friendship, professional, and sexual. Results indicated that "faculty roles were viewed as most appropriate by students when there was no confusion about the professional versus personal nature of the relationships...Social, friendship, and dating and sexual relationships, on the other hand, were viewed as more problematic," with sexual relationships rated as significantly less appropriate (Holmes et al., 1999). From their findings, Holmes et al. (1999) concluded, "it appears that students have rather clear views that relationships between faculty and students that have sexual overtones are inappropriate and that relationships consistent with the professional/academic role are appropriate."

Students' perceptions relating to the ethicality of student-faculty sexual intimacy have also been investigated. In their study, Skinner et al. (1995) asked undergraduate participants to assign ratings—from unquestionably not ethical to unquestionably ethical—to fifteen behavior items. The behaviors were categorized by Skinner et al. (1995) as overt ("both faculty and student are readily aware"), covert ("the student is likely to be completely unaware of the behavior"), and ambiguous ("the actions are not necessarily sexual, but may be related to sexual interactions"). These items ranged from hugging a student (ambiguous), to having sexual thoughts about a student (covert), to being sexually intimate with a student (overt). Overall, students reported that student-faculty intimacy was ethically inappropriate, "with at least 50 [percent] of the students rating 12 of the 15 behaviors as rarely ethical or unquestionably not ethical" (Skinner et al., 1999). In addition, they highlight student reactions to covert behavior items, reporting that while "these cognitive and affective behaviors can occur with no awareness on the part of the student," the students considered these to be "generally inappropriate and appeared to cause some discomfort to them" (Skinner et al., 1999).

The researchers also touched on an expected finding related to the ethical perceptions of student-invited intimacy. "Given the frequent resistance to classify student-faculty consensual sexual relationships as inappropriate," Skinner et al. (1999) remark, "we anticipated that the students would be most accepting of this student-initiated sexual interaction, a relationship intended to be clearly consensual. However, the reverse was found...Perhaps the participants believed that students are vulnerable and professors should recognize and respect this vulnerability, including showing restraint even if a student attempts to initiate sexual intimacy."

The results of an exploratory study show the classroom environment can be negatively impacted by student perceptions of faculty persons known to engage in multiple relationships. Chory and Offstein (2016) report "that when undergraduate students perceive their professor engages in behaviors characterized by simple socializing, alcohol consumption, and/or sexual activity with students, undergraduates predict that their own incivility in the professor's class is likely to increase. Students report that they are more likely to come to the multiple relationship professor's class under the influence of drugs and alcohol, to swear and use vulgarity in the class, and to disregard the instructor's rules and schedules." To avoid these disruptive effects, Chory and Offstein (2016) suggest that 1) "faculty should avoid sexual or drinking relationships with students," 2) "faculty should be friendly with students but not friends with them," and 3) encourage the use of "performance management principles" aimed to enhance student interaction and accountability, and to specify the instructor's roles as a model of professional conduct.

All considered, if students are assumed to be fully adult persons with agency, why not invest in their opinions? The majority have a negative view of student-faculty sexual involvement; therefore, I would contend that it actually undermines students' own beliefs about their personal and educational welfare by arguing in favor of professor-student sexual intimacy.

*

In the former section, I mentioned how research on professor-student sexual relationships is sparse. Most of the literature I've found is centered on their ethicality. There are a few studies on the prevalence of these relationships, but these are older, narrow in scope, and offer varying conclusions. I was unable to track down any empirical research regarding the social or psychological consequences for students following sexual intimacy—designated consensual or otherwise—with faculty persons.

Why not? A coworker once offered an answer after listening to my complaints during a smoke break. "The same people who'd do the research are from the same group who fuck their students," he scoffed. "They don't want to do any research that might show that what they're doing is wrong—and it probably would!"

Another reason for the gap in the literature could result from how these relationships are defined by researchers. Because of the power disparity between students and instructors, sexual intimacy is often categorized as sexual harassment, even if students felt the intimacy was welcomed at the time of reporting. Sexual harassment consists of sexualized verbal and physical conduct, and includes behaviors like the use of sexual epithets, name-calling, misuse of pornographic images, molestation and other forms of sexual contact, and rape (MacKinnon, 2016). This broad categorization has made it challenging to find information specific to student-professor sexual relationships: how often they occur, and whether they should be generally considered exploitative based on students' reactions.

Albeit sparse, the available data is pretty alarming.

Pope, Levenson, and Schover (1979) examined the responses of 481 anonymous individuals from the field of psychotherapy; twelve percent of teachers, four percent of supervisors, and three percent of administrators admitted to having had sexual contact with their students. "Of the female respondents who received their degrees within the last six years," Pope et al. (1979) emphasize that "25 [percent] had had sexual contact with their psychology educators," such as teachers and clinical supervisors. For women who'd had sex while students, 50 percent "disagreed that such activity could benefit both parties," and only two percent of all respondents affirmed that sexual relationships between students and their psychology teachers can be beneficial for both parties (Pope et al., 1979).

Glaser and Thorpe (1986) acquired 464 anonymous responses from women with backgrounds in clinical psychology, 17 percent of whom reported having had sexual contact with one or more educators with "the greater proportion of the contact occur[ring] prior to or during a professional working relationship." Respondents were asked their judgements of the sexual intimacy, which had substantially changed with time. "Although only 28 [percent] said they had experienced some degree of coercion at time of the contact, 51 [percent] now see some degree of coercion, and although 36 [percent] saw an ethical problem then, 55 [percent] see one now. Finally, 40 [percent] saw some hindrance to the working relationship then, but 51 [percent] see some hindrance now. Those changes match the current judgments of 95 [percent] of all respondents that any sexual contact between a student and an educator during a working relationship is likely to be coercive, harmful, and unethical to a considerable degree" (Glaser & Thorpe, 1986).

Miller and Larrabee (1995) came to similar conclusions. From a survey of 315 female counselors, six percent reported sexual contact with one or more educator or supervisor. These women also came to view these "as more coercive and more harmful to the working relationship than they did at the time" (Miller & Larrabee, 1995). The authors propose their change in perspective may result from a growing awareness of professional ethics after the counseling students graduated. Importantly, Miller and Larrabee (1995) also caution that students may rationalize the educator's sexual behaviors as acceptable if these are not clearly identifiable as harassment, explaining "if students willingly respond and become involved sexually, they may not perceive themselves to be harassed, especially if they're in awe of the educator or supervisor."

It's quite troubling that with time and additional life

experience, many students come to judge their involvement as less voluntary. Pope et al. (1979) also discovered that students who'd been sexually involved with an educator were at higher risk of repeating these behaviors once they became educators themselves (which I can't help comparing to statistics on child abuse victims who go on to perpetuate abuse as adults). But, the results of these studies come from surveys rather than interviews, so it's impossible to determine why respondents came to the conclusions they did.

I located two qualitative papers based on interviews with both faculty and students, discussing their relationships. Within each, the authors note some of the same limitations to their findings, including small sample sizes and the possibility of dishonest answers. They point out how few professors would admit they had pressured students for sex, as well as the unlikelihood of soliciting the participation of students who felt victimized. As a result, the authors of both studies stress that while their research saw little in the way of exploitation, they still recognize it as a potential within these relationships.

The first study drew on in-depth interviews with eleven students (eight female and three male) and fourteen faculty members (eleven male and three female). From the information they acquired, Skeen and Nielsen (1983) "tentatively conclude that student-faculty relationships are in many ways like other sexual relationships—i.e. based on similar interests, attitudes, and compatibility, as well as sexual attraction"—but what distinguishes them is the overlapping of public and private roles. For example, Skeen and Nielsen (1983) uncovered "some evidence of academic favoritism," such as "accepting a late paper" and "allowing a student to complete an independent study after the grade has been recorded." With respect to favoritism and its implications, the authors remark on the students' uneasiness and how this was reflected in their general attitudes toward student-faculty affairs. "When asked whether or not they thought such relationships were a good idea, the majority responded that they were not," Skeen and Nielsen (1983) confirm, further arguing, "this is precisely the issue which makes such a relationship problematic—that someone in a publicly scrutinized role is in a position to judge or evaluate another with whom he has an intimate relationship." Skeen and Nielsen (1983) further insist the appearance of mutual compliance doesn't refute the existence of abuse, adding how "a student may 'voluntarily' participate because s/he believes that otherwise there would be negative consequences." All told, despite focusing on the questionable effects of compounding public and private roles, the authors continue to recognize how the power disparity can influence students' judgement.

The second study, conducted by Bellas and Gossett (2001), involved ten professors (five male and five female) and fifteen students (all female); in total, the respondents represented twenty distinct relationships. On the issue of compromised objectivity, Bellas and Gossett (2001) found none of the relationships began until after the professor's supervisory role had concluded, and yet, "in six of the twenty relationships, students took additional classes and/or continued as advisees after becoming involved with professors."

Bellas and Gossett (2001) say they were "sympathetic to the concerns about student consent," and that "the issue of consent was clearly important in the minds of our respondents, but none of the students felt coerced to initiate or to sustain their relationships." When questioned about issues of power, all faculty respondents felt their relationship was equitable. On the other hand, "Students were more likely than professors to perceive inequities in their relationships. This was particularly true of students whose relationships had ended"—several of whom "cited power and control issues as contributing to the demise of the relationship" (Bellas & Gossett, 2001). Still, "only four respondents (three students and one female professor) said they would not participate in a consensual relationship again, all citing power differences as the major reason" (Bellas & Gossett, 2001).

"In general," Bellas and Gossett (2001) state "both faculty and student respondents tended to view their own relationships as exceptional or special" and "were glad that they had become involved." However, the majority of respondents "recognized the difficulties associated with these relationships and most advised others *not* to pursue them, particularly while in supervisory situations" (Bellas & Gossett, 2001). Finally, when asked their opinions of policies meant to regulate faculty-student consensual relationships, most professors and the majority of students supported university policies that prohibited romantic intimacy under supervisorial conditions.

One might assume these studies undermine my beliefs because the results aren't totally congruent with my own experiences. In fact, I feel this research is valuable because it highlights how the power discrepancy between parties is concerning, most often for the student. Instances of abuse don't have to be present for the power imbalance to negatively impress upon the low-power partner; the power disparity does, however, increase the potential for abuse.

The papers also mention conflicting interests, throwing doubt on the objectivity of a professor who actively evaluates the performance of a student with whom they've been sexually intimate. Special treatment of some kind is bound to happen. This is worrisome, given how instructor-student involvement can negatively influence third parties. As Mack (1999) says, "relationships between faculty and students do not happen in a vacuum." When a professor introduces sexuality to the educational process, "students are deprived of the mentoring trust that should foster their intellectual development and personal growth" (Mack, 1999). This extends beyond the couple, straining the trust and academic commitment of the professor's other students. The student-partner, too, can suffer from classmates' jealousy and judgments of their motivations in dating the faculty person.

What of the student-partner's own ability to remain objective as they attend classes, study, and do coursework? In response, Dziech and Hawkins (1998) state, "Human beings cannot easily separate work and school from the successes, frustrations, and failures of personal relationships; from the expectations, needs, and demands of spouses or lovers. It is ludicrous to assume a student will be able to maintain perfect calm while her professor-lover lectures on a Jack Updike novel if she suspects him of infidelity or fears he is about to reject her. Nor is it likely that one would be receptive to hearing about differential equations from a math professor with whom she's had a quarrel."

Dziech and Hawkins (1998) speak to further challenges faced by the student, as they strive to preserve their faculty-partner's acceptance: "If she falls short intellectually, she relinquishes the approbation of her lover as well as her teacher; if she fails to meet his expectations in bed, she will feel that not even brilliant academic performance can restore her tarnished image. Conversely, differentiating genuine academic achievement from favoritism becomes difficult. How can she know if an A means exceptional work, reward for compliance, or acknowledgement of an exceptional sexual accomplishment? And what about a D or an F?"

Considering these issues in total—the interference caused by a professor's power, the failure of objectivity, and the threats to the student's academic self-image—it's understandable most students report they wouldn't recommend dating faculty to their peers, even if they felt their own relationships were rewarding.

Ultimately, faculty-student relationships are far more complex and precarious than is conventionally understood. The professor may genuinely care for their student-partner and strive to promote equality in the relationship. But, there's no guarantee their efforts will result in fully realized autonomy on the part of the student—especially if the student continues to be within their radius of authority. No matter how exceptional the faculty-student couple may believe themselves to be, they cannot absolve themselves of their social context. No student can "consent" themselves out of the vulnerabilities defined by their lack of institutional power, just as no professor can love or appreciate them enough to subvert the influence of their authority over them. "To consent, one must be able 'to feel or perceive with'; and while equality of feeling between professors and students may arguably be possible, equality of perception clearly is not...The two may feel enormous physical, emotional, and even spiritual attraction; they may be compatible in every respect. But their perceptions of the relationship will inevitably differ because one hand and one hand only holds the pen...and so long as that is the case, the two cannot be regarded as equals" (Dziech & Hawkins, 1998).

I further believe, as Mack (1999) says, that "students should have the opportunity to learn in an atmosphere free from potential favoritism and sexual intimidation that can come with sexual relationships." I feel the potential for sexual intimidation is always present in professor-student relationships, but I also understand the "power differential, no consent" rationale, as Srinivasan (2020) puts it, doesn't fully articulate why these relationships are problematic. Furthermore, as social critic and scholar Andrew Delbanco (2012) asks, "What, exactly is at stake in college, and why should it matter how much or how little goes on there?"

The fundamental purpose of faculty-student contact is education. "At its core," Delbanco (2012) explains, "a college should be a place where young people find help for navigating the territory between adolescence and adulthood. It should provide guidance, but not coercion, for students trying to cross that treacherous terrain on their way toward self-knowledge. It should help them develop certain qualities of mind and heart requisite for reflective citizenship." Yet, these goals are greatly jeopardized when the helping relationship between faculty and students is overshadowed by a secondary personal relationship, and immediately sabotaged once sexuality is introduced. Regardless of whether the intimacy could be argued as consensual, when a professor has sexual contact with students, they deny them their right to a fair, well-rounded education and stunt their growth as future citizens and successful, healthy members of society. They have betrayed them and their principal duties as educators and mentors.

*

An increasing number of colleges and universities have adopted policies to restrict sexual relationships between their faculty and students. In an article from *Inside Higher Ed*, professor Tara Richards is quoted as saying, “There’s still wide variation in terms of policies” and the more successful institutions have a “proactive” approach, “taking into account their own student populations, norms and shared governance structures,” while less successfully, “institutions change their policies in response to incidents on their campuses or elsewhere” due to fears of liability (Flaherty, 2018).

I reckon most colleges fall into the latter category. Applying preventative measures isn’t something American institutions are very good at; hence, changes to policy and law generally come as a reaction to major events or public outcry. This may be, in part, because our culture largely suffers from the superstition that speaking a difficult truth will conjure it into existence. And when bad things do happen, we like to think of them as unique—as acts of god, even—rather than representations of the constructs around us and how these speak to our societal failures, including that of institutional indifference, neglect, or blind idealism.

My alma mater failed me because they had no established policies to regulate sexual relationships between faculty, staff, and students. This news stunned those who'd assumed the university had such policies, including members of the Faculty Senate—or so I was told. The promise of new policies offered some consolation, but consider how differently my complaint against Jack would have been handled if those policies were already in place.

As I drafted this text, some friends inquired about Title IX, the federal civil rights law which defines sexual harassment in higher education as illegal sex-based discrimination that deprives students of unfettered access to education. What are my thoughts on Title IX? Is it comprehensive enough? They also drew my attention to the Trump Administration's so-called "reforms," which went into effect in August 2020. One friend directed me to an article about the changes, urging, "Hurry and finish your book."

The truth is, I have little to say because my circumstances weren't found to be consistent with federal regulations. The language used by Title IX to define sexual harassment specifies *unwelcomed* sexualized speech and behaviors; it wasn't drafted in such a way to account for the complexities of discerning genuine consent when a power imbalance is present.

According to Title IX Coordinator Linda Barrow's interpretation of the law, my willingness to become romantically involved with Jack overrode any coercion on his part. Although I was groomed and manipulated into providing consent, I consented nonetheless. Dr. Barrow also resisted the view that Jack had created a hostile educational environment for me—even though he'd masturbated in front of me when he was supposed to have been instructing me, or made out with me at the conclusions of our meetings. I guess our private dating arrangement somehow made these in-office behaviors acceptable, but I certainly didn't learn a goddamn thing from them—except to deepen my sense of intimidation.

To rectify the limitations of Title IX, colleges and universities have been urged to implement their own policies to govern faculty-student sexual involvement. These policies tend to have the following goals: 1) "to protect the integrity of the school's educational mission through professional conduct standards," 2) "to protect the students and third parties," 3) "to protect the image and reputation of the school," and 4) "to avoid legal liability" (Richards et al., 2014). The regulations, however, differ between institutions, leading to "confusion among the university community as to what is considered acceptable and ethical behavior" (Richards et al., 2014). As relayed by Mack (1999), current policies may be classified into four basic types: "advisory policies that discourage but do not expressly prohibit faculty-student sexual relationships"; limited bans which forbid relationships when the professor has direct academic charge of the student; those that both discourage professors from entering relationships with students *and* prohibit relationships where the professor holds charge over the student; and complete bans on faculty-student sexual relations.

Through an analysis of 55 universities, Richards et al. (2014) uncovered that "although some policies were found to be more prohibitive than others, and the overwhelming majority of university policies"—98 percent—"acknowledged the issue of power differentials, all of the sampled universities contained loopholes that permitted consensual sexual relationships between faculty and students regardless of status... Even in instances where faculty knowingly engaged in prohibited behaviors, policies allowed for disclosure and alternative remedies for overlooking these indiscretions." Richards et al. (2014) report that "just over half of the sampled policies outlined consequences for violating the university's recommendations," and the majority "used ambiguous language regarding penalties, indicating that some consequence would be exacted but not defining any tangible punishment...The lack of clarity and consistency within policies omits any true sense of the risks associated with such behavior." Of the policies that proposed sanctions, many were concerned with the faculty person's failure to report the relationship rather than engaging in the relationship itself, which Richards et al. (2014) contend "tacitly implies university acceptance of such behavior."

It's rather shameful for universities to have policies that widely address students' diminished consent and the potential for exploitation, and remark on the damaging perceptions of unfairness and favoritism to third parties—but fail to hold faculty responsible to their reporting duties and refuse to dole out appropriate sanctions when these policies are violated. Simply drafting and enacting a policy is not enough; it must be comprehensive and actionable.

Earlier in this section, I drew from bell hooks's (2003) writings, and though I mostly disagree with her conclusions, she raises some noteworthy concerns about all students being regarded as potential victims and all educators as potential abusers, in addition to policy enforcement being used strictly to punish professors rather than empower students. In reference to her own sexual experience with a professor, hooks (2003) claims, "As a student, it was precisely silence and taboo that made coercion and exploitation more possible."

I firmly believe that knowledge acquisition is vital to individual and group empowerment. Educating students on matters related to sexual relationships with professors and their university's policies and reporting procedures will better equip them to make informed decisions about their academic experiences, and whether these should include sexual relations with instructors. If one cause of taboo is ignorance, then thorough training of both students and faculty could alleviate its influence; doing so would also address the "silence" about such relationships and their implications. However, since students lack institutional power compared to faculty, I don't feel the notion of them being viewed as potential victims can be helped. As such, professors may continue to be cast as potential abusers. Regardless, this can be offset by faculty who practice empathy for their students' circumstances, maintain professional boundaries, follow their university's policies, and refrain from sexual contact with students.

Just as friends have approached me about Title IX, I've also been asked to share my opinion on the best policy type. At first, I struggled to come up with an answer, hesitantly sharing the opinion of DeChiara (1988), who says, "No flat ban should apply to faculty-student relationships in which the teacher has no evaluative role. Not all faculty-student relationships present problems, and to ban them all would be unreasonably to deny to teachers and students one channel through which a mutually fulfilling relationship might arise." Even as the victim of professorial sexual exploitation, I remain a romantic at heart. Love is the only aspect of the human experience that can truly thwart life's inherent difficulties and give someone a sense of connection and purpose. And yet, for all its rewards, love is messy—and like all else, it doesn't occur in a vacuum.

I've adopted the opinion of Dziech and Hawkins (1998), who "bluntly" state that the college campus "is not a dating service. It is not the only and certainly not the best location for students and professors to seek potential mates. Students are on campus primarily to be educated, and faculty to teach and engage scholarly activity. Faculty contracts do not specify and students do not pay tuition for opportunities to engage in amorous adventures. When faculty-student romances are prohibited, educators are obliged to pursue sexual release with more appropriate partners, and students are less likely to engage in behaviors that places them at risk."

What of situations in which the faculty-partner has no supervisorial role over the student? Surely then, a sexual relationship involving the student's genuine consent is more probable, and therefore the potential for harm is lessened—right? To this point, Dziech and Hawkins (1998) assert, "it is impossible to ensure that the paths of a professor and his student-partner will never cross or never cast a shadow on the paths of others. Even when the faculty member does not bear direct responsibility for the student, there are always means by which he or she could exercise influence on the student's fate. If, for instance, a romance ends in serious acrimony and the student attends a class conducted by the ex-lover's best friend or office mate, the student may have very legitimate reasons to feel vulnerable. In very small departments or programs there is also a genuine likelihood that eventually the student would have no choice but to take a course from the partner in the failed relationship."

I prefer total bans on sexual relations between professors and students, as they are damaging to both faculty and students, and to institution of higher education. "Although bans cannot prevent amorous relationships, they do discourage them. They establish legal and ethical positions for faculty, administrators, and institutions. They communicate to the campus a required standard of behavior" (Dziech & Hawkins, 1998). In short, they send a message. Although prohibition is not prevention, it can offer safeguards that are "the best that beleaguered institutions can hope for as they struggle with more complexities and challenges than ever before" (Dziech & Hawkins, 1998).

Delbanco (2012) expounds on these challenges, writing that "the American college is going through a period of wrenching change, buffeted by forces—globalization; economic instability; the ongoing revolution in information technology; the increasingly evident inadequacy of K-12 education; the elongation of adolescence; the breakdown of faculty tenure as an academic norm; and, perhaps most important, the collapse of consensus about what students should know—that make its task more difficult and contentious than ever before." Certainly, higher education has much to contend with in order to progress in its mission. To remain relevant, permanent structures of the American landscape, universities must cultivate a reflexive and proactive institutional culture rooted in serving the needs of their consumers. This, quite frankly, can never be fully achieved so long as professors are permitted to endanger their students' physical, psychological, and intellectual well-being with sexual contact.

▪

After the events of 2016, I've developed this overbearing need for constant narration. During even a five-minute drive, the stereo talks. As I fold laundry, cook, or wash dishes, my laptop or phone babble loudly. I've consumed thousands of hours of audiobooks and podcasts. I've watched and rewatched countless taped lectures, movies, documentaries, and television shows—including *Mad Men*, which I've viewed in its entirety four times in the last few years.

Music has made a slow comeback, but it doesn't always cut it. Bereft of a plot or the anchor of a thesis, my thoughts diverge. Painful memories surface and bob like reckless buoys. But every so often, I give myself permission to remember, to sense it all over again.

Jack's eyes were a magnetic, icy blue. When he laughed, he sometimes snorted, which I think embarrassed him, but was actually rather adorable. If he was really tired, his voice took on a childish octave. Goofy, he was sometimes, and fidgety too. He tended to absent-mindedly tear up pieces of tape or paper and build odd, little structures during meetings or dinner engagements.

The particular curl of his lips as he spoke. The dense and bready feel of his flesh in my hands. How his beard's shadow sandpapered the skin on my nose and chin during feverish kissing. The faded purple bruises he left on my thighs with his teeth. I can still smell the laundry soap in his clothes. If I try, I can remember the taste of his breath—but I don't want to. Neither do I want to remember how he'd always rub his nose against my clitoris when he went down on me. I don't want to remember how the ceiling fan flapped noisily above as he weighed me down into the fibers of his mattress.

People have told me I should be angrier. I should have tried to get Linda Barrow fired. I should have inquired more lawyers, pressed harder for legal action.

Some said they'd always known JB was a creep. Good for them.

Others said I could have walked out. I could have said no. He was a serial cheater, maybe a sex-addict. What's the big deal? Everyone gets cheated on at some point. Men like him exist in the world, and I should have seen it coming. I should have known Jack was going to dupe, mind-fuck, rape, and abandon me.

Or they can't believe it. He was such a great guy. They can't imagine him squishing a bug, let alone treating numerous women like disposable meat puppets. It couldn't be that he did anything too awful. Perhaps he made mistakes—it happens. Magda, Phoebe, Irene, others, and I just handled it badly, blew it way out of proportion. There was something about us that cried out for Jack's behaviors, so really, it's our fault he hurt us—if you can even call it that.

They resist because they revered him. They credit him for their career paths and other successes—just as I had. On the verge of dropping out, he'd talked them into staying in class and pressing on. He wrote cover letters and references. He helped them apply for master's programs or find jobs after graduation. His motivations seemed calibrated to support his students and colleagues, not to harm them. That was unthinkable.

In the United States, we champion personal liberty, individualism, and choice. We like to think we have endless capacity to be contrary and resilient, and emphasize free will. We can't accept that, under the right conditions, we can bow to coercion and adopt attitudes and behaviors that result in personal costs. Instead, we promote the power of the individual to the extent that we blind ourselves to the sociopsychological pressures that can undermine our autonomy.

Similarly, we don't like to think about these issues. Learning about intimate partner abuse or exploitation is depressing. We lack patience for nuance, and we fear that the fact of someone else's misfortune might somehow contaminate us. So, we dismiss their woeful tales and swaddle ourselves with deluded biases. We blame them for their hardships, whether it be through their own misguided actions or due to some inherent personal defect. By believing people bring wrong upon themselves, we're confident we will dodge those struggles. But, avoiding the difficulties around us doesn't make them go away; it allows them to grow stronger, feeding off the darkness of our neglect. Ignorance only puts us at greater risk of ending up like those we sought to shut down.

I'm genuinely happy for the former students and colleagues whose interactions with Jack were pleasant and rewarding. What I or other survivors feel and believe doesn't need to redefine their perceptions of his treatment toward them. He didn't hurt you, but he hurt us. These truths can coexist.

I don't have all of the answers, though I think I have enough, to which these pages can attest. There are limitations to what I've covered, as with any research. Most notably, I can best speak to my own experiences, pondering, digging, and conclusions. I was also constricted by what materials I could access freely or with the help of friends in academia. With that being said, this text is an overview of subjects; it's not comprehensive. To fully appreciate the concepts and ideas I've relayed would require decades of avid research, resulting in volumes of work. This book is already on the longer side, and honestly, I'm tired and ready to move on to other, less emotionally-charged projects.

It's a little ironic, but in writing this, I've continued to follow Jack's direction. On occasion, he'd end lectures with a smile and a raised fist. "Okay gang," he'd announce, "fight the power!" Sometimes after releasing me from his grasp, he'd wipe his mouth dry with the back of his hand and open the office door. As I slipped past him into the hallway, he'd beam mischievously, saying, "Keep up the good work, Cal. Until next time, fight the power!"

Okay, Jack. Here's to blowing back the thick shades of societal cowardice and failure. Here's to fighting you and everything you represent: abuse of status and power, and academia's dirty, little secret. Here's to transcendence and survival. Here's to the end of silence.

REACT TO IT ALL

"In these hard times, you must be plucky and keep your head unbowed. The world belongs to the brave."

-Jenny Marx

"I am trying to describe these things not to relieve them in my present boundless misery, but to sort out the portion of hell and the portion of heaven in that strange, awful, maddening world… The beastly and the beautiful merged at one point, and it is that borderline I would like to fix, and I feel I fail to do so utterly."

-Vladimir Nabokov, *Lolita*

"The desire I feel is somehow not earthly-it's otherworldly, as in, I long for the other, for the life I could have led, there, or that one, there."

-Chelsea Hodson, "The End of Longing"

▪

It started snowing, so I was forced to stop jogging every quarter mile to wipe fog and snowflakes from my glasses. My nose dripped because I was also crying.

Eventually, I looked around and seeing no one, I flopped down on the curb and succumbed. I wept for a long time, and when it was over, I surveyed the streets again. But, it was fine; no one had seen me.

However, I wasn't fine. I couldn't tell if the cold sweats were because of the combined weather and exercise, or from the overwhelming churn of anxiety and paranoia. During this trek, I'd seen both a dead cardinal and, farther up the block, a dead mouse beside the sidewalk. Both times, I'd gasped and spit over my shoulder to ward off the evil eye.

I've always loved animals. Surely these were bad omens.

Then, I could smell death, and I ran from it. Gradually, much of my body slipped from existence. I forgot where my knees were, or that I had knees. Or ankles. But, I remained attached to my torso, and this was real to me—home to the maelstrom of aching rage, helplessness, and uncertainty. It hung above another place I'd forgotten, the place where he'd wormed his fingers, penis, and lies.

I spit again.

Somehow, the meat and bones of myself were dragged back to Alex's house. As I walked, my head clamored.

If I have to go to the hospital, then people will fucking understand and they'll start treating me seriously, as seriously as he hurt me. No one understands how much this hurts. I just need to wake up wake up, where am I where is the house?

Aloud, I spilled, "I cannot do this! It's too big and hurts too bad!"

Somehow, I stumbled upon the house, where I smoked a

cigarette on the porch and looked at funny pictures on my phone. This didn't work, so I tried stretching and taking slow, methodical breaths.

To no avail, the thoughts scratched, succeeding in their rule of my consciousness. A drawer opened, and I pulled a razor from a packet Alex's brother kept in the kitchen. Before commencing, I paused to listen. Alex was still asleep in the bedroom. It was still snowing outside. I was still alone.

I tugged the flesh of my belly over the kitchen counter. Rolls. Bread dough. Slicing challah for *kiddish*.

Made obvious by the countless zigzags of white, pinched skin, this wasn't just *like* ritual—it *was* ritual. But, I needed this time to be deep enough. As deep as the hurt ran. Deep enough to let it escape.

My hand swiped and swiped. The cuts bled so much that I packed a paper towel into the waistband of my athletic pants to control the flow. It wasn't what I'd wanted, however. The slashes were deep, but they were not deep enough, by my measure, to warrant medical intervention.

Coward, I thought, though not entirely with aim. I couldn't afford a trip to the emergency room anyway.

It was enough to clear my head. Within minutes of stashing the razorblade in my sewing kit, I calmly ate some almonds and watched a documentary.

*

Through the chill of another early afternoon, I pounded pavement again. This time, I'd glided into that meditative headspace one welcomes on a jog. I was feeling oddly analytical and embraced this.

In her follow-up letter, Linda Barrow had isolated a section of the diary entry wherein I'd described kissing Jack for the first time. Her opinion had been that this showed my consent, as I'd presumed Jack wouldn't have touched me if I hadn't initiated.

Mounting a hill, I realized something wasn't quite right. I rewound my memories, dissecting the initial visits to his house: walking there, being there, and walking home again. Something flickered and stalled. I stopped running, planted my feet under a tree beside the road, and probed my brain further.

My own diary had been inaccurate. I'd stupidly forgotten to include what now seemed like the most imperative detail.

During my very first visit to his house, he'd scooted across his couch to show me an article on his phone. His leg had squashed up against mine, and the closeness had made me uneasy.

I'd been wearing a handkerchief to conceal my hair. On my top half, I had on a polka-dot camisole, a long-sleeved red shirt, and a dark grey cardigan. Then, a pair of black leggings with warm socks scrunched at the ankles. And when I'd looked down, I saw it: splayed across my leg was a wide palm and shapely fingers tipped with short, clean fingernails.

Jack had put his hand on my thigh.

My limbs had stiffened, and he casually pulled away to reposition himself on the other side of the sofa.

Oh, but was I sure? Was I recalling this right?

Around two in the morning, I'd briskly tramped home through the cold blackness. I'd pondered it then too: *did this mean he likes me, or was this just meant as a friendly touch?* Maybe he really was just readjusting himself on the couch.

Later, during my third or fourth visit to his house—but before we'd kissed—hadn't he offered me a neck rub? Ah, yes!—and I'd submitted, shrugging down to a tank top and sitting between his legs so he could massage the ache from my shoulders. But, I hadn't journaled about this either.

Oh my god. *Cal, you utter fucking klutz.*

Walking home now, I laughed at my bone-headed forgetfulness, although I was also horribly shaken up.

What a brazen motherfucker. Of course, I kissed him first.

He'd summoned the initiation from me. He'd set the table, served me, and waited for me to take the first bite.

Damnit! Why hadn't I mentioned this before? Why had I failed to record such a momentous fact?

I found the bedroom light on. Alex was awake, and I approached him with my recollection. "I'm such an idiot," I mourned. "Why hadn't I fucking written about all of that? Linda could have read it, and maybe things would have been different. No wonder she decided that everything was consensual."

Alex was still groggy and rubbed his eyes before beckoning me into his lap. "So, you're forgetting something," he began patiently. "There was no policy, remember? It wouldn't have stopped Linda from saying what he did was okay—even though it wasn't—because there wasn't anything in the faculty policies against it."

"Oh. Right. I totally forgot about that." My distress dissipated, and my head slung into his shoulder. "Fuck. You're right. It wouldn't have made any difference."

He hugged me. "It's fucking shitty, but you did everything you could."

*

By springtime, my angst was amplified by a renewed sense of insecurity. I still couldn't shake the feeling I'd missed something—something I should have done, another person I should have talked to.

An earlier comment had been imbedded like a splinter, occasionally pricking me when I didn't work to ignore it: "The university mishandled your complaint."

Holding my breath, I tracked down the name of a professor who specialized in administrative policy and law. I puttered outside of his office until he trudged by. Then, I nervously swooped in, asking if he had a few minutes to chat.

Dr. Perry didn't know me. A half-eaten doughnut hung from his mouth. Nevertheless, he shrugged and bid me into the office. He relocated a stack of papers from a chair to his desk and motioned for me to sit. I gulped, leaving the door cracked.

To start, I introduced myself and acknowledged my part in the Jack Blair scandal and his subsequent resignation. At this, Dr. Perry's eyes crinkled with sympathy.

I expressed my disinterest in filing a lawsuit against the university, but said that for my own peace of mind, I wanted some insight into the politics of my complaint. I'd been told the school may have mismanaged it, in terms of how it followed an administrative chain after Linda Barrow concluded her investigation.

"Can you tell me your thoughts on the case?" I asked. "Like, based on your impressions, should I be... Should things have happened differently?"

Dr. Perry was expertly polite. His responses were shaped with jargon, though his tone was gentle. He paused every so often to ensure I was following along.

He said he approved of the way administration had behaved. Yes, it was unusual that Dr. Barrow referred my case to Dean Witterman for review. However, Dr. Perry thought this signaled Linda's level of concern about the situation. Instead of leaving it alone after closing the matter herself, she requested involvement from the same superiors who managed the conditions of Jack's employment.

Dr. Perry then explained why Jack was asked to resign as opposed to being fired. In some ways, this was a *better* outcome. If he'd been fired, Jack could have opted to fight the decision by suing on the basis of wrongful discharge, which may have allowed him to remain on campus while the suit played out. Really, Dr. Perry remarked, one could interpret Jack's resignation as an admittance of guilt.

Even without a policy to regulate student-professor relationships, Dr. Perry pointed out there *are* policies to hold professors accountable to competent, responsible, and honest conduct. Because Jack's actions displayed a lack of competency and were irresponsible and greatly disruptive, there was adequate cause for disciplinary action. Proof he'd been engaging in a sexual relationship with a student whom he evaluated was reason enough, regardless of whether the relationship was abusive. Everything else—his two-timing with colleagues, the other students he'd pursued or manipulated—just furthered the imperative to request his resignation.

Astonished by this, I shifted in my seat. "Oh—oh, I had no idea."

Dr. Perry smiled gingerly. "I hope this information gives you some equanimity."

"It does, thank you," I said earnestly. Then, flushed with embarrassment, I hurried away, permitting him to finish his doughnut and prepare for a meeting. Outside, I fell onto a bench and exhaled for what felt like the first time in weeks.

Okay, I thought. *Let it go.*

*

"How are you doing with everything?" asked Magda. We stood at the counter of a bookstore café, waiting for mugs of tea. Outside, the sun was high, and the afternoon was warm, yet I wrapped my hands around my cup, shuddering.

"It's weird," I admitted. "I'm dealing with a lot of post-trauma stuff, though it's gradually getting better. I haven't been having as many nightmares, but things are still rough. I still feel hypervigilant and jumpy around people. So, I haven't been getting out as much."

She pouted sympathetically. "That's hard. I'm sorry to hear that."

"Sometimes, I forget that it happened to me. Does that

make sense? Like, I've heard people talking about it on campus, and the first thought that comes to mind is 'yeah, I heard about that too!' And then, I'm like, wait—that was me. I'm the student who reported him."

"Oh, wow."

"It's just hard to believe, I guess."

We carried our tea to a table near the back of the café. Our chairs creaked loudly as we settled into them.

"What about you?" I asked.

"Jack's dead to me," Magda stated firmly. Her tone softened as she elaborated. "Well, I mean, I know he's not *actually* dead, but that's how I've been thinking of him. Really though, I don't think about him at all. He's just...dead to me."

I nodded, impressed with her ability to mentally box him in a coffin and shut him away. "And you haven't heard from him?"

"No, he's changed his phone number. The last time I tried to call him was back in January, and the number was out of service. I don't have anything to say to him, and anything he'd try to say would just be a pack of lies."

"Does anyone know where he is?"

Magda shook her head and swallowed a sip from her mug. "Nope. No one has heard from him."

"Damn. So, he cut everyone off and totally dipped out, huh? I guess you'd have to, if your true self was unveiled."

She shrugged. "Maybe. The last time I talked to him, he'd been freaking out over finances and said something about moving into a cheaper house in town, but I doubt he'll stay."

"I heard he was hanging around here, though."

"Really?" Magda stiffened.

I shared the rumors I'd heard on campus. One student told me their friend ran into Jack at a gas station, buying cigarettes. When I remarked that Jack didn't smoke, he laughed and said, "Yeah, well, if I were him, I'd start smoking." If Jack bought cigarettes, I thought, he'd probably done it for someone else to show *what a great guy he is.*

A couple of other students mentioned their friends had seen Jack "at the club," and he avoided them when approached. Someone said Jack had "drastically changed his appearance"—shaved his head and facial hair, and lost a bunch of weight—which gave me the willies. Zach Cantor had complained to my friend Troy about potentially seeing Jack's car a couple of times and how it'd freaked him out.

About a month before, I thought I'd seen his car too. I'd driven into the town where both Magda and Zach lived—and where Jack had been spotted—to visit a couple of friends. I pulled up to a stoplight near the highway exit ramp. Before proceeding, I noticed the car beside me as it drove away. It was the same color, make, and model of Jack's car. In a desperate panic, I'd impulsively jerked around the block to try to catch up with the mystery vehicle, but it was gone.

Magda shivered and smoothed the goosebumps from her upper arms. "Well," she hesitated, "I hope he's not around here. I haven't seen him and I don't want to."

*

I returned to the East Coast to visit Kamyar. I was smoking outside of the airport terminal when his sleek black car pulled up to the curb. He waited to hug me until after I'd blown the last drag over my shoulder and tossed the filter in the trash.

At his apartment, we snacked on chocolates and mandarins, and watched a stand-up comedy special. When we finally slipped into his bed, our bodies curled into one another. I opened to him, and it was perfect and safe. Afterward, I cried only a little while he washed up in the bathroom.

Morning came, and I rolled away from Kamyar, who continued to snooze. I drifted into the living room with a mug of instant coffee and a book I'd started reading on the airplane. Wrapped in a blanket I'd found on its backrest, I nestled into the sofa.

My eyes strayed from the book when I noticed the shimmer of a couple of hairs clinging to the blanket's weave. Furrowing my brow, I pinched them off and held them against the daylight that poured through the floor-to-ceiling windows.

I'd done this once before at Jack's townhouse. Spread over the floor beside his couch, I extracted threads of long, blonde hair from the carpet and absently wondered when he'd last vacuumed.

Now—*blonde or grey?* If blonde, I couldn't say. If grey, they may be Kamyar's, shed from the top of his head, where his hair was the longest. Or from his mother or one of his sisters.

I hastily concluded they were blonde, dropped them on the rug, and tried to pretend the discovery had never happened. For the remainder of my visit, I said nothing about it.

But after my first night back home, I awoke in a state of panic. Half-dressed and an hour late to work, I was slumped on the edge of my bed, sobbing uncontrollably. *Not him too*, I begged. My dearest friend and lover of over a decade.

All day, I stewed. I snapped at coworkers, only to blubber apologetically when their eyes widened, heads tilted with concern. Outside, I pressed myself against the building and sucked down cigarette after cigarette. I called Amber and Bevel for advice and rambled with choked paranoia.

Obviously, I had to confront Kamyar. I was on to him. I knew about the blonde woman, who was taller than me, thinner, and had more tattoos. Unlike me, she had perfect skin and shaved her armpits, legs, and vulva. She dressed impeccably, and maybe that's how they met—at the gym or a restaurant where she'd waited on Kamyar—after he'd complimented her shoes or blouse. Before either of them knew it, she was angled across his sofa while his tongue flicked its way across her flawless breasts and hard, flat stomach.

The office closed, and I sped home to ring Kamyar. "I know you're lying to me about seeing other women," I launched. "I don't understand why you wouldn't just tell me the truth. Is it just easier to lie than go into detail or something?"

His shock was palpable as he sputtered through the receiver. "What have I lied to you about? Where is all of this coming from?"

I described finding the hairs, their length and color. Internally, I shrieked at the thought that I might have to get tested for STIs again.

"Hold on," Kamyar urged. "Yes, I've had friends over. I didn't mention it because it didn't seem significant." He listed their names and explained how long he'd known them, how they'd met, and when he'd last seen them.

Shame blanketed me until my knees met the ground outside where I stood, chain-smoking with one hand and clutching my phone with the other. "Oh," I repeated. "Oh. Okay."

"Cal, why would I ever lie to you? Since day one, you've always said you wouldn't mind, as long as I was honest with you. You've encouraged me to meet other women. It's not happened, but I know that if it did, I could talk to you about it. I know you'd be happy for me."

"Right, of course."

"I'm sorry. Obviously, these kinds of details matter to you, so—"

"No. I'm sorry," I interjected. "I was drawing parallels where there weren't any. I've been totally unreasonable."

"No, I'm sorry too," he insisted. "I should try to communicate with you more. It would help with your anxiety, huh?"

"Yes, it would. I should work on it too. I haven't been easy to reach either."

After a pause, Kamyar said, "You've been through so much. Jack was so awful to you. I mean, that's what this is about, right?"

I crushed my cigarette into the chipped mug I kept outside for butts. Suddenly aware of the phantom knife between my ears, my glasses bounced on my nose as I rubbed my temples.

Yes, exactly! Well done, you paranoid fucking idiot. This is KAMYAR, for godssakes!

"Cal?"

"Hmm," I hummed. "Sorry. My head is killing me. Um, but yeah. This really has much more to do with Jack than with you or how we're doing. I didn't mean to conflate things."

"Oh, *azizam*," he sighed, "I wish I were there. I wish I could hold you right now."

I swallowed, rocking on my heels, and pressed my palms into my eyes. "I wish you could too."

*

I didn't have the stomach to pick up my diploma until about a year after I'd graduated. At the registrar's counter, I signed for it, and a manila envelope was presented to me.

"Here you go!" the assistant sang. "Congratulations!"

My face reddened, eyes sprang tears. I gulped and covered my face. This confused the assistant, who fussed over her desk for a box of tissues.

The involuntary, emotional outpouring was damn near humiliating. "I'm sorry," I managed. "I just have bittersweet feelings about it all now."

"Aw, I'm sorry to hear that! I hope it's nothing [the university] has done."

I blotted my tears with a tissue. "No, but we'll see how they react to it all."

She frowned at this, so—*what do people normally say when they do this?*—I waved flippantly. "It's fine," I said. "Thank you. I'll have to start looking for a nice frame."

My sniffling continued as I shuffled home. Once inside, I peeked at the document again.

"...confers upon Callow Louise Phoenix the degree of Bachelors of Arts with all of its rights, privileges, and responsibilities. Given under the seal of the University, this thirteenth day of May, two thousand and sixteen. Cum Laude."

My name was spelled correctly. The grade point average I'd wrestled to maintain through endless semesters was noted. One of the signatures at the bottom belonged to Dean Witterman.

Sighing, I slid the diploma back into the envelope and pulled open the top drawer of a spare dresser in the living room. Here, I'd stowed other significant relics from the last two years.

My graduation cap and gown. The ropes and medals. The learning disability assessment report. Copies of newspapers with the articles containing my first-hand statements. And finally, the letter from Linda Barrow, wherein she'd concluded my relationship with Jack was consensual and he hadn't created a hostile educational environment for me.

I left my diploma on top of the pile, shut the drawer, and walked away, shaking my head.

*

We were at a bar located in the city's former manufacturing district: me, Stephen, his girlfriend Jenna, and one of their classmates. Outside on the smoking porch, I threw my head back to exhale above the crowd and sipped water, occasionally using my straw to stab the soggy slice of lemon in the bottom of the cup.

Stephen slurred through a philosophical explanation of socially-conscious urban design. I patiently tried to follow along, though my eyes wandered to the profiles in the groups around us. A handful of people were rounding the stairs and stopped to bare their IDs to the bouncer. As they passed the doorway, I saw Jack.

Automatically, my hand shot up to clasp Stephen's arm; in doing so, I created a loud *slap!* Both Jenna and her friend broke from their conversation to swing their heads toward the sound. I must have looked affright. Blood drained from my face. My ears rang.

"What is it? What's the matter?" They followed my gaze to the man I was staring at. "*Who* is it?" they revised.

"It's...it's not him," I realized aloud.

Stephen had pushed a protective shoulder between me and the doorway. Jenna shoved him aside to face me squarely. Her nose hovered some inches from mine.

"What happened?" she asked.

"I thought I saw Jack, but it's not him."

"Why? How do you know it's not him? What's different about that guy?"

The man's image bobbed over her head. "It's not him," I echoed. "His complexion is darker. He has brown eyes. His face is too oval-shaped. He's bald, but I heard Jack had changed his appearance, so I wasn't sure."

"Why did you think it was Jack? Does Jack dress like that?"

"Yeah, he wears button-ups and dark jeans. But, he'd never wear jeans that tight."

Jenna snickered, whispering, "Does he wear *Italian shoes* like that motherfucker?"

The man now sat behind us at a table near the back of the porch. His legs were crossed; one shoe dangled into the walkway: black and brown wingtips, with narrow, tight laces.

I chortled, "Yes, actually! He does. Goddamn it."

"What a piece of shit. They're both assholes and they don't even realize." Jenna's smile sparkled with sympathetic hatred.

The four of us were now staring at the man. Sensing the burn of our scrutiny, he glanced up and frowned as we all looked away.

I hung my head at the floor. "That poor bastard. He has no idea I'm over here hating him and he's not even Jack."

"Fuck him," Jenna dismissed, waving her glass. "Fuck them both. Who cares?" She straightened her shoulders. "Are you okay? Better now?"

"Yes, thank you."

"The trick is to see the differences," she explained. "When

you're having a flashback or being triggered, you can snap out of it by focusing on what's different from the thing or situation that traumatized you."

In unison, she and Stephen drew me into a hug that smothered the last of the throbbing panic in my chest. Our conversations picked back up, but my thoughts swam, disconnected. I continued to steal peeks at the man and his shoes.

One evening, I'd stood beside Jack in his closet as he removed a box from the top shelf. Inside was a pair of vintage-inspired black boots with hooked eyelets and thin black laces. I recognized them; he'd worn them to class when I'd taken Intro with him, six years earlier. "Why don't you wear them anymore?" I'd asked.

He kept them because he'd worn them in Poland, while he toured the grounds at Auschwitz. After leaving what remains of the camp, he said he took off those boots and never wore them again. They were now a hallowed keepsake, a stark reminder of human tragedy—something that inspired him and his work as both an artist and a sociologist.

At the time, I thought this gesture was utterly beautiful. My bones had hummed with admiration.

Now, as I lit another cigarette, turned to blow the smoke over the railing, and gazed into the twilit industrial cityscape—I knew better. His story was bullshit. It was exactly the kind of thing you would tell a sentimental Jewish girl to win her over, to capture her heart.

*

Another year had bloomed and retreated by the time I received final word from Dean Witterman. Those twelve months had been streaked with tumultuous, unforeseen developments—the most positive being that Alex and I now shared an apartment with my cats and seven jam-packed bookshelves.

I'd spent this particular afternoon cooking, baking, and

washing up as I went along. The following day was Alex's birthday, and mine the day after that. I'd made a carrot cake to mark the occasions, alongside a dinner of alfredo primavera.

Here and there, Alex wandered by the kitchenette to offer help and was shooed away. But after hours on my feet, I was ready to surrender. Once the carrot cake was frosted, I called to the bedroom, "Babe, I'm dying."

Alex appeared in the doorway. "What can I do?"

I beckoned to him with a knife coated in cream cheese frosting. Alex purred and plucked it from my grasp. After giving its blade a long, pleasurable lick, he offered me a taste.

I shook my head. "Will you stir the alfredo for me, please? I'm fucking wiped."

He took over, permitting me to collapse into the armchair in front of my desk. I can't say why I decided to check my student email just then, except that it had been a while since I'd done so. Expecting to delete spam messages or announcements that no longer applied to me, I apathetically signed in.

An email from Dean Witterman was listed at the top of my inbox.

I gasped and sat upright. My knees knocked loudly against the desk. From far away, I heard Alex exclaim, ask a question, but I couldn't manage a response. Transported, my eyes locked onto the contents of the computer screen; the rest of me hovered above.

Jul 28, 2018 at 8:06 AM

Cal,

I know this seems like a long time coming, but I wanted to let you know that the [university] Board of Regents passed a policy this week. I've attached a copy to this email. It is a comprehensive policy that covers both consensual relationships and familial relationships.

Please note that section [0.0] states:

> [0.0] No University Employee or affiliate shall enter into a consensual relationship with any student or student-athlete currently enrolled at the University whom they teach, manage, supervise, advise, or evaluate in any way.

As I think I mentioned to you before, the policy went through much review and took longer to get approved than I had anticipated and had hoped. But I do think it is a good policy. [When the Vice President] presented the item to the Board for approval, [they] mentioned that the other [nearby] universities were also revisiting their policies and [they] thought our new policy would be a model for them. As Dean, I will work to make sure that faculty are aware of the new policy.

I believe your courage instigated this new policy and I thank you for that. It is a policy that will ensure [the university] provides a fair and safe environment for students, faculty, and staff. I also know that the circumstances surrounding this were at great cost to you. I hope you have continued to heal and move forward.

I hope you are doing well and enjoying your summer. I wish you all the best!

I slowly returned to my body. Tears were collecting in tiny puddles above my cheeks. A weight on my upper arm bent my head, and I saw Alex's hand. He spoke in a velvet rumble.

I gaped at him. "Wha—what?"

He'd skimmed the email from over my shoulder. "Babe, this is great. Are you okay? Are you happy with it?"

"Yes, I... It's golden."

He knelt, encouraging my face into the front of his T-shirt. "You did it, honey."

"I did it!" I echoed, now sobbing outright. "This was the final part, the thing I've been waiting for."

"Good timing, just before your birthday."

"No shit!" I laughed.

Alex lifted me from the chair with a kiss, and we resumed our dinnertime activities. It was getting dark outside, and neither of us had eaten all day.

Later, I slipped out onto the balcony with my laptop. By the time my response was sent, the moon had breezed above the horizon, its silhouette caught in the black, spindled outlines of nearby trees.

Jul 30, 2018 at 11:24 PM

Dean Witterman,

I understand it's a time-consuming process to make policy changes in any institution. I really appreciate your work on this and for keeping your word. I'm happy with the policy, and this definitely brings me peace of mind. It cannot alter what's been done to me, but it assures me, nonetheless.

Thank you for acknowledging my trauma. I'm still working with a counselor and continue to address my mental health. My biggest hurdle has been learning to be more patient with myself, especially when bad days stretch into bad weeks.

It's been far from easy.

You know, I do love [the university]. I never felt Dr. Blair's abuses were reflective of any sanctioned attitudes held [there]. With the exception of any memories pertaining to him, my overall impressions of [the university] are positive. I'm a better, wiser, and more balanced person because of it. Your support, as well as the support of [other faculty and staff], has progressed my appreciation. Thank you for taking me seriously, for hearing me and believing me. Thank you for your part in pushing these policy changes through. I feel they will make students safer and hopefully deter exploitation in the future, god willing.

Thank you. Thank you so much. This comes as a huge relief to me.

I read my reply to Alex when he came outside to check on me. "What do you think?" I asked. "Was I too heavy-handed with the PTSD reference?"

"Nah, no way. I mean, you're being honest, and they should know this is still affecting you. That wasn't even the tip of the iceberg."

Attracted to its hazy blue, moths and gnats bounced against my laptop's screen. I brushed them away and closed the display. "It's after midnight now," I noticed aloud, smiling. "Happy birthday."

"Thanks," Alex mumbled, deadpan.

"You're old now."

"So are you. An old Jewish woman."

"It's true. Thirty going on eighty-six. Old, grumpy potato—that's me."

"Cutie potato," Alex corrected, and leaned down to kiss me.

We stepped from the balcony into our living room. Filburt, who'd been watching us through the glass, meowed and ran in the direction of the bathroom. Gojira blinked at us from her perch on the sofa's backrest.

"I know it's super late now, but do you want some cake?"

Alex *pfft*-ed. "Fuck yeah, I want some cake. What kind of question is that?"

I turned into the kitchenette and gasped. "Oh my god! One of the cats has been at the cake!"

Alex hurried over to see. A haphazard spot of speckled brown cake glistened on the far left corner, licked clean of frosting. "Wow," he concluded plainly.

"It's not that bad. I think I can cover that area with what's left." I extracted a knife from the silverware drawer before pausing. "I wonder which cat it was."

"When was the last time you saw Gojira jump up on the counter? It was totally Filburt."

"Well, to be sure, why don't you go sniff his face to see if he smells like cream cheese?"

"I'm not going to do that."

"Then, get out of the kitchen so I can focus on salvaging this cake, ya fuck."

Murmuring lighthearted curses, Alex padded away. Moments later, he called from the bedroom. "Hey, I just smelled Filburt," he reported. "He smells like a cat."

Laughing wildly, I caught myself before accidentally piercing the cake with a diagonal jerk. My giggles subsided, and the remaining frosting was mustered into the bald patch. Eventually, it looked just as it had before Filburt's gluttonous assault.

*

Cody marveled, "You're not the same person from before."

I swayed in my seat as his big red truck navigated a traffic circle, and looked at him curiously, somewhat stunned.

He rushed to clarify. "I don't mean that in a bad way, like I didn't like who you were before. Of course, I liked who you were before, since I asked to marry you. You're just different now—the new and improved Cal."

The truck bounced into the parking lot next to my building and settled into a pair of yellow lines. Cody cut the engine and sank into a comfortable slouch. Ahead of us, blue-green hills curled into the horizon, polka-dotted by twinkling lights and divided by the long, black belt of a nearby highway.

I poked my arm through the window to pinch the cherry from my cigarette. "Our relationship changed me a lot, in its aftermath," I stated frankly. "Actually, I feel like the changes in my personality could be measured this way: me, before meeting Alex, then after my relationship with you, and now, after what Jack did."

"I think you've handled things beautifully. You seem very calm, considering."

Me, calm? Compared to two or three years ago, sure, totally—almost night and day.

"I guess I prefer to focus on those unintended, positive consequences. Like, Alex and I are closer now than we've ever been. I'm glad I didn't pursue academia. I love my job; I love working with recovering addicts. I never would have imagined that's what I'd end up doing, but I think it suits me." With a shrug, I got to the point. "I'm just *grateful*," I gushed. "I have a lot to be grateful for, and I refuse to be too miserable to acknowledge that. God knows, I'm traumatized, but I don't have to be *paralyzed* by my trauma. I won't give Jack or anyone else the satisfaction. Fuck that."

"That's right!" Cody lifted his palm to high-five me before giving me a quick hug. "I'm proud of you. You're doing great—have a great way of looking at everything."

I thanked him and slid back into my seat.

"I hope I didn't..." He hesitated, weighing his words. "Well,

I just—I hope I'm not up there with what Jack did. I still feel terrible about a lot of things that happened between us."

"God, no," I grunted. "At least with you, it was *real*. We were genuinely in love. I'm glad we're still friends. And I'm *really* happy with Alex. I'm going to marry that poor bastard."

"Good! You should. He's a good man."

At this, we mirrored smiles. No irony was lost.

We embraced again.

As I exited the truck, *I love yous* were exchanged, and I walked on, sneakers crunching over the parking lot. At the point where the asphalt gave way to the sidewalk in the courtyard, I paused to watch Cody's truck vanish around the building. Seconds expired as I lingered there, pressed against the parking garage like a shadow, wondering if I wasn't, in fact, completely full of shit.

Grateful. Calm and grateful. Who am I kidding?

Yet, who would I be if this weren't true, and I'd allowed myself to be withered down by the hot stew of my anguish? A pitiful, guarded creature, addicted to my distress, traversing the present through a haze of bad memories. Turning myself into salt every day, for looking back. Stripped of the ability to recognize that sometimes, there *is* beauty and goodness in the otherwise godforsaken maelstrom of life.

I didn't deserve such a fate, so why unnecessarily prolong the torment some sick fuck imposed on me? Yes, I still ached. Yes, I was altered—scathed. Torn and gutted, I'd struggled to adapt to living in a constant state of internal screaming, as if all of my *kishkas* had been replaced with lungs. But over time, I'd learned how to breathe normally again, to carefully dial the volume down, down, down.

Summer was bowing to autumn. Another eventful twelve months had passed since I'd heard from Dean Witterman and the policy changes went into effect, and nearly three years since I'd reported Jack. And sure enough, that obnoxious cliché about time and healing proved to be a reliable truth.

I was, in general, okay. Changed, calm and grateful—not great, but still okay.

After letting myself into the apartment, I threw my purse into a chair and went to see the rest for myself.

I removed my big owl glasses and leaned into the bathroom mirror. A couple of new grey hairs glittered within the unruly, half-loops of my eyebrows. Severed by the fold of a floral headscarf, wrinkles crept across my forehead and into my temples. I tried to relax my face and smooth my features, but the wrinkles remained like tracks in baked clay. The fatty crescents hanging from my nose to frame my mouth also seemed more pronounced.

I wore it in my face, just as I wore it throughout my brain. But, I had to admit that much was left well-enough alone. Most of me, really.

Even at the age of thirty-two, my face was speckled with acne. I was still five-foot-three inches tall, and weighed around one hundred and fifteen pounds. My ribs and collarbones probed the flesh around them, while I carried a loathsomely squishy belly at my waist. Tree-thick and stumpy, my legs were the same. Layers of zigzagged pink, purple, and white scars still puckered the expanse of my left arm, sides and abdomen, thighs and legs. Atop this battered flesh, my skin still exhibited the same tattoos, as well as navel, facial, and ear piercings. The same menorah necklace hung from the stiff column of my neck.

When I spoke, I was still teased for my culturally confused speech. The mostly Midwestern dialect of my surroundings, with exaggerated vowels to match my father's East Coast origins. The Yiddish I'd absorbed from him and others, and the Hebrew I'd picked up in *shul*. The same slips in diction and pronunciation which hinted at the long months I'd spent living in England as a teenager.

Beyond this, what could be seen or heard, what was true before persisted. I still took showers just to feel warm and encapsulated, and slept with Meyer, the teddy bear Mom had hand-sewn and given to me on my twelfth birthday. I still ate the same foods, listened to the same music, and watched the same movies and television shows. My favorite books were still *Jane Eyre*, *The Jungle*, and *Catherine, Called Birdy*.

Friends, family, and partners continued to love me and be loved by me. I was still sober. I was still writing.

Cal and the Hebrew name Binah—me. Me, the wounded kitten. A casualty of existing, of being female-bodied, of being ethnically and culturally other, and of dwelling in perpetual poverty. A prey to anxious fright and idiosyncratic phobias—still terrified of change, responsibility, and failure.

This reflection, that young woman: me. I am. I was. There, then, here, now—me. Mostly left alone, intact—*me?*

Yes, goddamn it. Yes.

Epilogue

At the conclusion of the spring 2017 semester, Eleanor Parsons stepped down as head of the sociology department. I suspect the move was ordered by administrators; however, she'd told me the decision had been hers. "It's just my time," she'd said.

Eleanor has since passed away. May her memory be a blessing.

During the summer of 2017, university officials declined to renew Phoebe Kosel's teaching contract. Their excuse was insultingly poor; she was simply informed that the department wanted "to move in another direction." Without protest, she immediately packed up her office and left campus.

She and her family now live in the Northwest. She no longer works in higher education.

Connie was asked by administration to take early retirement in the spring of 2018. She agreed and is no longer employed at the university.

Despite being a tenure-track professor, Zach Cantor's position was terminated prior to the start of the 2018–19 academic year. In confidence, he said their decision was a relief. Zach has since left Kansas, but continues to work in academia and appears to be doing all right.

Before the start of the spring 2017 semester, Magda was granted medical leave. Complications arose subsequently, and she was forced to vacate her position. She'd been tenured and taught at the university for almost ten years.

Magda now lives and teaches in the Pacific West. We've stayed in touch, and she's doing well.

Both Tracy Hines and Anna McNeil are still employed by the university.

In 2019, Irene graduated with honors. Soon after, she and her fiancé bought a house together and were married the following year. She and I remain friends.

Over the last few years, Jack Blair has moved several times in Kansas and Nebraska. Since his departure from the university, he's coauthored two textbooks and has collaborated with law enforcement as a consultant and patrol officer. He has also been employed as a grant writer, youth and family advocate, and domestic violence prevention specialist. I've found no evidence that he's still teaching or employed in higher education at this time.

My last sighting of him occurred in January 2017, while jogging around the perimeter of the university's campus. Jack pulled out of the parking lot ahead of me and turned into the street. He stared ahead as he drove past, feigning ambivalence. I pounded the cement, shoulders back, and glared razors through the passenger-side windows as he sped by. I know he saw me; it was evident in the frustration engraved in the clench of his jaw.

I continued my trek and didn't look back.

*

I returned to college in 2018 and after three years, I successfully passed the state licensing exam in substance use disorder counseling. I'm grateful to serve clients in the same outpatient treatment center wherein I rediscovered myself as a recovering person.

My darling kitty Gojira suddenly passed away in January 2020. To stem Filburt's mourning, I talked Alex into adopting a new companion from a local no-kill cat shelter: a five-year-old black cat with emerald eyes. We named her Bergamia and love her dearly.

Alex proposed in October 2019 and two years later, we held a costume party wedding shit-show (as described on our invitations). About two hundred dear friends and family members bore witness as Alex and I stood beneath a *chuppah* and exchanged statements of infinite commitment. I wore a black silk dress with metallic beading discovered at a thrift store by my best friend Amber. Alex wore a costume, emulating the painter Bob Ross. Rabbi Alpert officiated.

I've never known such joy as I did that day, when I married my *b'sherter.*

During the summer of 2018, I started hand-sewing another quilt. Someday, I'll finish it.

References

1. Errors of Cognition

Batmaz, Sedat, Sibel Kocbiyik, Özden Yalçınkaya-Alkar, & Mehmet Hakan Turkcapar.(2016). Cognitive distortions mediate the relationship between defense styles and depression in female outpatients. *The European Journal of Psychiatry, 30* (4), 237–247.

Beck, Aaron T., & Pretzer, James. (2005). A cognitive perspective on hate and violence. In R.J.Sternberg (Ed.), *The psychology of hate.* Washington, DC: American Psychological Association.

Burkett, James P., & Young, Larry J. (2012). The behavioral, anatomical and pharmacological parallels between social attachment, love and addiction. *Psychopharmacology*, 224 (1),1–26.

Dare, Brandon A., Rosanna E. Guadagno, & Nicole Muscanell. (2013). Commitment: The key to women staying in abusive relationships. *Journal of Interpersonal Relations, Intergroup Relations, and Identity, 6*, 58–64.

DeAngelis, Tori. (2008). The two faces of oxytocin: Why does the 'tend and befriend' hormone comes into play at the best and worst of times? *Monitor on Psychology*. Retrieved November 23, 2019, from https://www.apa.org/monitor/feb08/oxytocin

Dutton, Donald G., & Painter, Susan L. (1981). Traumatic bonding: The development of emotional attachments in battered women and other relationships of intermittent abuse.*Victimology: An International Journal, 6* (1-4), 139–155.

Dutton, Donald G., & Painter, Susan L. (1993). Emotional attachments in abusive relationships: A test of traumatic bonding theory. *Violence and Victims, 8* (2), 105–20.

Festinger, Leon. (1957). *A theory of cognitive dissonance.* Stanford, CA: Stanford University Press.

Gardner, Daniel. (2008). *The science of fear: Why we fear the things we shouldn't–and put ourselves in greater danger*. New York, NY: Dutton (Penguin Group).

Goffman, Erving. (1961). *Encounters: Two studies in the sociology of interaction*. Indianapolis, IN: Bobbs-Merrill Company, Inc.

Guzmán, Yomayra F., Natalie C. Tronson, Vladimir Jovasevic, Keisuke Sato, Anita L. Guedea,Hiroaki Mizukami, Katuhiko Nishimori, & Jelena Radulovic. (2013). Fear-enhancing effects of septal oxytocin receptors. *Nature Neuroscience, 16* (9), 1185–1187.

Hentschel, Uwe, Juris G. Draguns, Wolfram Ehlers, & Gumund Smith. (2004). Defense mechanisms: Current approaches to research and measurement. In U. Hentschel, G. Smith, J.G. Draguns, & W. Ehlers (Eds) *Defense mechanisms: Theoretical, research and clinical perspectives*. Amsterdam, the Netherlands: Elsevier B.V.

Howard, Jonathan. (2018). *Cognitive errors and diagnostic mistakes: A case-based guide to critical thinking in medicine*. New York, NY: Springer Publishing Company

Inaba, Darryl S., & Cohen, William E. (2014). *Uppers, downers, all arounders*, eighth edition. Medford, OR: CNS Productions, Inc.

Lewis, Todd F. (2014). *Substance abuse and addiction treatment*. Upper Saddle River, NJ: Pearson Education.

Mook, Douglas. (2004). *Classic experiments in psychology*. Westport, CT: Greenwood Press.

Nicholson, Shannon B., & Lutz, David J. (2017). The importance of cognitive dissonance in understanding and treating victims of intimate partner violence. *Journal of Aggression, Maltreatment & Trauma, 26* (5) 475–492.

Rationalization. (n.d.). In *American Psychological Association dictionary of psychology*. Retrieved November 5, 2018, from https://dictionary.apa.org/rationalization

Smith, Eliot R., Diane M. Mackie, & Heather M. Claypool. (2014). *Social psychology*, fourth edition. New York, NY: Psychology Press.

Tavris, Carol, & Aronson, Elliot. (2007). *Mistakes were made (but not by me): Why we justify foolish beliefs, bad decisions, and hurtful acts.* New York, NY: Houghton Mifflin Harcourt.

Trivers, Robert L. (2011). *The folly of fools: The logic of deceit and self-deception in humanlife.* New York, NY: Basic Books.

2. Manipulation and Psychological Abuse

American Psychiatric Association. (2013). *Diagnostic and statistical manual of mental disorders*, fifth edition. Arlington, VA: American Psychiatric Association.

Barhill, Anne. (2014). What is manipulation? In C. Coons and M. Weber (Eds.) *Manipulation: Theory and practice.* New York, NY: Oxford University Press.

Bhattacharjee, Yudhijit. (2017). Why we lie: The science behind our deceptive ways. *National Geographic.* Retrieved March 27, 2018 from https://www.nationalgeographic.com/magazine/2017/06/lying-hoax-false-fibs-science/

Bifulco, Antonia, & Moran, Patricia. (1998). *Wednesday's child: Research into women's experience with neglect and abuse in childhood, and adult depression.* New York, NY: Routledge.

Brown, Laura S., & Freyd, Jennifer J. (2008). PTSD criterion A and betrayal trauma: A modestproposal for a new look at what constitutes danger to self. *Trauma Psychology, Division 56, American Psychological Association, Newsletter, 3*, 11–15.

Buss, David M., Mary Gomes, Dolly S. Higgins, & Karen Lauterbach. (1987). Tactics of manipulation. *Journal of Personality and Social Psychology*, 52 (6), 1219–1229.

Ellin, Abby. (2019). *Duped: Double lives, false identities, and the con man I almost married.* New York, NY: Public Affairs.

Freyd, Jennifer J., Bridget Klest, & Carolyn B. Allard. (2005). Betrayal trauma: Relationship to physical health, psychological distress, and a written disclosure intervention. *Journal of Trauma & Dissociation, 6* (3), 83–103.

Gorin, Moti. (2014). Towards a theory of interpersonal manipulation. In C. Coons and M.Weber (Eds.) *Manipulation: Theory and practice*. New York, NY: Oxford University Press.

Govier, Trudy. (1998). *Dilemmas of trust*. Montreal & Kingston, Canada: McGill-Queen's University Press.

Marshall, Linda L. (1996). Psychological abuse of women: Six distinct clusters. *Journal of Family Violence, 11* (4), 379–409.

Marshall, Linda L. (1999). Effects of men's subtle and overt psychological abuse on low-income women. *Violence and Victims, 14* (1), 69–88.

Marshall, Linda L. (2000). *SOPAS: Subtle and Psychological Abuse of Women Scale* [Measurement instrument]. Retrieved December 3, 2017, from http://www.midss.org/content/subtle-and-overt-psychological-abuse-women-scale-sopas

McCornack, Steven A., & Levine, Timothy R. (1990). When lies are uncovered: Emotional and relational outcomes of discovered deception. *Communication Monographs*, 57, 119–138.

Royse, David. (1994). *How do I know it's abuse?: Identifying and countering emotional mistreatment from friends and family members*. Springfield, IL: Thomas Books.

Salamon, Michael J. (2011). *Abuse in the Jewish community: Religious and communal factors that undermine the apprehension of offenders and the treatment of victims*. Jerusalem,Israel: Urim Publications.

Sinnamon, Grant. (2017). The psychology of adult sexual grooming: Sinnamon's seven stage model of adult sexual grooming. In W. Petherick & G. Sinnamon (Eds.), *The psychology of criminal and antisocial behavior: Victim and offender perspectives*. London, England: Academic Press.

Steffens, Barbara A., & Rennie, Robyn L. (2006). The traumatic nature of disclosure for wives of sexual addicts. *Sexual Addiction & Compulsivity, 13*, 247–267.

3. Rape

Allison, Julie A., & Wrightsman, Lawrence S. (1993). *Rape: The misunderstood crime.* Newbury Park, CA: SAGE Publications.

Basile, Kathleen C. (2005). Sexual violence in the lives of girls and women. In K.A. Kendall-Tackett (Ed.), *Handbook of women, stress, and trauma.* New York, NY: Brunner-Routledge.

Bisson, Jonathan I. (2007). Post-traumatic stress disorder. *BMJ: British Medical Journal, 334*(7597), 789–793.

Bourke, Joanna. (2007). *Rape: Sex, violence, history.* Great Britain: Virago Press.

Burgess-Jackson, Keith. (1999). A theory of rape. In K. Burgess-Jackson (Ed.), *A most detestable crime: New philosophical essays on rape.* New York, NY: Oxford University Press.

Fields, Erica L., & Kirchoff, Alisha L. (2011). Date rape. In W.J. Chambliss (Ed.), *Crime and criminal behavior.* Los Angeles, CA: SAGE Publications.

Foa, Edna B., & Rothbaum, Barbara Olasov. (1998). *Treating the trauma of rape: Cognitive behavioral therapy for PTSD.* New York, NY: Gilford Press.

Freedman, Estelle B. (2013). *Redefining rape: Sexual violence in the era of suffrage and segregation.* Cambridge, MA: Harvard University Press.

Hansson, Desirée. (1992). What is rape trauma syndrome? *Occasional Papers Series,* 4-92. Cape Town, South Africa: Institute of Criminology, University of Cape Town.

Kilpatrick, Dean G., Lois J. Veronen, & Connie L. Best. (1985). Factors predicting psychological distress among rape victims. In C.R. Figley (Ed.), *Trauma and its wake: The study and treatment of post-traumatic stress disorder (Vol 1).* Bristol, PA: Brunner/Mazel.

Peterson, Kirtland C., Maurice F. Prout, & Robert A. Schwarz. (1991). *Post-Traumatic Stress Disorder: A clinician's guide.* New York, NY: Springer Science+Business Media.

Resick, Patricia A., & Schnicke, Monica K. (1996). *Cognitive processing therapy for rape victims: A treatment manual*. Newbury Park, CA: SAGE Publications.

Snyder, James J., & Dishion, Thomas J. (2016). Introduction: Coercive social processes. In J.J. Synder and T.J. Dishion (Eds.), *The Oxford handbook of coercive relationship dynamics*. New York, NY: Oxford University Press.

Terry, Karen, & Cling, B.J. (2004). Megan's Law: New protections against sex abuse. In B. J. Cling (Eds.), *Sexualized violence against women and children*. New York, NY: Guilford Press.

United States Department of Justice. (2012). An updated definition of rape. Archives. Retrieved February 7, 2018, from https://www.justice.gov/archives/opa/blog/updated-definition-rape

4. Psychopathy

American Psychiatric Association. (2013). *Diagnostic and statistical manual of mental disorders*, fifth edition. Arlington, VA: American Psychiatric Association.

Blair, James, Derek Mitchell, & Karina Blair. (2005). *The psychopath: Emotion and the brain*. Malden, MA: Blackwell Publishing.

Carnahan, Thomas, & McFarland, Sam. (2007). Revisiting the Stanford Prison Experiment: Could participant self-selection have led to the cruelty? *Personality and Social Psychology Bulletin, 33* (5), 603–614.

Cleckley, Hervey M. (1988). *The mask of sanity: An attempt to clarify some issues about the so-called psychopathic personality*, fifth edition. Augusta, GA: Emily S. Cleckley.

Crawford, Amy. (2012). The pros and cons of being a psychopath. *Smithsonian Magazine*. Retrieved March 21, 2019, from https://www.smithsonianmag.com/science-nature/the-pros-to-being-a-psychopath96723962

DeCelles, Katherine A., Joshua D. Margolis, Scott D. DeRue, & Tara L. Ceranic. (2012). Does power corrupt or enable? When and why power facilitates self-interested behavior. *Journal of Applied Psychology*, 97 (3), 681–689.

Hare, Robert D. (1999). *Without conscience: The disturbing world of the psychopaths among us*. New York, NY: Gilford Press.

Haslam, S. Alexander, & Reicher, Stephen. (2017). Tyranny: Revisiting Zimbardo's Stanford Prison Experiment. In J.R. Smith and S.A. Haslam (Eds.), *Social psychology: Revisiting the classic studies*, second edition. Thousand Oaks, CA: SAGE Publications Inc.

Hervé, Hugues. (2007). Psychopathy across the ages: A history of the Hare psychopath. In H. Hervé and J.C. Yuille (Eds.), *The psychopath: Theory, research, and practice*. Mahwah, NJ: Lawrence Erlbaum Associates, Inc.

Kantor, Martin. (2006). *The psychopath of everyday life: How antisocial personality disorder affects all of us*. Westport, CT: Praeger Publishers.

Kosson, David. (2013). *Psychopathy, antisocial personality disorder, and underlying mechanisms*. Retrieved June 30, 2017, from https://www.youtube.com/watch?v=XIOFe5cFDg4

Lilienfeld, Scott. (2016). *The search for successful psychopathy*. Retrieved July 16, 2017, from https://www.youtube.com/watch?v=1zjt4GCC7Ck

Resnick, Brian. (2018). Philip Zimbardo defends the Stanford Prison Experiment, his most famous work. *Vox*. Retrieved September 21, 2019, from https://www.vox.com/science-and-health/2018/6/28/17509470/stanford-prison-experiment-zimbardo-interview

Schouten, Ronald, & Silver, James. (2012). *Almost a psychopath: Do I (or does someone I know) have a problem with manipulation and lack of empathy?* Center City, MN: Hazelden Publishing.

Zimbardo, Philip G. (1971). The power and pathology of imprisonment. Congressional Record. (Serial No. 15, October 25, 1971). Hearings before Subcommittee No. 3, of the Committee on the Judiciary, House of Representatives, 92nd Congress, First Session on Corrections, Part II, Prisons, Prison Reform and

Prisoners' Rights: California. Washington, DC: U.S. Government Printing Office.

5. Obedience to Authority

Biddle, Bruce J. (1986). Recent developments in role theory. *Annual Review of Sociology, 12* (1), 67–92.

Blass, Thomas. (2000). The Milgram paradigm after 35 years: Some things we now know about obedience to authority. In T. Blass (Ed), *Obedience to authority: Current perspectives on the Milgram paradigm*. Mahwah, NJ: Lawrence Erlbaum Associates.

Burger, Jerry M. (2009). Replicating Milgram: Would people still obey today? *American Psychologist*, 64 (1), 1–11.

Elms, Alan C. (2009). Obedience lite. *American Psychologist*, 64 (1), 32–36.

Hofling, Charles K., Eveline Brotzman, Sara A. Dalrymple, Nancy Graves, & Chester M. Pierce. (1966). An experimental study in nurse-physician relationships. *Journal of Nervous and Mental Disease, 143* (2), 171–180.

Irons, Richard, & Schneider, Jennifer P. (1999). *The wounded healer: Addiction-sensitive approach to the sexually exploitative professional.* Northvale, NJ: Jason Aronson Inc.

Kelman, Herbert, & Hamilton, V. Lee. (1989). The My Lai massacre: A military crime of obedience. In D.M. Newman and J. O'Brien (Ed.), *Sociology: Exploring the architecture of everyday life*, eighth edition. Thousand Oaks, CA: Pine Forge Press.

Martin, Robin, & Hewstone, Miles. (2003). Social-influence processes of control and change: Conformity, obedience to authority, and innovation. In M.A. Hogg and J. Cooper (Eds.),*The SAGE handbook of social psychology*. London, England: SAGE Publications.

Milgram, Stanley. (1963). Behavioral study of obedience. *The Journal of Abnormal and Social Psychology*, 67 (4), 371–378.

Milgram, Stanley. (1974). *Obedience to authority: An experimental view.* New York, NY: Harper & Row.

Perry, Gina. (2012). *Behind the shock machine: The untold story of the notorious Milgram psychology experiments.* New York, NY: The New Press.

Plummer, Ken. (2010). *Sociology: The basics.* New York, NY: Routledge.

Reicher, Stephen, & Haslam, S. Alexander. (2017). Obedience: Revisiting Milgram's shock experiments. In J.R. Smith and S.A. Haslam (Eds.), *Social psychology: Revisiting the classic studies.* Thousand Oaks, CA: SAGE Publications Inc.

Runciman, Walter G. (2000). *The social animal.* Ann Arbor, MI: University of Michigan Press.

Sheridan, Charles. L., & King, Richard G. (1972). Obedience to authority with an authentic victim. *Proceedings of the Annual Convention of the American Psychological Association, 7*, 165–166.

Schaefer, Richard T. (2009). *Sociology Matters*, fourth edition. New York, NY: McGraw-Hill.

Slater, Mel, Angus Antley, Adam Davison, David Swapp, Christoph Guger, Chris Barker, Nancy Pistrang, & Maria V. Sanchez-Vives. (2006). A virtual reprise of the Stanley Milgram obedience experiments. *PLoS ONE*, 1 (1): e39.

Tolbert, Pamela S., & Hall, Richard H. (2009). *Organizations: Structures, processes, and outcomes*, tenth edition. Upper Saddle River, NJ: Pearson Education Inc.

Vandenburgh, Henry. (2004). *Deviance: The essentials.* Upper Saddle River, NJ: Pearson Prentice Hall.

6. Helping Professionals and the Ethics of Sexual Boundaries

American Association of University Professors. (2009). Statement on professional ethics. Retrieved July 13, 2019, from https://www.aaup.org/report/statement-professional-ethics

American Medical Association. (2016). Code of medical ethics: opinion 9.1.1. Retrieved July 13, 2019, from https://www.ama-assn.org/delivering-care/ethics/code-medical-ethicsprofessional-self-regulation

American Psychological Association. (2017). Ethical principles of psychologists and code of conduct. Retrieved July 13, 2019, from https://www.apa.org/ethics/code/?item=10#707

Biaggio, Maryka, Tana L. Paget, & Sue M. Chenoweth. (1997). A model for ethical managementof faculty-student dual relationships. *Professional Psychology: Research and Practice, 28* (2), 184–189.

Bouhoutsos, Jacqueline, Jean Holroyd, Hannah Lerman, Bertram R. Forer, & Mimi Greenberg. (1983). Sexual intimacy between psychotherapists and patients. *Professional Psychology: Research and Practice, 14* (2), 185–196.

Branstetter, Steven A., & Handelsman, Mitchell M. (2000). Graduate teaching assistants: Ethical training, beliefs, and practices. *Ethics & Behavior, 10*, 27–50.

Corey, Gerald, Marianne S. Corey, Cindy Corey, & Patrick Callanan. (2015). *Issues and ethics in the helping professions*, ninth edition. Stamford, CT: Cengage Learning.

Dziech, Billie W. & Weiner, Linda. (1990). *The lecherous professor: Sexual harassment on campus*, second edition. Chicago, IL: University of Illinois Press.

Eichenberg, Christiane, Monika Becker-Fischer, & Gottfried Fischer. (2010). Sexual assaults in therapeutic relationships: Prevalence, risk factors and consequences. *Health*, 2 (9), 1018–1026.

Garrett, Tanya. (2002). Inappropriate therapist-patient "relationships." In R. Goodman and D. Cramer (Eds.), *Inappropriate relationships: The unconventional, the disapproved, and the forbidden.* Mahwah, NJ: Lawrence Erlbaum Associates, Inc.

Irons, Richard, & Schneider, Jennifer P. (1999). *The wounded healer: Addiction-sensitive approach to the sexually exploitative professional.* Northvale, NJ: Jason Aronson Inc.

Kitchener, Karen S. (1988). Dual role relationships: What makes them so problematic? *Journal of Counseling & Development, 67*, 217–221.

Kolbert, Jered B., Barbara Morgan, & Johnston M. Brendel. (2002). Faculty and student perceptions of dual relationships within counselor education: A qualitative analysis. *Counselor Education and Supervision, 41*, 193–206.

National Association of Social Workers. (2017). Code of ethics. Retrieved July 13, 2019, from https://www.socialworkers.org/About/Ethics/Code-of-Ethics/Code-of-Ethics-English

National Association of State Directors of Teacher Education and Certification. (2015). Model code of ethics for educators. Retrieved July 13, 2019, from https://www.nasdtec.net/page/MCEE_Doc#PrinIII

Pope, Kenneth S., & Vasquez, Melba J.T. (2011). *Ethics in psychotherapy and counseling: practical guide*, fourth edition. Hoboken, NJ: Jack Wiley & Sons, Inc.

Rabbinical Council of America. (2018). Code of conduct. Retrieved July, 13, 2019 from https://rabbis.org/pdfs/Code_of_Conduct_3_13_2018.pdf

Rape, Abuse & Incest National Network. (2018). Sexual exploitation by helping professionals. Retrieved August 3, 2018, from https://www.rainn.org/articles/sexual-exploitationhelping-professionals

Sassler, Sharon, Katherine Michaelmore, & Jennifer A. Holland. (2016). The progression of sexual relationships. *Journal of Marriage and Family, 78* (3), 587–597.

7. Professor-Student Sexual Intimacy: Attitudes, Outcomes, and Policy

Arnett, Jeffrey J. (2015). *Emerging adulthood: The winding road from the late teens through the twenties*, second edition. New York, NY: Oxford University Press.

Barbella, Lisa. (2010). Hot for teacher: The ethics and intricacies of student-professor relationships. *Sexuality & Culture, 14* (1), 44–48.

Bellas, Marcia L., & Gossett, Jennifer L. (2001). Love or the "lecherous professor": Consensual sexual relationships between professors and students. *The Sociological Quarterly*, 42 (4),529–558.

Chory, Rebecca M., & Offstein, Evan H. (2016). Too close for comfort? Faculty-student multiple relationships and their impact on student classroom conduct. *Ethics & Behavior, 28* (1), 23–44.

DeChiara, Peter. (1988). The need for universities to have rules on consensual sexual relationships between faculty members and students. *Columbia Journal of Law and Social Problems, 21*, 137–162.

Delbanco, Andrew. (2012). *College: What it was, is, and should be*. Princeton, NJ: Princeton University Press.

Ei, Sue, & Bowen, Anne. (2002). College students' perceptions of student-instructor relationships. *Ethics & Behavior*, 12 (2), 177–190.

Dziech, Billie W., & Hawkins, Michael W. (1998). *Sexual harassment in higher education: Reflections and new perspectives*. New York, NY: Routledge.

Flaherty, Colleen. (2018). Academe sees a new wave of faculty-student relationship restrictions in the era of Me Too. *Inside Higher Ed*. Retrieved from https://www.insidehighered.com/news/2018/05/24/academe-sees-new-wave-faculty-student-relationship-restrictions-era-me-too

Glaser, Robert D., & Thorpe, Joseph S. (1986). Unethical intimacy: A survey of sexual contact and advances between psychology educators and female graduate students. *American Psychologist, 41* (1), 43–51.

Holmes, Deborah L., Patricia A. Rupert, Stephanie A. Ross, & Wendy E. Shapera. (1999). Student perceptions of dual relationships between faculty and students. *Ethics & Behavior, 9* (2), 79–107.

Hooks, bell. (2003). *Teaching community: A pedagogy of hope*. New York, NY: Routledge.

Kitchener, Karen S. (1988). Dual role relationships: What makes them so problematic? *Journal of Counseling & Development, 67*, 217–221.

Mack, Margaret H. (1999). Regulating sexual relationships between faculty and students. *Michigan Journal of Gender and Law, 6* (1), 79–112.

MacKinnon, Catharine A. (2016). In their hands: Restoring institutional liability for sexual harassment in education. *The Yale Law Journal, 125* (7), 2038–2105.

Miller, Gary M., & Larrabee, Marva J. (1995). Sexual intimacy in counselor education and supervision: A national survey. *Counselor Education & Supervision, 34* (4), 332–343.

Pope, Kenneth S., Hanna Levenson, & Leslie R. Schover. (1979). Sexual intimacy in psychology training: results and implications of a national survey. *American Psychologist, 34* (8), 682–689.

Richards, Tara N., Courtney Crittenden, Tammy S. Garland, & Karen McGuffee. (2014). An exploration of policies governing faculty-to-student consensual sexual relationships on university campuses: Current strategies and future directions. *Journal of College Student Development, 55* (4), 337–352.

Skeen, Richard, & Nielsen, Joyce M. (1983). Student-faculty sexual relationships: An empirical test of two explanatory models. *Qualitative Sociology, 6* (2), 99–117.

Skinner, Linda J., Melissa K Giles, Sue Ellen Griffith, Michael E. Sonntag, Kenneth K. Berry, & Robert Beck. (1995). Academic sexual intimacy violations: ethicality and occurrence reports from undergraduates. *Journal of Sex Research, 32* (2), 131–143.

Srinivasan, Amia. (2020). Sex as a pedagogical failure. *The Yale Law Journal, 129* (4), 1100– 1146.

Acknowledgments

I'm so fortunate to have a community of friends and kin. I'm especially grateful for the following persons for their care and support: Mikki, Andy, Sam, Amy, Nicole, Stephen, Naomi, Zahra, Irene, Caleb, Mark, Cody, David, Pat, Ashley, Mariah, Ava, Richard, Ashanti, Wes, Troy, Carlos, Kat, Daniel, Aaron, Tina, Mama Annette, Joe, Beth, Taylor, Jessica, Yalitza, Madi, Verlisa, Jeff, Will, Joanna, Rebecca, Martel, Brooke, Aubrey, Courtney, Carrie, Matt, Megan, Beckie, Maryam, Marvin, Israel, Jeffery, Thea, Sara, Joey, Jenn, Brian, Nancy, Rick, Brock, Tania, Tara, Kody, Morgan, Chris, Josh, Carmen, Steven, Doni-Marie, Haley, Donna and Scott, Carly, Dusty, Michelle, Diane, Dave and Deb, the Foxy By Proxy Revue, Rabbi Doug Alpert, my bubbe Judy, my precious mother Kathryn, and my counselors Heather, Sonya, Marie, and Wendy.

I'm indebted to the university faculty and staff who've been my friends and allies, such as Grace, Connie, Charles, Phoebe, Zach, Rachel, and those whom I can't mention for privacy's sake. You know who you are, and my heart is heavy with thanks.

Thanks also to Christie, Sasha, and the other helping professionals who supplied me with validation and guidance when I needed it the most.

I'm part of a family of exceptional writers and fellow creative weirdos. For their encouragement and kindness, I'd like to recognize Charlie J. Eskew, Louise Krug, Dennis Etzel Jr., Jason Allen, Barrett Bowlin, Christine Neulieb, Elizabeth Earley, Donald Quist, Kali VanBaale, Johnathan Penton, Rosalyn Spencer, Jose A. Rodriguez, Amy Fleury, Chad Abushanab, Will Donnelly, Gary Jackson, Lisa Hase-Jackson, Eric McHenry, Karen Bjork Kubin, p.e. garcia, Bernadette Roe, Alyse Bensel, Wendy Taylor Carlisle, Tara Stillions

Whitehead, Ruben Quesada, Joseph M. Hess, Kevin Rabas, Hina Ahmed, Val Killpack, Colin Katchmar, Sam Reichman, Jenny Molberg, Nick Demske, Abby E. Murray, Miranda Weiss, Lawrence Welsh, Rajiv Mohabir, Marya Hornbacher, Sarah Smarsh, and the loving fellowship of Sober AWP. Thanks, also, to Sandy Longhorn, director of the C.D. Wright Women Writers Conference. Excerpts from this manuscript were presented at the 2018 event.

Special thanks to Cynthia Lewis for her time, advice, and interest in my story.

I'm eternally grateful to the staff of Atmosphere Press, who believed in the importance of this book and were supportive and patient through every stage of the publication process.

To those exceptional beings I consider soulmates—Bevel, Kamyar, Drew, Nick, and Huascar—thank you for loving me and growing with me, despite the odds we've shared. I love you so, so much, to the extent that it sometimes defies rationale.

To my loving and loyal husband Alex and life partner Amber—I could not be without you. You are my life's saviors, renewing my sense of purpose and keeping the blood moving uninterrupted through my veins. I love you more than language can qualify.

Above all, I'd like to acknowledge Magda, my sister woman and fellow survivor. I love you, Magda. May you continue to demonstrate resilience and beauty in all of your endeavors.

In blessed memory of my grandma Carol Brunner Rutledge, whose own memoir was the first I ever read—I wish you could see what I've accomplished in your literary wake, but I trust you'd be proud.

About Atmosphere Press

Founded in 2015, Atmosphere Press was built on the principles of Honesty, Transparency, Professionalism, Kindness, and Making Your Book Awesome. As an ethical and author-friendly hybrid press, we stay true to that founding mission today.

If you're a reader, enter our giveaway for a free book here:

SCAN TO ENTER
BOOK GIVEAWAY

If you're a writer, submit your manuscript for consideration here:

SCAN TO SUBMIT
MANUSCRIPT

And always feel free to visit Atmosphere Press and our authors online at atmospherepress.com. See you there soon!

About the Author

Cal Louise Phoenix is a multi-genre writer and licensed substance use disorder counselor. She is thriving in her native Kansas. *Studies in Lechery* is her first full-length book.

Made in the USA
Monee, IL
27 August 2024

63970268R00225